C000009020

Corfu
& the Ionians

Cadogan Guides
West End House, 11 Hills Place,
London, W1R 1AH, UK

The Globe Pequot Press
6 Business Park Road, PO Box 833, Old Saybrook,
Connecticut 06475–0833

Copyright © Dana Facaros 1994, 1999
Illustrations © Suzan Kentli 1993, 1995

Reprinted 1999

Book design by Animage
Cover photographs © James Davies
Maps © Cadogan Guides, drawn by Map Creation Ltd

Editing: Mary-Ann Gallagher
Proofreading: Linda McQueen
Indexing: Judith Wardman

Series Editor: Rachel Fielding

ISBN 1–86011–915–8

A catalogue record for this book is available from the British Library

Printed in Great Britain by
The Cromwell Press, Trowbridge.

About the Author

Dana Facaros is a professional travel writer. Over the past fourteen years she has lived in several countries, concentrating on the Mediterranean area. In collaboration with her husband Michael Pauls she has written more than twenty Cadogan Guides on, amongst others, Italy, Spain, France and Turkey. Her roots, however, are in the Greek Islands; her father comes from Ikaria. Dana's guide to all the Greek Islands, now in its seventh edition, was first published in 1979.

Acknowledgements

A big *efcháristo parapolí* to my ever-affable hosts extraordinaire and experts on the Greek condition, Michael and Brian; to my cousin Filia for everything, to Claudia for her expert updating. Also a round of applause to Mary-Ann for her diligent editing.

Please Help Us Keep This Guide Up to Date

We have done our best to ensure that the information in this guide is correct at the time of going to press. But places and facilities are constantly changing, and standards and prices fluctuate. We would be delighted to receive any comments concerning existing entries or omissions. Authors of the best letters will receive a copy of a Cadogan Guide of their choice.

Contents

Topics

Athens and Piraeus

Corfu/Kérkyra

The Islands

Maps

The Greeks call the Ionians the *Eptánissa*, the Seven Islands, and they stand out as remarkably among the country's 3000 islands as the seven stars of the Pleiades stand out in beauty among the constellations in the night sky. Strategically scattered down the west coast of Greece, from lush Corfu overlooking the mountains of Albania down to Kýthera at the southern end of the Peloponnese, the seven have always

Introduction

been among the most beloved and coveted pieces of property in the country: Corinthians, Romans, Goths, Byzantines, Normans, Angevins, Venetians, Turks, Frenchmen, Russians, and the British have won the right to call them their own, until 1864 when the British, in a rare act of generosity, presented them to Greece.

The stomping grounds of Odysseus and Nausicaa, the seven Ionian islands have been lumped together politically since Byzantine times. They share a unique history, and character, most notably marked by the five centuries of Venetian rule. They are more luxuriant than the Greek island stereotype of arid rocks piled with sugar cube villages; the Ionians are swathed in olive groves, pines and cypresses and bathed in a soft golden light very different from the sharp, clear solar spotlight that shines on the Aegean. In temperament, too, the Seven Islands beg to differ: they are more gentle and lyrical, less prone to the extremes that bewitch and bedazzle the rest of the country. They also get more rain, especially from late October to March, but it too has a good side in the breathtaking bouquet of wild flowers in the spring and autumn, especially on Corfu, a paradise for botanists.

Yet for all that they have in common, each of the seven major Ionians has a strong, distinct personality of its own. Ferry and even flight connections between the islands are improving every year, and now—at least in the summer—you can, with relative ease, visit six of them if you like. The inhabitants used to divide their archipelago into two groups: the olive-growing islands (Corfu, Paxí and Lefkáda) and the currant-growers (Kefaloniá, Ithaca and Zákynthos), whose inhabitants, at least according to themselves, are more intelligent and industrious. Beautiful and distant **Kýthera**, the island of Aphrodite and cradle of half the Greeks in Melbourne, Australia, remains the exception to the rule: an island out of time, aloof from the crowds and charter flights, and becoming trendy because of it.

Luxuriant **Corfu**, of course, is one of the reigning queens of Greek tourism, with its gorgeous beaches and historic town, accurately described in the British Press as a 'Venice without canals, Naples without the degradation.' Corfu is large enough to absorb the invader, but suffers from pockets of mass package tourism of the least attractive type. Far from the lager lout ghettos, however, it has charming mountain villages and a scattering of quiet beaches, and enough natural beauty to forgive its sins. Next to Corfu, bijou **Paxí** with its many sheltered coves is a favourite of sailors; completely covered with olive groves, it attracts a sophisticated but low-key set, and sandy beaches are only a short boat ride away on little **Antípaxi**.

Lovely, fertile **Zákynthos**, the favourite of the Venetians, is the second most visited island of the seven. Unfortunately it has lost much of its original character owing to earthquakes and package tourism. It does have, besides a very swinging nightlife, stunning scenery, and you can avoid much of the tourist faldirol altogether by sticking to the quieter villages and taking off on your own to explore.

Kefaloniá, the biggest and most mountainous of the seven, offers an astonishing variety of scenery and moods: beautiful beaches, magnificent scenery, forests, wine, two delightful caves, and plenty of character, all enjoyed by a quarter of the visitors who fill Zákynthos. **Lefkáda**, too, offers a fine mixture of rugged scenery, typical villages, good restaurants and swimming, as well as some of the finest hang-gliding and watersports in Greece. Rugged but friendly **Ithaca**, lacking the sumptuous beaches and sophistication of its sisters, is a great place to get away from it all, to ramble about places associated with Odysseus' famous homecoming; it is still a very Greek island, if that's what you're looking for, and one of the nicest of all.

Travel

Getting There and Around

The bible of travel to and around Greece is the *Greek Travel Pages*, updated monthly. Consult a copy at the National Tourist Organization or a travel agency specializing in Greece, or check out the GTP website: *http://www.hellas.de/gtp*.

By Air

'The air and sky are free,' Daedalus told son Icarus as he planned their ill-fated winged escape from Crete. They aren't free any more, but you can fly for less if you look around. As competition increases in Europe, don't automatically presume charter flights with their restrictions are your best buy; flying the Greek national carrier, Olympic Airways, opens up very reasonable onward prices to island airports. Students or anyone under 26 will find the most bargains (*see* p.6). The good news is that you can fly 'open jaws' into one Greek airport and out of another. The bad news is that a Greek airport tax (£20 at the time of writing) is added on to some ticket prices.

Charter Flights to Athens or the Ionian Islands

Charter flights to Athens are frequent in the summer from Europe, less frequent from North America, and non-existent from Australasia. Europeans also have the luxury of charter flights direct to the islands of Corfu, Kefaloniá, Zákynthos, and to the mainland airports of Aktion and Préveza (for Lefkáda) from London Gatwick, Luton, Glasgow, Cardiff, Newcastle, Manchester, Belfast, and Dublin. Check the travel sections in the major weekend papers, *Time Out*, or the *Evening Standard* for last-minute discounts on unsold seats, or get advice from your local travel agent or the specialists listed below. Most UK charters run from May to mid-October but some firms feature early specials in March and April depending on when Greek Easter falls, usually from London Gatwick and Manchester.

Charter tickets have fixed outward and return dates with as often as not departure and arrival times in the wee hours. They are also governed by several restrictions. Tickets are valid for a minimum of 3 days and a maximum of 6 weeks and must be accompanied by an accommodation voucher stating the name and address of the hotel, villa or campsite; you don't really have to stay there. Although a formality, every so often there is a crackdown aimed at what the Greeks consider undesirables flouting the law. Because they subsidise airline landing fees they want to prevent charter flights being used as a cheap way to get to other countries, in this case Albania. If you come to Greece on a charter, you may visit any neighbouring country for the day, but not stay overnight, at the very real risk of forfeiting your return ticket home. Travellers with stamps from previous holidays in Turkey will not be barred entry, but if you have Turkish Cypriot stamps check with the

Passport Office before you go. Returning from Greece, make sure you confirm your return flight three days prior to departure.

Scheduled Flights from the UK and Ireland to Athens

Scheduled flights direct to Athens operate several times daily from London on **Olympic**, **British Airways**, and **Virgin Atlantic. EasyJet** fly from Luton and offer very reasonable fares (return flights start at £140). East European companies like **Czech Airlines** also fly to Athens and can work out cheaper in season, but you may have to wait for hours for connections in Prague and supply your own drinks and peanuts. Apex and Superpex flights offer substantially reduced fares, with flights from London to Athens ranging from £190 low season to £280 high season. They must, however, be paid for instantly and are not refundable or flexible. Rates range from £212 return midweek in low season to £298 weekends in high season. Scheduled flights from Ireland to Athens on Olympic and Aer Lingus fly via Heathrow and tend to be considerably pricier than charters.

Olympic Airways	London ✆ (0171) 409 3400
	Dublin ✆ (01) 608 0090
British Airways	London ✆ (0181) 897 4000
	Belfast ✆ (0345) 222111
	Dublin ✆ (1 800) 626 747
Aer Lingus	Belfast ✆ (01232) 314844
	Dublin ✆ (01) 844 4777
Virgin Atlantic	London ✆ (01293) 747747
easyJet	UK ✆ (0990) 292929
Czech Airlines	London ✆ (0171) 409 3400

discounts and special deals

Alefcos Tours, ✆ (0171) 267 2092. Olympic Airways consolidator.

Avro, ✆ (0181) 715 0000. Charter and scheduled flights to Athens and major islands from London Gatwick and Luton; also from Manchester, Glasgow, Cardiff, Newcastle and Birmingham.

Balkan Tours, ✆ (01232) 246 795. Charter flights direct from Belfast.

Delta Travel, ✆ (0161) 272 8455; ✆ (0151) 708 7955; ✆ (0121) 471 2282. Manchester-based agents for scheduled flights from Heathrow, Manchester and Birmingham to Athens; wide range of island charters.

Island Wandering, ✆ (01580) 860733. Reasonable schedules to Athens, island packages and 'open jaws' routes, using Olympic Airways flights.

Joe Walsh Tours, ✆ (01) 676 3053. Budget fares from Dublin.

Eclipse Direct, ✆ (01293) 554400; ✆ (0161) 742 2277. Flights from Gatwick, Manchester, Birmingham.

Sunset Air Fares, ✆ (01204) 701 111. Bolton-based agent with charters to the islands.

Teleticket, ✆ (01293) 567640. Good for excess charter seats from Gatwick to Athens: cheap but often excruciatingly early arrivals.

Trailfinders, London, ✆ (0171) 937 5400; Bristol, ✆ (0117) 929 9000; Birmingham, ✆ (0121) 236 1234; Manchester ✆ (0161) 839 6969; Glasgow, ✆ (0141) 353 2224. One of the best for finding affordable flights.

WT Holidays, ✆ (01) 789555. Charter flights from Dublin.

Scheduled Flights from North America

Olympic, TWA and **Delta** offer daily nonstop flights from New York to Athens in the summer; Olympic also flies direct to Athens from Atlanta, Boston, and Chicago several times a week, depending on the season, and offers connecting flights from Dallas, Detroit, Houston, Los Angeles, Miami, Philadelphia, San Francisco and Washington DC; from Canada, Olympic flies direct to Athens from Toronto and Montreal, with connecting flights from Vancouver and Calgary. Usually cheaper **Tower Air** flies direct from New York to Athens two or three times a week. American economy fares (Apex and Superapex/Eurosavers, booked at least three weeks in advance) range from $760 return New York–Athens in low season to $1200 high season; Canadian economy fares to Athens from Toronto or Montreal range from $1020 low season $1350 high season. When ringing around, take into consideration the large discount Olympic offers its international passengers on flights to the islands; at the time of writing, only $100 US will take you on to any domestic destination in Greece.

From many cities in the USA and Canada, European airlines such as **KLM** or **Czech Airlines** offer the best deals to Greece. If you have more time than money, get a cheap or standby flight to London and once there hunt up a cheap ticket to an island (*see* above) although this may be a headache in July or August.

Olympic Airways	USA, ✆ (800) 838 3600	
	Canada:	Montreal ✆ (514) 878 9691
		Toronto ✆ (416) 920 2452
Delta:	USA, ✆ (800) 241414	
Air Canada	Canada, ✆ (800) 555 1212	
	USA, ✆ (800) 776 3000	

KLM:	USA, ☏ (800) 374 7747
	Canada, ☏ (800) 361 5330
Tower Air:	USA, ☏ (800) 34 TOWER
TWA:	USA, ☏ (800) 892 4141
Czech Airlines	USA, ☏ (800) 223 2365
British Airways	USA, ☏ (800) 247 9297
	Canada, ☏ (800) 668 1055

discounts and special deals

New Frontiers, USA, ☏ (800) 366 6387. Canada, in Montréal, ☏ (514) 526 8444.

Travel Avenue, USA, ☏ (800) 333 3335.

Air Brokers International, USA, ☏ (800) 883 3273. Discount agency.

Council Charter, USA, ☏ (800) 223 7402. Charter specialists.

Homeric Tours, USA, ☏ (800) 223 5570, ✉ 753 0319. Charter flights and custom tours.

Last Minute Travel Club, USA, ☏ (800) 527 8646. Annual membership fee gets you cheap standby deals.

Encore Travel Club, USA, ☏ (800) 444 9800. Scheduled flight discount club.

Scheduled Flights from Australasia

Olympic flies at least twice a week direct to Athens from Melbourne and Sydney, and if their fares aren't the cheapest, consider the discounts the Greek carrier offers international passengers on its domestic flights. Other carriers such as Qantas, Singapore Airlines, Aeroflot, KLM, Thai Airways, British Air, and Gulf Air. Prices in low season (Nov–Mar) average around $2000 low season, $2350 at other times. There are no direct flights from New Zealand, but Air New Zealand, Qantas, Singapore Airways or Alitalia will get you there with only one stop en route. If you can pick up a bargain flight to London, it may work out cheaper to take that and find a discount flight from there (*see* above).

Olympic Airlines	Sydney and Brisbane, call toll-free ☏ (008) 221 663;
	Melbourne, ☏ (008) 9331448; Adelaide,
	☏ (008) 331 448; (no office in New Zealand)
Thai Airways	Australia, ☏ (1 800) 422 02
	Auckland, ☏ (09) 377 3886
British Airways	Sydney, ☏ (9258 3300)
	Auckland, ☏ (09) 356 8690

Singapore Airlines	Sydney, ☎ (02) 9236 0144
	Auckland, ☎ (09) 379 3209
KLM	Australia, ☎ (1 800) 505 474
Aeroflot	Sydney, ☎ (02) 9233 7911
Alitalia	Sydney, ☎ (02) 9247 1308
	Auckland, ☎ (09) 366 1855
Qantas	Sydney, ☎ (02) 957 0111
	Auckland, ☎ (09) 357 8900
Air New Zealand	☎ (649) 303 5826
Gulf Air	Sydney, ☎ (02) 9321 9199

discounts and special deals

Flight Centres, Sydney, ☎ (02) 9241 2422; Melbourne, ☎ (03) 650 2899; Auckland, ☎ (09) 209 6171; Christchurch, ☎ (03) 379 7145 and other branches.

Brisbane Discount Travel, in Brisbane, ☎ (07) 3229 9211.

UTAG Travel, Sydney, ☎ (02) 956 8399, and branches in other Australian cities.

Budget Travel, Auckland, toll free ☎ (0 800) 808 040.

From Africa

Olympic flies three times a week from Johannesburg by way of Nairobi to Athens; in Johannesburg ☎ (880) 4120, ✆ 880 7075; Cape Town, ☎ (021) 230 260, ✆ 244 166; in Nairobi, ☎ 219 532.

Domestic Flights to the Islands

Flights from Athens to Corfu, Kýthera, Kefaloniá, Zákynthos, and Aktion and Préveza (for Lefkáda) can be booked in advance through **Olympic**; as many planes are small, do this as far in advance as possible. And because planes are small, baggage allowances (15kg) tend to be enforced—unless you've bought your ticket abroad, when you're allowed all 23kg. Children under twelve go half-price. In the summer planes make the short hop between Kefaloniá and Zákynthos.

Student and Youth Travel

If you're under 26 or a full-time student under 32 with an **International Student Identity Card** to prove it, you're eligible for **student/youth charters**; these are exempt from the voucher system and are often sold as one-way tickets, enabling you to stay in Greece longer than is possible with a regular charter flight. Students under 26 are sometimes eligible for discounts on scheduled flights as well; especially with Olympic Airways who currently offer 25% discount to ISIC card holders on all connecting flights from Athens to the islands.

Young people of Greek origin (age 10–15) may be eligible for Gold Card discounts (contact your country's Greek National Tourist Office). Specialists in youth and student travel include:

Campus Travel, 52 Grosvenor Gardens, London, ☎ (0171) 730 3402; with branches at most UK universities: Leeds, ☎ (0113) 246 1155; Bradford, ☎ (01274) 383261; Bristol, ☎ (0117) 929 2494; Manchester, ☎ (0161) 833 2046; Edinburgh, ☎ (0131) 668 3303; Birmingham, ☎ (0121) 414 1848; Oxford, ☎ (01865) 242067; Cambridge, ☎ (01223) 324283. Runs own youth charters to Athens in summer.

STA Travel, 86 Old Brompton Road, London, SW7 3LH or 117 Euston Road NW1 2SX, ☎ (0171) 361 6161; Bristol, ☎ (0117) 929 4399; Leeds, ☎ (0113) 244 9212; Manchester, ☎ (0161) 834 0668; Oxford, ☎ (01865) 792800; Cambridge, ☎ (01223) 366966, and many other branches in the UK; in the **USA,** New York city, ☎ (212) 627 3111; outside New York ☎ (1 800) 777 0112. In **Australia**, Sydney ☎ (02) 9212 1255, elsewhere ☎ (1 800) 637 444

USIT, Aston Quay, Dublin 2, ☎ (01) 679 8833; Cork, ☎ (021) 270 900; Belfast, ☎ (01232) 324 073; Galway, (091) 565 177; Limerick (061) 415 064; Waterford, (051) 72601. **Ireland**'s largest student travel agents.

Council Travel, 205 E. 42nd St, New York, NY 10017, ☎ (800) 743 1823. Major specialist in student and charter flights; branches all over the **USA**. Also in the **UK**, 28 Poland St, London W1V 3DB, ☎ (0171) 437 7767.

Travel Cuts, 187 College St, Toronto, Ontario M5T 1P7, ☎ (416) 979 2406. **Canada**'s largest student travel specialists; branches in most provinces.

Children and Pregnancy

Free child places on package holidays and discount air fares for tiny travellers vary from company to company. Get a good travel agent, trawl through the brochures and read all the small print. The big package operators geared to family holidays like Thomson offer a wide range of child discounts and seasonal savers with in-resort amusements, kiddie clubs and baby-sitting as well as deals for children under twelve in hotels and teenagers up to seventeen in self-catering accommodation. On some UK charter flights infants under two travel free on a full fare-paying adult's lap, while on others you may be charged £15–£20 for the baby, or 10% of the adult fare. Children from two to twelve cost between 25%–65%, and over twelve you'll have to fork out full fare. On international Olympic flights you'll pay 67% of the adult fare for children aged two to twelve, 10% for infants under two, while under-12s go for half-fare on all domestic flights. Watch out for birthdays; if your toddler has crossed the magic two-year-old age barrier by the return journey you'll have to pay for another seat. Note that many airlines won't let single mothers travel with two infants, although you may get through the restriction by having one on your lap and one in a car seat; explain your position when you book in case they are adamant on the one child per adult rule or turn you away at the check-in.

If you're pregnant, think before you fly. Although Greek hospitals have improved in recent years, you should make sure your insurance covers repatriation. Most airlines will carry women up to 34 weeks of pregnancy—Olympic even later—but you will have to provide a doctor's certificate after 28 weeks to prove you are well enough to fly. Again, check when you book.

Getting to and from Ellinikon Airport, Athens

Athens' Ellinikon Airport is divided into three terminals: East Terminal (used by some charters, all non-Olympic international airlines and Air Greece), West Terminal or Olympiki, used for all Olympic Airlines flights, both international and domestic, and the Charter Terminal; if you're on a charter double check to make sure you go to the right one. Express bus 091 connects all three terminals to central Athens, stopping in front of the Post Office in Sýntagma Square and from Stadíou Street by Omónia Square every 20 minutes between 5.21am and midnight and every hour at night from 1.12am–4.12am. Fares are 160dr from 7am to 11.30pm, 200dr otherwise. From Karaiskaki Square in Piraeus, express bus no.19 goes to the airport's three terminals every hour from 6am to midnight, and at 2.30am and 5am. The same buses will take you from terminal to terminal, or catch a taxi (under 1000dr). For more on taxis and getting around Athens, *see* pp.76–7.

There's a **left luggage** facility in the Olympic airport, and another at the international airport, down at the far end beyond the charters' hall.

essential airport numbers (✆ 01–)

East Terminal	✆ 969 4111
West Terminal	✆ 926 9111
Charter Terminal	✆ 997 2581

airlines in athens (✆ 01–)

Aeroflot	14 Xenofóndos, ✆ 322 0986, 📠 323 6375
Air Canada	10 Óthonos, ✆ 322 3206, 📠 323 1057
Air France	18 Vouliagmenis, Glyfáda, ✆ 960 1100, 📠 960 1457; airport ✆ 969 9334
Air Greece	22 Filellínon, ✆ 324 4457, 📠 324 4479; airport ✆ 960 0646

Air Zimbabwe	22 Filellínon, ✆ 324 5415, 🖷 324 5446
Alitalia	577 Vouliagmenis, Argyroupoulis, ✆ 995 9200, 🖷 995 9214; airport ✆ 961 3621
American Airlines	15 Panepistimiou, ✆ 331 1045
British Airways	10 Óthonos, ✆ 890 6666, 🖷 325 5171; airport ✆ 961 0402
Continental Airlines	25 Filellínon, ✆ 324 9300
Czech Airlines	15 Panepistímiou, ✆ 323 0174
Cyprus Airways	10 Filellínon, ✆ 324 7801, 🖷 324 4935; airport ✆ 961 0325
Delta	4 Óthonos, ✆ 331 1668, 🖷 325 0451; airport ✆ 964 8800
Iberia	8 Xenofóndos, ✆ 323 4523; 🖷 324 0655; airport ✆ 969 9813
KLM	22 Voúlis, ✆ 988 0177; airport ✆ 969 9733
Lufthansa	East Terminal, ✆ 369 2200, 🖷 363 6881
Malev	15 Papepistímiou, ✆ 324 1116
Olympic	96 Syngroú, among many branches; reservations ✆ 966 6666, 🖷 966 6111. Information ✆ 936 3363
Qantas	East Terminal, ✆ 969 9323
Sabena	41c Vouliagmenis, Glyfáda, ✆ 960 0021; 🖷 0219; airport ✆ 961 3903
SAS	E. Terminal, ✆ 960 1003, 🖷 960 1306; airport ✆ 961 4201
Singapore Airlines	9 Xenofondos, ✆ 323 9111, 🖷 325 4326; airport ✆ 961 2815
South African Airways	8 Merlin, ✆ 361 7278, 🖷 362 7433
Swissair	4 Óthonos, ✆ 323 5813, 🖷 322 5548; airport ✆ 961 0203
Thai Airlines	1 Sekeri St, ✆ 364 7610, 🖷 364 7680; airport ✆ 960 0607

TWA	8 Xenofóndos, ✆ 322 6451, 📠 322 8973; airport ✆ 961 0012
United Airlines	5 Syngrou, ✆ 924 2645, 📠 922 9268
Virgin Atlantic	8–10 Tzireon, Makrigiánni, ✆ 924 9100, 📠 9144; airport ✆ 960 1461

By Train

The obvious and most benign way to reach the Ionian islands is by way of Italy, either from Venice or Ancona if you prefer to spend your time on deck, or from Brindisi if you prefer to save a bit of money and spend the time sitting on a train. Check on trains from Britain with British Rail International, ✆ (0990) 848 848; some ferries give discounts to passengers holding rail passes.

Domestic Trains

train routes for the islands

Athens–Pátras	(for Ionian Is.)	7 a day
Athens–Kalamáta	(for Kýthera)	8 a day

In Athens, the railway station is Laríssa Station, Deligiánni Street, ✆ 362 4402. In Piraeus, the station for Kalamáta and the Peloponnese is near the Piraeus–Athens metro on Aktí Kalimassióti.

By Coach

London to Athens

Taking a coach from London to Thessaloníki or Athens is always a possible alternative for those who decide that a train trip is too expensive or too easy a route to travel. It is rarely cheaper than a standby flight, and takes 4 days instead of 4 hours, but it's a chance to see Munich, Belgrade and other fine bus terminals en route. **Eurolines**, 52 Grosvenor Gardens, Victoria, London SW1W 0AU, ✆ (0171) 730 8235, make the journey from London to Athens for around £218 return if you're over 26; there's a £12 saving if you're under 26. Departures from London are on Friday mornings in July, August and September only. **Olympic Bus Ltd**, 70 Brunswick Centre, London WC1 1AE, ✆ (0171) 837 9141 offers 2½-day journeys from London to Athens via Brussels and Italy for a mere £50 one-way, or £100 return, departing London on Friday evenings. In Greece, you'll find agencies selling bus tickets on the most obscure islands, as well as in Athens; **Filellínon Street** near Sýntagma Square is Athens' budget travellers' boulevard, so check there.

Domestic Buses

The domestic bus service in Greece is efficient and regular, and still a bargain. Bus services from Athens relevant to this book are as follows:

Athens to	No. daily	Terminal	✆	Duration
Gýthion (for Kýthera)	4	Kifissoú	512 4913	4½hrs
Kefaloniá	4	Kifissoú	525 0785	8hrs
Kérkyra (Corfu)	2	Kifissoú	512 9443	11hrs
Lefkáda	4	Kifissoú	525 0108	5½hrs
Pátras (for Ionians, Italy)	16	Kifissoú	513 6185	3hrs
Zákynthos	3	Kifissoú	512 9432	7hrs

To get to the terminal at **100 Kifissoú Street** (✆ 512 4910) take bus no.051 from Omónia Square (Zinonos and Menandroú Sts).

In August, reserve seats in advance on the long-distance buses if you can. Note that Lefkás is joined to the mainland by a bridge, which is good to remember if you want an island and the ferries aren't running due to strikes or bad weather.

There never seem to be enough buses on the islands in the summer, nor is it customary to queue. However, you will not be left behind if it is humanly possible for you to squeeze on. If you can wake up in time, you will find that buses are rarely crowded early in the morning.

By Sea

The most common sea route to Greece is from Italy, with daily ferry services from Ancona and Brindisi, and frequently from Bari and Venice. Ancona to Pátras takes a day and a half; Brindisi ferries connect with the night train from Rome and arrive in Pátras the next morning. Passengers are usually allowed a free stopover in Corfu if that island is not their ultimate destination, before continuing to Igoumenítsa or Pátras, but make sure it is noted on your ticket.

In the summer, reserve in advance, especially if you bring a car (most travel agents can do this for you). Students and young people can get a discount of up to 20%. Discounts of up to 30% on car prices are also offered when buying a return ticket. As a rule, the costlier the ferry, the faster it sails (Minoan, for instance, takes only 22 hours from Ancona to Pátras).

If you're in a big big hurry, **Catamaran Ferry Lines** (86 Filonos St, 18546 Piraeus, ✆ 429 3903, ✆ 452 3624) link Brindisi with Corfu and Igoumenítsa in under four hours.

Italy–Greece Ferries

The fares listed below are approximate 1999 prices in drachmas for an airline-type seat, one way, in low/high season; there are even cheaper deck class tickets, while cabins are considerably dearer. As a general rule, cars under 4.25m cost a few thousand drachmas more than the low season seat prices listed below; double that price for taking a car in high season. Hellenic Mediterranean is the first to get its itineraries on the Internet, in English, at *http://www.hml.it/indexen.htm*.

Ports	Seat Prices	Company
Ancona–(or Venice)–Corfu–Pátras & Brindisi–Corfu–Igoumenítsa	11,500/23,400dr 8000/14,000dr	Strinzis Lines 26 Aktí Possidónos,Piraeus ✆ 422 5000, @ 422 5265
Ancona–Pátras & Trieste–Corfu–Igoumenítsa–Pátras	14,200/25,800 dr 16,500/27,500dr	ANEK Lines 54 Amalías, Athens ✆ 323 3481, @ 323 4137
Ancona–Pátras (20 hrs)	18,800/24,800dr	Superfast Ferries 157 Alkyonidon,Voúla, Athens ✆ 969 1100, @ 1190
Ancona–Igoumenítsa–Corfu–Pátras & Brindisi–Corfu–Igoumenítsa & Venice–Igoumenítsa–Corfu–Kefaloniá–Patras	17,000/27,200dr 9000/16,000 dr price on application	Minoan Lines 2 Vass. Konstantinoú, Athens ✆ 689 8340, @ 689 8344
Ancona–Igoumenítsa–Pátras & Bari–Igoumeníts–Ancona–Heráklion (Crete) in July/Aug	14,000/19,500dr 10,000/16,000dr	Marlines 38 Aktí Possidónos, Piraeus ✆ 411 0777, @ 411 7780
Brindisi–Corfu–Igoumenítsa–Pátras Brindisi–Kefaloniá–Páxi–Zákynthos–Pátras	6400/17,500dr price on application	Hellenic MediterraneanLines PO Box 80057, Piraeus ✆ 422 5341, @ 422 5317
Bari–Igoumenítsa–Pátras	11,500/17,400dr	Ventouris Ferries 5 Nikodímou, Athens ✆ 324 0071
Brindisi–Corfu–Igoumenítsa	7000/13,400dr	Fragline 5a Réthymnou, Athens ✆ 821 1285, @ 821 3095
Brindisi–Corfu–Igoumenítsa–Pátras	11,900/15,800dr	Adriatica 85 Aktí Miaoúli, Piraeus ✆ 429 0487, @ 429 0490

Ferries to the Islands

Comfort on Greek ferries has improved by leaps and bounds in recent years, especially the long-haul ferries: shops, video rooms, air-conditioning, disco bars, slot machines and small swimming pools are added attractions to the old pleasures of lazily watching passing islands, feeling the sea breeze (or tempest, if the wind kicks up), looking out for dolphins during the day or shooting stars at night. Most island ferries have three classes: the first, or 'distinguished' class, with a plush lounge and private cabins (these often cost as much as flying); the second class, often with its own lounge as well, but smaller, porthole-less cabins, segregated by sex, not recommended for claustrophobes; and third or tourist class, which offers access to typical large rooms full of airline-type seats and the deck and the snack bar area. As a rule the Greeks stay inside and the tourists stay out—on warm summer nights in particular this can be the most pleasant alternative, especially if you have a sleeping bag. Drinking water is never very good on the boats, but all sell bottled water, beer, coffee, and soft drinks (for about twice as much as on shore). Biscuits and cigarettes complete the fare on the smaller boats, while the larger ones usually offer sandwiches, self-service dining or full meals (usually adequate and fairly priced) served in a dining room.

Although Athens' port Piraeus is the busiest in Greece, the only Ionian island it serves is Kýthera. The main port for the Ionian islands is Pátras in the Peloponnese, linked by bus and train from Athens, although you'll do better catching one of the aforementioned buses that coincide with the smaller ferry ports.

The National Tourist Office publishes a free weekly list of ship departures, both abroad and to the islands; for serious island-hoppers, ask for their free booklet, *Greek Travel Routes: Domestic Sea Schedules*. At the same time, be aware that any number of factors (weather, health emergencies and unforeseen repairs) can throw timetables out of the window, so if you have to catch a flight home allow for the eccentricities of the system and leave a day early to be safe. For the latest information on departures and arrivals, ring the relevant port authorities (*limenarchíon*). Numbers are listed for each island. For mainland departures numbers are:

Piraeus Port Authority ✆ (01) 422 6000 (for ferry schedules) or ✆ (01) 451 1311

Pátras Port Authority (for the Ionian Islands) ✆ (0613) 41002

Always keep your ticket with you on a Greek ship, in case of a 'ticket control', a comedy routine necessitated by the fact that the crew doesn't always check tickets when passengers board. Instead, after one or two pleas on the ship's loudspeaker system for passengers without tickets to purchase them forthwith, you suddenly find all the doors on the boat locked or guarded by bored but obdurate sailors, while bands of officers rove about the boat checking tickets. Invariably mix-ups occur: children are separated from their parents, others have gone to the WC, someone has left a ticket with someone on the other side of the immovable sailor, crowds pile up at the doors, and stowaways are marched to the purser's office.

Prices are still reasonable for passengers but rather dear for cars. All ships and hydrofoils are privately owned, and although the Greek government controls prices some will charge more for the same journey, depending on the facilities offered, speed, etc. In most cases children under the age of 4 travel free, and between 4 and 10 for half-fare. Buying a ticket on board will cost 20% more. In the summer, especially in August, buy tickets well in advance if you have a car or want a cabin. Refunds are given only if the ship never arrives.

Hydrofoils and Catamarans

There are several fleets of hydrofoils, several catamarans, and the occasional 'sea jet' thumping over the Greek seas, and new lines are added every year. Most services run throughout the year but are considerably less frequent between November and May. As a rule hydrofoils travel at least twice as fast as ferries and are twice as expensive. In the peak season they are often fully booked, so buy tickets as early as you can. In a choppy sea, a trip may leave you saddle-sore, and beware, if the weather is very bad, they won't leave port.

Tourist Excursion Boats

These are generally slick and clean, and have become quite numerous in recent years. They are usually more expensive than the regular ferries or steamers, but often have schedules that allow visitors to make day trips to nearby islands (though you can also take them one way), and are very convenient, having largely taken the place of the little caique operators, many of whom now specialize in excursions to remote beaches.

By Car

Driving from London to Athens (and taking the ferry from Italy to Greece) at a normal pace takes around 3½ days. Don't even consider driving down unless you are planning to spend a few weeks on one or two islands, and if that's the case the smaller the better, both for squeezing the car on to the ferry, and for negotiating the sometimes very narrow village roads.

Alternatively, there are countless rent-a-car firms on the islands; most are family-run, and fairly reliable (asking around a bit will usually reveal who the stinkers are). If an island has a lot of unpaved roads and not a lot of competition, prices tend to be higher; at the time of writing, hiring a small car varies between 10–15,000dr a day in the summer, and open-air Jeeps at least a third more. Most require that you be at least 21, some 25. Read the small print of your contract with care (look out for mileage limits, etc.), and don't be surprised if you have to leave your driving licence as security. In the off season, negotiate. Arriving at a car hire agent's with a handful of brochures from the competition has been known to strengthen one's bargaining position. Fuel at the time of writing is around 230dr a litre; unleaded (*amólivdi*) a wee bit less.

An **International Driving Licence** is not required from EU citizens. Other nationals can obtain an international licence at home, or at one of the Automobile Club offices in Greece (ELPA), by presenting a national driving licence, passport and photograph. The minimum age is 18 years.

The Motor Insurance Bureau at 10 Xenofóntos Street, Athens, ✆ (01) 323 6733, can tell you which Greek insurance company represents your own, or provide you with additional cover for Greece.

The **Greek Automobile Club** (ELPA) operates a breakdown service within 60km (40 miles) of Athens and Pátras: dial ✆ 104. If you belong to an automobile club at home, breakdown service is free anywhere.

Customs formalities for bringing in a car are very easy and usually take very little time. You are allowed a year of free use of the car in Greece, and after that can apply for a 4-month extension. North Americans and Australians are allowed 2 years. If you leave Greece without your car, you must have it withdrawn from circulation by a customs authority.

ELPA has a list of lawyers who can offer free legal advice on car problems. They also have a 24-hour information number useful to foreign motorists; call ✆ 174, and speak English.

While driving in the centre of Athens may be a hair-raising experience, the rest of Greece is fairly easy and pleasant. There are few cars on most roads, even in summer, and most signs, when you're lucky enough to find one, have their Latin equivalents. Traffic regulations and signalling comply with standard practice on the European Continent (i.e. driving on the right). Crossroads, tipsy tourists, Greeks arguing and gesticulating at the wheel, and low visibility in the mountains are probably the greatest hazards.

Where there are no right-of-way signs at a crossroads, give priority to traffic coming from the right, and always beep your horn on blind corners. If you're exploring, you may want to take a spare container of petrol along, as stations can be scarce on the ground (especially on the islands) and only open shop hours. There is a speed limit of 50km per hour (30mph) in inhabited areas.

By Motorbike and Moped

Motorbikes and even more popular mopeds are ideal for the islands in the summer. It almost never rains, and what could be more pleasant than a gentle thyme-scented breeze freshening your journey? Scooters (the Greeks call them *papákia*, 'little ducks', supposedly for the noise they make) are both more economical and more practical than cars. They can fit into almost any boat and travel paths where cars fear to tread. Rentals are not expensive, and include third party insurance coverage in most cases. You will have to have a valid driving licence (for Americans, this means an international one). For larger motorbikes (anything over 75cc) you may be asked to show a motorcycle driver's licence. The down-sides: many of the bikes are poorly maintained, many of the roads are poorly maintained, and everyone takes too many risks: hospital beds in Greece fill up each summer with casualties, both foreign and Greek (check your insurance to see if you're covered). Most islands have laws about operating motorbikes after midnight (the 'little ducks', often stripped of their mufflers, tend to howl like a flock of Daffys and Donalds on amphetamines) but they are as enforced as often as the helmet requirement. Actually, no: you do see Greeks wearing helmets, but only on their elbows, which, judging by the way they drive their machines, must be where they keep their brains. Literally hundreds of people, nearly all young, are killed every year in Greece. Be careful.

By Bicycle

Cycling has not caught on in mountainous Greece, either as a sport or as a means of transport, though you can usually hire an old bike in most major resorts. Trains and planes carry bicycles for a small fee, and Greek boats generally take them along for nothing.

Hitch-hiking

Greek taxi drivers have recently convinced the government to pass a law forbidding other Greeks from picking up hitchhikers. As with the aforementioned helmet-wearing law, this is regarded as optional, but it is true that you may find hitching slow going; perhaps because of the law, motorized holidaymakers now seem to stop and offer more rides than the locals. The Greek double standard produces the following percentages for hopeful hitch-hikers:

Single woman: 99% of cars will stop. You hardly have to stick out your thumb.
Two women: 75% of cars will find room for you.
Woman and man: 50%; more if the woman is pretty.
Single man: 25% if you are well dressed with little luggage; less otherwise.
Two men: start walking.

Entry Formalities

All **European Union** members can stay indefinitely. The only reason you would need special permission to stay would be for working or if complicated banking procedures were involved requiring proof of residence; contact the Aliens Bureau: 173 Leof. Alexandrás, 11522 Athens, ✆ 646 8103.

The formalities for **non-EU tourists** entering Greece are very simple. American, Australian and Canadian citizens can stay for up to 3 months in Greece on presentation of a valid passport. South Africans are permitted 2 months. If you want to stay longer, take your passport 20 days before your time in Greece expires, to the Aliens Bureau or your local police station, and be prepared to prove you can support yourself with bank statements and the like.

If you overstay your 3 months, be prepared to pay a fine of 22,200dr.

Specialist Holidays

A complete list is available from the **National Tourist Organization of Greece** (*see* pp.41–2).

in the UK

British Museum Tours, 46 Bloomsbury Street, London, WC1B 3QQ, ✆ (0171) 323 8895. Different archaeological guided tours every year.

Cox & Kings, Gordon House, 10 Greencoat Lane, London, SW1P 1PH, ✆ (0171) 873 5000; 🖷 630 6038; *Cox.Kings@coxkings.sprint.com*. Botanic holidays on Corfu.

Explore Worldwide, 1 Frederick Street, Aldershot, Hants, GUII ILQ, ✆ (01252) 344161. Ionian island treks.

Filoxenia, Sourdock Hill, Barkisland, Halifax, West Yorkshire, HX4 0AG, ✆ (01422) 371796, 🖷 310340. Cookery on Corfu and painting groups in Kýthera.

Greco-File, ✆ (01422) 375999. Expert advice on where to go, flights and 'couture' holidays to unusual islands for the discerning traveller.

Greek Islands Club, 66 High Street,Walton-on-Thames, KT12 1BU, ✆ (01932) 220477, 🖷 229346; USA and Canada ✆ (1 800) 394 5577; *http.// www.vch.co.uk/villas/*, e-mail *info@vch.co.uk*. Helpful and friendly with choice villas and a range of activity holidays on the Ionian islands (even Kýthera), including modern Greek, cuisine, bird-watching, wild flowers, music and wine-making.

Norfolk and Suffolk Wildlife Trust Holidays, Dudwick House, Buxton, Norwich, NR10 5HX, ✆ (01603) 278296. Join members of the Norfolk and Suffolk Wildlife Trust on botany and bird-watching trips to Corfu.

Peligoni Club, PO Box 88, Chichester, West Sussex, PO20 7DP ✆ (01243) 511499. A one-off, friendly, English-run sailing and windsurfing club on the northeast coast of Zákynthos. *See* p.212.

Peng Travel, 86 Station Road, Gidea Park, Romford, Essex, RM2 6DB, ✆ (01708) 471832. Naturist holidays in Crete.

Peregrine Holidays, 40–41 South Parade, Summertown, Oxford, OX2 7JP, ✆ (01865) 511642. Wildlife and walking tours.

Solos Holidays Ltd, 41 Watford Way, London, NW4 3JH, ✆ (0181) 951 2800. Singles group holidays in four-star hotels in Zákynthos, Corfu, and Kefaloniá, for independent people in the 30–49 and 50–69 age brackets. Also spring and autumn rambling breaks in Corfu.

Swan Hellenic Ltd, 77 New Oxford Street, London, WC1A 1PP, ✆ (0171) 800 2200. Cultural, archaeological and art history tours and cruises.

Travel Companions, 110 High Mount, Station Road, London, NW4 3ST, ✆ (0181) 202 8478. Vera Coppard can match you up with a kindred spirit, for a £40 fee, if you don't want to travel alone.

in the USA/Canada

Aegean Visions, 26 Sixth St, Suite 260, Stamford, CT, 06905, ✆ (203) 667 2524, toll free (800) GREECE97, ✆ 969 0799. Scuba-diving, hiking, archaeological, alternative living.

Avenir Adventures, 1790 Bonanza Drm Suite 207, Park City, UT 84060, ✆ (800) 367 3230. Expeditions by land and sea for small groups.

Cloud Tours, 645 5th Avenue, New York, NY 10022, ✆ (212) 753 6104, toll free ✆ (800) 223 7880, ✆ 980 6941. Scuba-diving, biking, honeymoon tours, women's groups, religious history tours and many others.

IST Cultural Tours, 225 West 34th Street, Suite 913, New York, NY 10122, ✆ (212) 563 1202, toll free ✆ (800) 833 2111, ✆ 594 6953. Customized tours including yacht cruises and lectures on archaeology.

Our Family Abroad, 40 W. 57th St, Suite 430, New York, NY 10019, ✆ (212) 459 1800, toll free (800) 999 5500, ✆ 581 3756. Gay and lesbian tours.

Peddlers Destination & Adventures International, 8489 Crescent Drive, Los Angeles, CA 90046, ✆ (213) 659 7267, (800) 695 4599, 📠 (213) 650 6902. Island cycling tours.

The Greek Island Connection, 418 E. 14th Street, Suite 3, New York, NY 10009, ✆ (212) 674 4072, toll free (800) 241 2417, 📠 674 4582. Archaeology, cooking, hiking, biking, gay and lesbian, religion.

in Greece

Hellenic Society for the Study and Protection of Dolphins and Whales, 201 Thessalias St, 13231 Petroúpolis, Athens. Study cruises in the Ionian sea, keeping tabs on the dolphin population.

The Path of Avatar, Corfu, ✆ (00 30) 663 51845. Consciousness-raising (in English) with Nayana Gabriele Keller Jutta Weyck.

Disabled Travellers

Many of the Greek islands, with their ubiquitous steps and absence of suitable transport, would put severe constraints on visitors in chairs, and ferry and hydrofoil access is difficult.

Major islands such as Corfu and Rhodes and many smaller ones that receive lots of visitors (such as Skíathos, Zákynthos and Kos) have hotels with facilities—the Greek National Tourist Office has a list.

In the UK, several of the big package holiday companies like **Thomsons** have some suitable tours. Contact **RADAR**, 12 City Forum, 250 City Rd, London, EC1V 8AS, ✆ (0171) 250 4119 or **Tripscope**, ✆ (0181) 994 9294 for advice and referrals.

In the USA a similiar service is provided by the **Travel Information Service**, Moss Rehabilitation Hospital, 1200 W. Tabor Red, Philadelphia, PA 19141, ✆ (215) 456 9600 and the **Society for the Advancement of Travel for the Handicapped**, 347 Fifth Avenue, Suite 610, New York, NY 10016, ✆ (212) 447-SATH, 📠 725 8253. **New Directions**, 5276 Hollister Ave, Suite 207, Santa Barbara CA 93111, ✆ (805) 967 2841, 📠 964 7344.

In Canada, the **Jewish Rehabilitation Hospital**, 3205 Place Alton Goldbloom, Montréal PQ H7V 1R2 is a good source of travel info.

In Greece, contact **The Panhellenic Association for the Blind**, 31 Veranzérou St, 10432 Athens, ✆ (01) 522 8333, 📠 522 2112 or **Association Hermes**, Patriárchou 13, Grigouiou E, 16542 Argyroúpolis, ✆ (01) 996 1887.

Yachting, Sailing and Flotilla Holidays

Are we sailing straight, or is the shore crooked?

old Greek proverb

One of the great thrills of sailing the Ionian sea is the variety of places to visit in a relatively short time, with the bonus that nowhere are you far from safe shelter or harbours with good facilities for yachtsmen. There is little shallow water, except close to the shoreline, few currents and no tides or fog. The islands and mainland provide a virtually inexhaustible supply of secluded coves and empty beaches, even at the height of the tourist season. The Greek National Tourist Organization has initiated a programme of rapid expansion in the face of mounting competition from Turkey and Spain; facilities are being improved and new marinas are being constructed throughout the country.

Individual island maps show main yacht supply stations and ports of entry and exit. Greek weather guarantees near-perfect sailing conditions. The only real problem you'll encounter is the strong winds in parts of the country at certain times of the year, notably April to October, when most yachtsmen are at sea. The Ionian Sea and the west coast of the Peloponnese are affected by the *maistros*, a light-to-moderate northwest wind which presents itself in the afternoon only. Less frequently there are westerly winds, from moderate to strong, to the west and south of the Peloponnese. To the south of Attica, and east of the Peloponnese, the sea is to a great extent sheltered by land masses and it is not until summer that the menacing *meltémi* blows. The Aegean Sea is affected by a northwest wind in the south, and a northeasterly in the north, and when the *meltémi* blows in August and September, it can reach force eight, testing all your skills at the helm.

If you wish to skipper a yacht anywhere within the Greek seas, consult the *Compile Index Chart of Greek Seas*, otherwise known as *XEE*, published by the Hellenic Navy Hydrographic Service. Basically it is a map of Greece divided into red squares, each with an index number, from which you can select the appropriate charts and order them accordingly. For non-Greeks, you can buy what is known as *XEE 64*, a booklet of abbreviations explaining the signs on the charts, with texts in English and Greek.

You also need the Pilot book A, which cost 2500dr and covers the Ionian Sea, Corinthian Gulf and North Peloponnese shores in great detail, from South Albania to Kýthera, describing geographical data, possible dangers, and the present state of transportation and communication. All ports, marinas and visible inland features are mentioned, including where to obtain fresh water and fuel. The Hydrographic Service constantly updates the books and sends additional booklets to authorized sellers and to all port authorities, where you may consult them. The nautical charts

Average wind speeds (in knots) during the months April to October

Area	April	May	June	Jul	Aug	Sept	Oct
Kýthera (Kýthera)	NE 9.8	W 8.2	W 7.8	NE 7.4	NE 8.2	NE 9.0	NE 10.6
N. Ionian (Corfu)	SE 2.9	WSE 2.6	W 2.9	NWW 2.6	NW 2.6	SE 2.3	SE 2.6
N.Ionian (Argostóli)	NW 5.8	NW 5.0	NW 5.4	NW 5.8	NW 5.4	NWN 4.4	NWNE 5.0
S. Ionian (Zákynthos)	N 9.8	NEN 9.4	NE 9.8	N 10.2	NNE 9.8	N 9.0	NE 10.2
S.Ionian (Methóni)	W 11.8	W 11.0	W 11.4	W 11.8	W 11.0	W 10.2	NE 9.8

are updated using the latest, most sophisticated, methods, and follow standardized dimensions. They are on a 1:100,000 scale for bigger areas and 1:750,000 for ports. Heights and depths are given in metres with functional conversion tables for feet and fathoms.

Further information is provided in booklets called *Notes to Mariners*, published monthly and available for consultation at port authorities. These give information on any alterations to naval charts you have purchased for your voyage. Besides all this there is the Navtex service. A special department of the Hydrographic Service keeps you informed about the weather or any special warnings for the day, through telex, or Navtex. The text is in Greek and English, and there are four re-transmission coastal stations covering the Greek seas. Weather forecasts for yachtsmen are broadcast at intervals throughout the day on VHF Channel 16 (in Greek and English); security warnings are also broadcast on this channel, e.g. dangerous wrecks, lights not in operation, etc.

The following is a list of **bunkering ports and supply stations** in Greece where fuelling facilities and other provisions may be obtained:

Adámas (Mílos)*, Aegina, Ag. Nikólaos (Kéa), Ag. Nikólaos (Crete)*, Alexandroúpolis*, Álimos Marína, **Argostóli** (Kefaloniá)*, Chíos*, **Corfu Port***, Ermoúpolis (Sýros)*, Flísvos Marína, Goúvia Marína*, Gýthion*, Chalkís*, Chaniá (Crete)*, Hýdra, Itéa*, Kalamáta*, Kálymnos, Kamáres (Sífnos)*, **Kapsáli** (Kýthera), Kastellórizo, Kástro (Ándros), Katákolo*, Katápola (Amorgós), Kavála*, Kými (Évia), Korínthos*, Kos*, Lákki (Léros), Lávrion*, **Lefkás**, Liméni (Máni), Linariá (Skýros), Mýrina (Límnos)*, Mytilíni*, Monemvásia, Mýkonos*,

Náfpaktos, Náfplion*, Náxos, Néa Róda, Paléa Epidávros, Paleokastrítsa, Párga, Parikía (Páros), Pigádia (Kárpathos), Pílos*, Póros, Pórto Koufó, Pórto Ráfti, Préveza*, Rhodes (Mandráki)*, Skála (Pátmos)*, Skiáthos*, Skópelos, Spétses, Thessaloníki Marína*, Thessaloníki Port*, Tínos, **Váthi** (Ithaca)*, Vólos*, Vouliagméni Marína, **Zákynthos***, Zéa Marína.

* indicates official ports of entry and exit, where there are port, customs and health authorities, as well as immigration and currency control services. Others are: Égion, Gerakini (Chalkidikí), Glyfáda, Igoumenítsa, Herákleon, Kimássi (Évia), Pátras, Pérama, Pithagórion and Vathí (Samos), Dáfni (Agion Óros), Elefsína, Fíra (Santoríni), Ivira (Agion Óros), Kalí Liménes (Crete), Drépanon (Achaía) and Stilí (Lamia).

Yachts entering Greek waters must fly the code flag 'Q' until cleared by entry port authorities. Upon arrival the port authority (*Limenarchíon*) issues all yachts with a transit log, which entitles the yacht and crew to unlimited travel in Greek waters. It also allows crew members to buy fuel, alcohol and cigarettes duty-free. It must be kept on board and produced when required, and returned to the customs authorities on leaving Greece at one of the exit ports. Permission is normally given for a stay of 6 months, but this can be extended. Small motor, sail or rowing boats do not require a '*carnet de passage*', and are allowed into Greece duty-free for 4 months. They are entered in your passport and deleted on exit. For more information, apply to the Greek National Tourist Organisation, 4 Conduit Street, London W1R 0DJ, ✆ (0171) 734 5997, who produce a useful leaflet called *Sailing the Greek Seas*.

Anyone taking a yacht by road is strongly advised to obtain boat registration documentation from the DVLA, Swansea SA99 1BX, ✆ (0792) 783355. The Royal Yachting Association, R.Y.A. House, Romsey Road, Eastleigh, Hampshire SO5 4YA, ✆ (0703) 629962, is a useful source of yachting information.

Yacht Charter

Chartering yachts is very popular these days, and, as the promotional literature says, can be cheaper than staying in a hotel (if you have enough friends or family to share expenses). Between the various firms there are over a thousand vessels currently available in all sizes, with or without a crew (though without a crew—bareboat charter—both the charterer and another member of the party must show proof of seamanship: a sailing certificate or letter of recommendation from a recognized yacht or sailing club). There are various options: motor yachts (without sails), motor sailors (primarily powered by motor, auxiliary sail power) and sailing yachts (with auxiliary motor power). The Greek National Tourist Organisation has a list of Greek charter firms, or contact **The Hellenic Professional Yacht Owners Association**, Zéa Marína A818 536, Piraeus, ✆ 452 6335, ✆ 452 6335 and

℗ 428 0465, and **Greek Yacht Brokers and Consultants Association**, 11 Poseidonos Av., Alimos, ℗ (01) 985 0122, 105 57 Athens, ℗ 323 0330. In the UK, the **Yacht Charter Association**, 60 Silverdale, New Milton, Hampshire BH25 7DE, ℗ (01425) 619004, supplies a list of its recognized yacht charter operators and offers advice on chartering overseas.

Flotilla and Sailing Holidays

If you want to float among the islands on the wine-dark sea, but don't own your own yacht, or lack the experience to charter one, a flotilla holiday may be just the answer. A growing number of flotilla companies offer one- or two-week sailing holidays, some of which will take on instructing even the most inexperienced sailors (usually beginning with a week based on land). High season prices for a fortnight's holiday range from £550 per person to £9000 per head, on a four-person yacht. The yachts have 4–8 berths (there are shared boats available for couples and singles) and sail in flotillas, usually from six to a dozen yachts, supervised by a lead boat, with experienced skipper, engineer and social hostess. Plenty of free time built in.

operators

Agemennon Yachts, 213B Karaiskaki St., 26222 Pátras, Greece, ℗/✉ (00 30) 61 344009, *skp@hi way.gr*. Yacht charters.

BUOYS Cruising Club, 8 Chase Side, Enfield, Middlesex EN2 6NF, England, ℗ (0181) 367 8462. Charters from Athens.

Euroyacht, 22 Akti Themistokleous, 18536 Piraeus, Greece, ℗ (00 30) 1 428 1920, ✉ 1 428 1926. Bareboat or crewed sail or motor boats, and flotilla sailing.

Ghiolman Yachts, 7 Filellinon St, Athens, ℗ 323 3696. Besides yachts, can supply mobile phones, helicopters, planes, and even put private islands at your disposal.

Grecian Holidays, 75 The Donway West, Don Mills, Ontario M3C 2E9, Canada, ℗ (800) 268 6786, ✉ (416) 510 1509.

Greek Island Cruise Centre, 4321 Lakemoor Dr., Wilmington, NC, 28405, USA ℗ (800) 341 3030. Yacht charters.

Just Boats, Kontakali 49100 Corfu, Greece, ℗ (00 30) 661 90932, ✉ 90837, *root@ just_boats.ker.forthnet.gr*. Crewed and bareboat yachts, flotilla holidays, caiques.

Interpac Yachts, 1050 Anchorage Lane, San Diego, CA, 92106 USA, toll free ℗ (888) 99 YACHT. Crewed power or sail yacht charters.

The Moorings, 188 Northdown Road, Cliftonville, Kent CT9 2QN, England ✆ (01843) 227140. Offers charters from Corfu.

McCulloch Marine, 32 Fairfield Road, London E3 2QB, England ✆ (0181) 983 1487. Offers charters from Athens.

Odysseus Yachting Holidays, 33 Grand Parade, Brighton BN2 2QA, England ✆ (01273) 695094. Flotilla holidays.

Sovereign Sailing, 120 St George's Road, Brighton, BN2 1EA, England, ✆ (01273) 626284. Flotilla holidays.

Sunsail, The Port House, Port Solent, Portsmouth PO6 4TH, England, ✆ (01705) 210345, for dinghies, flotillas, tuitional sailing and watersports.

Valef, 22 Aktí Themistokléous, Piraeus, Greece, ✆ (01) 428 1920, ✉ 428 1926 (in the USA: 7254 Fir Rd, PO Box 391, Ambler, Pa 19002, ✆ (800) 223 3845; in Canada, Islands in the Sun Cruises, 10441 124 St, Edmonton, Alberta, T5N 1R7, ✆ toll free (800) 661 7958. *VALEF@ix.netcom.com*, *http//ValefYachts.com*). One of the largest and most reputable firms, with more than 300 crewed yachts, accommodating 4–50 people from $300 to $8000 a day.

Windstar Cruises, Standard House, 15–16 Bonhill St, London, EC2P 2EA, England, ✆ (0171) 628 7711. Yacht charters.

World Expeditions Ltd, 7 North Road, Maidenhead, Berkshire, SL6 1TL, England, ✆ (01628) 74174. Yacht charters.

Womanship, Learn to Sail Cruises For and By Women, USA, ✆ (800) 324 9295. North American company specialising in women-only flotilla holidays in the Greek islands.

Yacht Agency Rhodes, 1 Vyronos & Canada, P.O. Box 393, 85100 Rhodes, Greece, ✆ (00 30) 241 22927, ✉ 241 23393, *yar@cn.forthnet.gr*. Yacht charters.

yacht repair yards

And in case something goes wrong...

Corfu: ✆ (0661) 39 578. **Glýfada (Athens):** ✆ (01) 894 7353. **Pátras:** ✆ (061) 423830. **Piraeus Marina Zéa:** ✆ (01) 428 4100. **Préveza:** (0682) 23014/26 593.

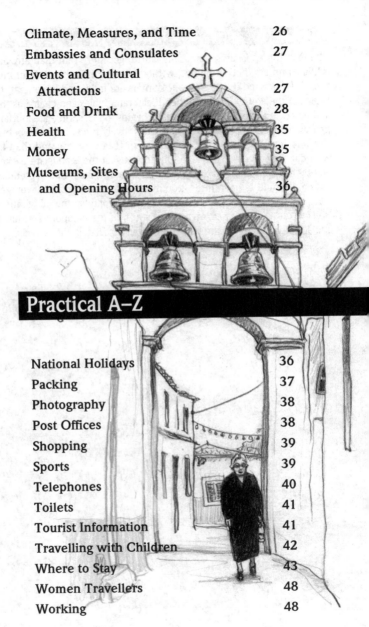

Practical A–Z

Climate, Measures, and Time

The lush Ionian islands, especially Corfu, get more rain than any part of Greece, while summers tend to be hot, without the natural air-conditioning provided by the *meltémi* wind in the Aegean. Winters are mild, and in general the wet season begins at the end of October when it can rain 'tables and chairs' as the Greeks say, and peters out in early April. It usually begins to feel spring-like in March, when the first wildflowers appear, and an especially lovely time to come is between mid-May and mid-June: the flowers are still out, the sea is warm, and the nights are alive with dazzling firefly displays. In July and August the islands are packed to the gills, and there's something happening 24 hours a day; from mid-September to October, the crowds and temperatures drop, but the sea is still warm (average temperature 21C, or 70F) and the lusher islands enjoy a second 'spring' of wildflowers. Kýthera isolated on its lonesome down to the south of the Peloponnese, has a much drier and sunnier climate, of the type more often associated with Greece.

Average Daily Temperatures

	Athens		Corfu		Kýthera	
	F°	C°	F°	C°	F°	C°
Jan	48	11	50	10	54	12
Feb	49	11	51	10	54	12
Mar	54	12	52	12	56	13
April	60	16	60	15	61	17
May	68	20	66	19	68	20
June	76	25	71	21	74	23
July	82	28	78	27	76	25
Aug	82	28	78	26	76	25
Sept	76	25	74	23	74	23
Oct	66	19	66	19	68	20
Nov	58	15	58	15	63	18
Dec	52	12	54	12	58	14

Two uniquely Greek **measurements** you may come across are the *strémma*, a Greek land measurement (1 *strémma* = ¼ acre), and the *oká*, an old-fashioned weight standard, divided into 400 *drams* (1 *oká* = 3lb; 35 *drams* = ¼lb, 140 *drams* = 1lb).

'God gave watches to the Europeans and time to the Greeks,' they say; if you need more precision, **Greek time** is Eastern European, two hours ahead of Greenwich Mean Time, and seven hours ahead of Eastern Standard Time in North America.

Embassies and Consulates

Australia: 37 D. Soútsou, 115 21 Athens, ✆ 644 7303, ✉ 644 3633.

Canada: 4 I. Gennadíou, 115 21 Athens, ✆ 725 4011, ✉ 725 3994.

Ireland: 7 Vass. Konstantínou, 106 74 Athens, ✆ 723 2771, ✉ 724 0217. Also *see* **Corfu**, p.107.

New Zealand: 24 Xenia, 115 28 Athens ✆ 771 0112.

Netherlands: 5–7 Vas. Konstantínou, Athens, ✆ 723 9701. Also *see* **Corfu**, p.107.

South Africa: 60 Kifissías, 151 25 Maroússi, ✆ 680 6459, ✉ 689 5320.

United Kingdom: 1 Ploutárchou Street, 106 75 Athens, ✆ 723 6211, ✉ 724 1872. Also *see* **Corfu**, p.107.

USA: 91 Vassilías Sofías, 115 21 Athens, ✆ 721 2951, ✉ 645 6282.

Events and Cultural Attractions

Besides the big religious and national holidays, the Ionian islands offer a wide range of other events in the summer. Each island has a section on its own particular feast days; below is a list of more ambitious annual events. Dates squirm around a lot; ring the National Tourist Organization a month or two before the event to pin them down.

February

Carnival, Zákynthos and Kefaloniá.

June

Theatre Competition, young writers present their plays on Ithaca.

June–September

Athens Festival. International culture. Modern and ancient theatre, jazz, classical music and dance, often with visiting British companies, in the stunning setting of the Herodus Atticus Odeon beneath the Acropolis. Also a wide range of performances at the Lycabettus Theatre, Lykavitós Hill, including the **International Jazz and Blues Festival** in late June.

Epídávros Festival in the Peloponnese. Ancient Greek drama under the stars in an authentic setting, so take a cushion or something to sit on. Special buses from Athens. Festivals Box Office, 4 Stadíou Street, Athens, in the arcade, © 322 1459.

July

Ithaca Music Contest. Modern Greek composers show off their work.

August

Zákyntheia, Zákynthos cultural events.

International Folklore Festival, Lefkáda, with groups from around the world.

Wine Festivals, Zákynthos, with music and celebrities.

August–September

International Meeting of Medieval and Popular Theatre, Zákynthos.

Kefaloniá International Choral Music Festival, Lixoúri. Gathering of Greek and foreign choirs, symphony orchestras and folk dance groups.

Classical Music Festival, Paxí, with international musicians.

September

Corfu Festival, with classical music concerts and other events.

Robolo Festival, wine festival at Omala, Kefaloniá.

Food and Drink

Life's fundamental principle is the satisfaction of the needs and wants of the stomach. All important and trivial matters depend on this principle and cannot be differentiated from it.

Epicurus, 3rd century BC

Epicurus may have given his name to gourmets, but in reality his philosophy was an economical one that advocated maximizing the simple pleasures of life: rather than continually seek novelty and delight in ever more extremes, Epicurus suggests, make a plate of bread and olives taste sublime by fasting for a couple of days. In that way modern Greeks are all epicureans: centuries of occupation and extreme poverty have taught them to relish food more than cuisine, and they eat with great zest and conviviality. Meals are not about scaling gastronomic heights, but a daily reminder to the Greeks of who they are and what their country has to offer—fish from the seas, lamb from the valleys, fresh herbs and honey from the mountains, wild young greens from the hills, olives, fruits and nuts from the groves. The method of cooking these things is often quite simple; Turkish and Italian influences remain strong, just as they do in the language. What's more, recent studies show that Greek food not only tastes good, but is remarkably good for you, too.

For all that, Greece has acquired a poor reputation for food. In the 1970s, the relatively few restaurants that existed, especially on the islands, were overrun. Standards fell as they tried to cope with the influx of people; standards fell even lower when making as much money as possible in a few short months became the overriding consideration. Neither did the first generation of taverna owners in the tourist age see any reason to improve; the masses, mostly travelling on a shoestring, seemed content with cheap village salads, reheated moussaká, kebabs, taramosaláta and more kebabs, often served in a kind of caricature of Greekiness (plastic grapes and Zorba, Zorba, Zorba). Others, like the hotel owner in Páxos who dished out tinned brussels sprouts with everything, struggled haplessly to please middle-aged customers from the pale north who swore that they couldn't abide garlic or even olive oil, which in Greece is close to nectar (guide books used to train their readers to say 'WHORE-is LA-thi, parakaLO'—'without oil, please').

While too many tourist tavernas still grind out greasy grub, advertised with plastic idiotic photos of food sun-blasted over the years into greenish plates of flaking scabs (no wonder that they have to hire obnoxious touts who drag in clients from the street!), their days seem to be numbered, as diners have come to know and expect better. The new generation of taverna owners are making a concerted effort to offer real Greek cooking, reviving recipes handed down from mother to daughter, recipes very much based on what's in season: vegetables like butter beans, green beans and okra in rich tomato and olive oil sauces; *briáms* of aubergines and courgettes; beetroot with hot garlic *skordaliá* dip; stuffed, lightly battered courgette flowers; prawns in filo parcels; octopus *stifádo*; beef stew with baby onions; lamb grazed on mountain herbs baked with fresh dill, yoghurt and lemon; ragout of snails, and whitebait so fresh they're almost wriggling. A simple sun-ripened Greek tomato in August, sprinkled with fresh oregano and anointed with olive oil from the family grove, is enough to jump-start the old taste buds. Just try to reproduce the same sensation back home.

One criticism levelled at Greek food is that it's served cold. It usually is, and that's because Greeks believe tepid food is better for the digestion than hot in the summer (once you get used to it, you realize that many dishes are actually tastier once they're left to cool in their own juices). The pace of life is different as well. There's no rush. Lunches begin late and stretch long into the afternoon and dinners into the small hours. While we tend to shovel down quick dinners in front of the TV, the gregarious Greeks eat to enjoy, to relax, to talk. A night out with friends in a taverna is the best entertainment going.

vegetarians

Of all the people in the European Union, the Greeks now eat the most meat per capita, but they also eat most cheese, more than even the French, and follow only the Italians in eating pasta. Basically they just eat a lot, which means there are plenty of dishes for vegetarians, a wide range of pulses and *ladera* (fresh vegetable main courses cooked with olive oil, invented for the many Orthodox fasts) and salads from artichokes to aubergines as well as okra, beetroot leaves, spinach-style greens with lemon and in some places *cápari*, pickled caper plant which looks like prunings from a rose bush but tastes delicious. There are delicate cheese and spinach pies in flaky filo pastry, and pasta dishes and pizzas up to Italian standards, thanks to the influx of those pickiest of all diners; stuffed peppers and tomatoes; deep-fried courgettes; *dolmádes*, sometimes using cabbage leaves instead of vines.

If you're a vegetarian or used to buying pre-packed, sanitized meat, it's worth pointing out that in many parts of Greece, especially the remoter islands, food comes on the hoof, on the wing or in the net. It's not uncommon to see a kid or sheep despatched near a taverna by day and then turn up on the menu at night. Bunnies hopping round the village also hop into the pot, the family pig turns into sausages, free-range chickens end up being barbecued and after a while the washing line of drying octopus becomes part of the scenery.

Eating Out

So how can you find a good place to eat? As always, follow the locals. Greek families aren't going to throw away hard-earned cash on tourist food. If you're hungry for something a cut above taverna fare, keep an eye open for restaurants that have made an effort to revive traditional Greek décor, austere but colourful with handpainted signs, painted chairs, weaving and so on; their owners usually prove to be just as serious about reviving traditional recipes in the kitchen.

Greek eating places are divided into five categories. **Tavernas** and *estiatória* (restaurants) are found everywhere and the differences between them tend to get a bit blurred. But you'll generally find the *estiatório* has a wider menu and is a bit more upmarket. Tavernas are more like family-run bistros and can range from shacks on the beach to barn-like affairs called *Kéntrikos* that provide music in the evening. There may not be a menu as such. The waiter will reel off what's on or even invite you to have a look for yourself. Mine host may have some special fish, a lobster or 'dish of the day'. Homemade English translations may leave you more baffled than ever (*see* **Topics**); the **menu decoder** on pp.221–3 may help.

A typical Greek meal begins with a basket of bread and a range of starters that everyone shares: *taramosaláta*, *tzatzíki* (cucumbers and yoghurt), prawns, feta cheese, little cheese or spinach pies, *saganáki* (fried cheese sprinkled with lemon), greens in olive oil and lemon sauces, green beans, okra or butter beans in sauce or fried courgettes and aubergines. These are followed by a shared salad and potatoes, and a main course that you eat on your own—fish, pasta, an oven dish ('ready dishes', moussaká, stuffed vegetables, etc.), or else meat, lamb, pork, beef or kid, either stewed, baked in a casserole (*stifádo*, *kokinistó*, veal *youvétsi* with tear-drop pasta are typical) or freshly grilled (*tis óras*, 'the On Times'), chops (*brizóles*), lamb cutlets (*paidhákia*), souvláki (kebabs), meatballs (*keftédes* or *sousoukákia*), sausages (*lukániko*), or chicken (*koutópolou*, usually free-range). Greeks eat very little duck; if offered 'Quacker', you'll get rolled oats. Desserts are rare outside tourist places, although you may find some fresh watermelon or yogurt; Greeks make lovely sweets, puddings, cakes, and ice creams (just look at the displays in any **zacharoplasteío** or pastry shop) but tend to eat them in the late afternoon with a coffee after the siesta, or in the early evening, hours before dinner.

At the seaside you'll find the fish tavernas, **psarotavérnes**, specializing in all kinds of seafood from freshly fried calamari, shrimps, giant prawns, to red mullet, swordfish, bream and sardines. Ironically, fish is expensive, because of depletion of stocks in the Med, but you can find cheapies like fresh whitebait (*marídes*), cuttlefish stew (*soupiá*), small shrimps (*garídes*), sometimes cooked in feta cheese, and fish soups like *psarósoupa* or spicy *kakavia*, a meal in themselves with hunks of fresh bread and a bottle of wine. When eating fish soup it's customary to remove the fish, put it on a plate, drink the broth, then tuck into the fish. Note that each type of fish has its own price, and portions are priced by weight.

If you're a red-blooded **meat eater** then head for the nearest **hasapotavérna**, which is a grill room attached to a local butcher's shop. Not that common, they offer fresh meat of all kinds, kebabs, home-made sausages and sometimes delicious stews, usually served by the butcher's assistant in a bloodstained apron for added carnivorous effect. The **psistariá** is another version of the theme specializing in chicken, lamb, pork or *kokorétsi*, a kind of lamb's offal doner. You may even find a **mageiria**, simple home-cooking places with old-fashioned pots simmering on the stove , often only open for lunch. Other kinds of eateries in Greece need no introduction: the pizzeria (often spelled *pitsaria*) and in big towns and major resorts, American fast fooderies, along with Goody's, the main Greek clone, and mom-and-pop attempts at the same.

A pitcher or bottle of tap water comes with each meal, and most Greeks order wine or beer. Note that when dining with Greeks it's customary to pour wine for each other—always guests first—and drink constant toasts, glasses chinking—*steen yámass*, good health to us, *steen yássou* or *yássas*, good health to you. By all means clink glasses, but on no account bring your glass down on another person's (unless your intentions for the evening are entirely dishonourable). If a man does it to your glass, it's best to say '*yámass*' and act dumb, unless you want to take him up on it.

Eating out in Greece has always been something of a movable feast. Because of the intense heat in summer, Greek families tend to eat late lunch at home, followed by their siesta or *mesiméri*. Then its back to work, and around 8 or 9pm, it's time for the evening *vólta* or stroll to see and be seen, catch up on the news, and decide where to go. Greeks eat late, rarely before 10pm, and meals can go on into the small hours. The children are there (they too nap in the afternoon) and are more than welcome—babies are rocked, toddlers crawl under the table and the older children get up to goodness knows what. Dinner is often boisterous, punctuated with fiery discussions, maybe bursts of song or dance. The more company round the table the merrier, and the more likely your meal to turn into a spontaneous cabaret that no organized 'Greek Night' can match. You may even get your table whipped away from under you in a dancer's jaws. *Kalí órexi! Bon appetit!*

prices

A **Greek menu**, *katálogos*, usually has two-tier prices—with and without tax; you pay the highest. **Prices** are fixed according to category, although there can be seasonal fluctuations when they jump, especially at Easter and in August. If you suspect you're being ripped off, the system makes it easier to complain. If you eat with the Greeks, there's no Western nit-picking over who's had what. You share the food, drink, company and the bill, *to logariasmó*, although hosts will seldom let foreign guests part with a drachma. A new law designed to catch tax evaders insists that you take a receipt (*apóthexi*); the police make periodical checks. An average taverna meal—if you don't order a major fish—usually runs at around 2500–3000dr a head with generous carafes of house wine (*see* below). Prices at sophisticated restaurants or blatantly touristy places tend to be a bit higher, and places on remote islands can be just as costly because of extra transport prices. Quite a few places now offer set price meals with a glass of wine (often for under 2000dr) some for two people, some better than others. In the 'Eating Out' sections of this book, any price given is per person with house wine.

kafeneíons and cafés

Every one-mule village will have at least one **kafeneíon**, a social institution where men (and increasingly women, although they're still outnumbered) gather to discuss the latest news, read the papers, nap in hard wooden chairs, play cards or backgammon and incidentally drink coffee. Some men seem to live in them. They are so essential to Greek identity that in at least one instance, on Skópelos, when real estate interests threatened the last old *kafeneíon* with extinction, the town hall opened one for its citizens. The bill of fare features Greek coffee (*café hellinikó*), which is the same stuff as Turkish coffee, prepared to order in 40 different ways, although *glykó* (sweet), *métrio* (medium) and *skéto* (no sugar) are the basic orders. It is always served with a glass of water. '*Nes*' aka Nescafé with condensed Dutch milk has by popular tourist demand become available everywhere, though Greeks prefer their instant coffee whipped and iced (*frappé*)—and it's lovely on a hot day. Tea will be a pot of hot water and a bag. Soft drinks, *tsikoúdia* (rakí), brandy, and *ouzo* round out the old-style *kafeneíon* fare.

Newer cafés (those with the cushy soft plastic chairs under awnings) usually open much earlier and close much later than *kafeneíons*. They are good places to find various kinds of breakfast, from simple to complete English, with rashers, baked beans and eggs, and attempts at cappuccinos. They also serve mineral water (try the sparkling IOΛH), ice cream concoctions, milkshakes, fruit juices, cocktails, pastries, and thick Greek yoghurt (cow, sheep or goat's milk) and honey. They are also a traditional place to stop for a late-night Metaxa; the more stars on the label (from three to seven), the smoother and the higher the price.

bars (barákia) and ouzeriés

Nearly every island has at least one trendy music bar, usually playing the latest hit records and serving fancy cocktails as well as standard drinks. These establishments come to life at cocktail hour then again around midnight, when everyone has spent the day on the beach and the earlier part of the evening in a taverna. Bars used to close at dawn, although in 1994 the Greek government decreed a 2am weekday closing, claiming that the nation was nodding off at work after a night on the tiles. In general bars are not cheap, sometimes outrageously dear by Greek standards, and it can be disconcerting to realize that you have paid the same for your Harvey Wallbanger as you paid for your entire meal half an hour before in the taverna next door. Cocktails have now risen to beyond the 1000dr mark in many bars, but before you complain remember that the measures are triples by British standards. If in doubt stick to beer (Greece has a new brand to try, Mythos), *ouzo*, *suma* (like *ouzo*, but often sweeter—each island makes its own), wine and Metaxá (Metaxá and Coke, if you can stomach it, is generally about half the price of a rum and coke). One unfortunate practice on the islands is the doctoring of bottles, whereby some bar owners buy cheaper versions of spirits and use them to refill brand-name bottles.

Just when it seemed time to write the obituary on a grand old Greek institution, the **ouzerie**, it has come back with a vengeance. The national aperitif, *ouzo*—the *rakí* drunk by the Byzantines and Venetians, inexplicably renamed *ouzo* in the 18th century from the Latin *usere*, 'usable'—is clear and anise-flavoured, and served in small glasses or a *karafáki* holding about three or four doses which many drinkers dilute and cloud with water. It is cheap and famous for making its imbibers optimistic. As the Greeks look askance at drunkenness—as they did in ancient times, when they cut their wine with water and honey—*ouzo* is traditionally served with a little plate of snacks called *mezédes* which can range from grilled octopus, nuts, olives, chunks of cheese and tomatoes to elaborate seafood platters; for an assortment, ask for a *pikilía* (usually translated as '*seafood various*'). Similar to *ouzeriés* are **mezedopoieíons**, specializing in these Greek tapas, where you can build up an entire meal, sometimes from a hundred choices on the menu, and wash them down with wine or beer.

Wine

The country's best-known wine, **retsína**, has a very distinctive taste of pine resin. In ancient times, when the Greeks stored their wine in clay amphorae sealed airtight with resin; the disintegration of the resin helped prevent oxidation in the wine and lent it its distinctive flavour. It is an acquired taste, and many people can be put off by the pungent odour and sharp taste of some bottled varieties. Modern *retsínas* show increasingly restrained use of resin; all *retsínas* are best appreciated well-chilled. Draught *retsína* (*retsína varelísio*) can be found only on some islands, but in Athens it is the accepted, delicious accompaniment to the meal. Retsína is admirably suited to Greek food, and after a while you may find non-resinated wines a rather bland alternative. Traditionally it comes to the table in chilled copper-anodized jugs, by the kilo (about a litre), or *mesó kiló* (half) or *tétarto* (250ml) and served in small tumblers. Etiquette requires that they are never filled to the brim or drained empty; you keep topping up your companions' glasses, as best you can.

Ordinary red and white **house wines** are often locally produced bargains—ask for *krasí varelísio* (barrelled wine) or *krasí chíma* (loose wine). These wines are nearly always better than fine, though you may be unlucky and get one that's a stinker; if you're suspicious, order a *tétarto kiló*. Kefaloniá produces the best wines on the Ionian islands, especially Robolo, marketed through Greece. On Ithaca try the red wine, and on Zákynthos look for Verdea, a white wine with green tints that when kept in casks tastes something like sherry, ranging from 14–16° proof.

Greece also produces an ample selection of medium-priced red and white wines in bottles. They tend to be highly regionalized, each island and village offering their own varieties made from indigenous grapes; forget the tyranny of Cabernet Sauvignon and Chardonnay. All the principal wine companies—Boutari, Achaia-Clauss, Carras, Tsantali—have made strides to improve the quality in the past decade, investing heavily in new equipment and foreign expertise, and it shows; even that humblest of bottles (and Greece's best-seller) Deméstika has become very acceptable of late, and bears little resemblance to the rough stuff that earned it some unflattering sound-alike nicknames. Look out for the nobler labels; Boutari Náoussa is an old-style, slightly astringent red, while Boutari's Grande Réserve is their best red; Lac des Roches is their most popular white on the islands. Peloponnesiakos from Achaia-Clauss is an easy-drinking, light white wine which is faddishly popular at the moment anywhere within exportable distance of the Peloponnese. From Carras, Château Carras is a Bordeaux-style red wine made from the Cabernet Sauvignon and Merlot grapes; if you're lucky you might find Carras Limnio, one of Greece's most distinct red wines. Boutari's Santoríni is their finest island white, while in Rhodes CAIR supplies Greece with its sparkling *méthode traditionelle* white, Caïr. Emery produces some good whites including Villare. The most noble red wines come from Nemea, and are superb with roast lamb.

In recent years small bottle-producers have become very fashionable with the wine-drinking elite. Some of these are superb; others deserve obscurity. But for the most part you are unlikely to come across them in the average taverna. If you're a wine buff, it's worth seeking them out from local recommendations in wine shops (*kávas*) and high-class restaurants.

Health

At the bare minimum there is at least one doctor (*iatrós*) on every island with more than a couple of hundred people, whose office hours are from 9 to 1 and from 5 to 7. On bigger islands there are hospitals which are open all day, and outpatient clinics, open in the mornings. EU citizens are entitled to free medical care; British travellers are often urged to carry a Form E111, available from DSS offices (apply well in advance on a form CM1 from post offices), which will admit them to the most basic IKA (Greek NHS) hospitals for treatment; but this doesn't cover medicines or nursing care. In any case, the E111 seems to be looked on with total disregard outside Athens; expect to pay up front, and get receipts so you can be reimbursed back home. As private doctors and hospital stays can be very expensive, you should take out a travel insurance policy. You should make sure your holiday insurance has adequate repatriation cover; Greek hospitals have improved by leaps and bounds but as it's still common for families to supply food and help with the nursing, you may feel neglected. Non-Europeans should check their own health policies to see if they're covered while abroad.

Greek general practitioners' fees are usually reasonable. Most doctors pride themselves on their English, as do the pharmacists (found in the *farmakeío*), whose advice on minor ailments is good, although their medicine is not particularly cheap. If you forgot to bring your own condoms and are caught short, they are widely available from *farmakeío* and kiosks, with lusty brand names such as 'Squirrel' or 'Rabbit'. If you can't see them on display, the word *kapótes* (condom) gets results. You can also get the Pill (*chápi antisiliptikó*), morning-after Pill and HRT over the pharmacy counter without a prescription. Be sure to take your old packet to show them the brand you use. For some reason Greeks buy more medicines than anyone else in Europe (is it hypochondria? the old hoarding instinct?) but you shouldn't have to. The sun is the most likely cause of grief, so be careful, hatted and sun-screened. If you find the olive oil too much, Coca Cola or *retsína* will help cut it. Fresh parsley is good for stomach upsets. See pp.63–5 for possibly unkind wildlife. If anything else goes wrong, do what the islanders have done for centuries: pee on it.

Money

The word for **bank** in Greek is *trápeza*, derived from the word *trapézi*, or table, used back in the days of money-changers. On all the islands with more than goats and a few shepherds there is some sort of banking establishment, or, increasingly, at least an automatic teller. If there's no bank, travel agents, tourist offices or post offices will change cash, traveller's cheques and Eurocheques. If you plan to spend time on a remote island, such as Schinoússa, it is safest to bring enough drachmae with you. Beware that small but popular islands often have only one bank, where exchanging money can take forever: beat the crowds by going at 8am, when the banks open (normal banking hours are 8–2, 8–1.30 on Friday). The number of 24-hour **automatic cash-tellers** on the islands grows every year: some accept one kind of credit card and not another (VISA is perhaps the most widely accepted). You can also use these to withdraw cash at banks. Major hotels, luxury shops and resort restaurants take cards (look for the little signs) but smaller hotels and tavernas certainly won't.

Traveller's cheques are always useful even though commission rates are less for cash. Major brands (Thomas Cook and American Express) are accepted in all banks and post offices; take your passport as ID, and shop around for commission rates.

Running out? Athens and Piraeus, with offices of many British and American banks, are the easiest places to have money sent by cash transfer from someone at home—though it may take a few days. **American Express** may be helpful here; their office in Athens is 2 Ermou St, right by Sýntagma Square, ✆ 324 4975, and there are branches on Corfu and Pátras.

The Greek drachma (abbreviated dr, in Greek δρχ) is circulated in coins of 100, 50, 20, 10, and 5dr. and in notes of 100, 500, 1000, 5000 and 10,000dr.

Museums and Archaeological Sites and Opening Hours

Significant archaeological sites and museums have regular admission hours. Nearly all are closed on Mondays, and open other weekdays from 8 or 9am to around 2pm, although more important sites now tend to stay open later, until 4 or 5pm. Hours tend to be shorter in the winter. On the other hand, churches are often open only in late afternoon (from 6 to 7pm), when they're being cleaned. Students with valid ID often get a discount on admission fees. These are usually between 400 and 1000dr; more expensive ones are listed as such in the text.

National Holidays

Most businesses and shops close down for the afternoon before and the morning after a religious holiday. If a national holiday falls on a Sunday, the following Monday is observed. Orthodox Easter is generally a week after Roman Easter.

1 January	New Year's Day	*Protochroniá*; also *Ag.Vassílios* (Greek Father Christmas)
6 January	Epiphany	*Ta Fóta/ Theofánia*
February–March	'Clean Monday' (precedes Shrove Tuesday, and follows a three-week carnival)	*Katharí Deftéra*
25 March	Annunciation/ Independence Day	*Evangelismós*
late March–April	Good Friday	*Megáli Paraskeví*
	Easter Sunday	*Páscha*
	Easter Monday	*Theftéra tou Páscha*

1 May	Labour Day	*Protomayá*
40 days after Easter	Pentecost (Whit Monday)	*Pentikostí*
15 August	Assumption of the Virgin	*Koímisis tis Theotókou*
28 October	'Ochí' Day (in celebration of Metaxás' 'no' to Mussolini)	
25 December	Christmas	*Christoúyena*
26 December	Gathering of the Virgin	*Sináxi Theotókou*

In Greece, Easter is the equivalent in significance of Christmas and New Year in northern climes, the time when far-flung relatives return to see their families back home; it's a good time of year to visit for the atmosphere, feasts and fireworks. After Easter and May 1, spring (*ánixi*—the opening) has offically come, and the tourist season begins. Festival dates for saints' days listed in the text vary over a period of several given days, or even weeks, owing to the Greek liturgical calendar's calculations for Easter; check these locally. It's also worth remembering that the main partying often happens the night *before* the saint's day.

Packing

Even in the height of summer, evenings can be chilly in Greece, especially when the *meltémi* wind is blowing. Always bring at least one warm sweater and a pair of long trousers, and sturdy and comfortable shoes if you mean to do any walking—trainers (sneakers) are usually good enough. Plastic swimming shoes are handy for rocky beaches, often the haunt of those little black pincushions, sea urchins; you can easily buy them near any beach if you don't want to carry them around with you. Greeks are inveterate night people: bring ear plugs if you don't want to hear them scootering home under your hotel window at 4am.

If you travel in August without any reservations, consider bringing a sleeping bag, just in case your destination is all full up. Serious sleeping-baggers should also bring a Karrimat or similar insulating layer to cushion them from the gravelly Greek ground. Torches come in very handy for moonless nights, caves and rural villages. Note that the **electric current** in Greece is mainly 220 volts, 50Hz; plugs are continental two-pin. Buy an adaptor in the UK before you leave, as they are rare in Greece; North Americans will need adaptors and transformers.

On the pharmaceutical side, bring extras of any prescription drug you need, just in case—other items, such as seasickness remedies, sunscreen, insect repellent, women's sanitary towels and sometimes Tampax, tablets for stomach upsets and aspirin are widely available in pharmacies and even kiosks, but on remote islands you'll need to seek out the *farmakeío*; if there's no pharmacy, you've had it. Soap, washing powder, a clothes line, a knife for picnics and especially a towel are essential budget traveller's gear. A photo of the family and home is always appreciated by new Greek friends.

Let common sense and the maxim 'bring as little as possible and never more than you can carry' dictate your packing; work on the theory that however much money and clothing you think you need, halve the clothes and double the money.

Photography

Greece lends herself freely to photography, but a fee is charged at archaeological sites and museums. For a movie camera of any kind, including camcorders, you are encouraged to buy a ticket for the camera; with a tripod you pay per photograph at sites, but cameras (especially tripod-mounted ones) are not allowed in museums, for no particular reason other than the museum's maintaining a monopoly on its own (usually very dull) picture stock. 35mm film, both print and slide, can be found in many island shops, though it tends to be expensive and the range of film speeds limited. Disposable and underwater cameras are on sale in larger holiday resorts. Large islands even have one-hour developing services.

The light in the summer is often stronger than it seems and is the most common cause of ruined photographs; opting for slow film or filters will help. Greeks usually love to have their pictures taken, and, although it's more polite to ask first, you should just go ahead and take the photo if you don't want them to strike a pose. You should avoid taking pictures (well, who would want to anyway?) of the aircraft, military installations and barracks, communications systems on mountain tops, and military look-out posts. If you have an expensive camera, it never hurts to insure it. Above all, never leave it alone. Although Greeks themselves very rarely steal anything, other tourists are not so honest.

Post Offices

Signs for post offices (*tachidromío*) as well as postboxes (*grammatokivótio*) are bright yellow and easy to find. Post offices (which are also useful for changing money) are open from Monday to Saturday 7.30am to 8pm; on small islands they may shut for lunch. Stamps (*grammatósima*) can also be bought at kiosks and in some tourist shops, although they may charge a small commission. Be warned that postcards can take up to three weeks to arrive at their destinations, while anything in an envelope will usually get there in a week or so, depending on the route. If you're in a hurry, pay extra for an express service. To send a package, always go to an island's main post office. If you do not have an address, mail can be sent to you poste restante to any post office in Greece, and picked up with proof of identity (you'll find the postal codes for all the islands in the text, which will get your letters there faster). After one month all unretrieved letters are returned to sender. In small villages, particularly on the islands, mail is not delivered to the house but to the village centre, either a *kafeneíon* or bakery.

Shopping

Official shopping hours in Greece are: Mon, Wed 9–5; Tues, Thurs and Fri 10–7, Sat 8.30–3.30 and Sun closed; in practice, tourist-orientated shops stay open as late as 1am in season. Leather goods, gold and jewellery, traditional handcrafts, embroideries, and weavings, onyx, ceramics, alabaster, herbs and spices and tacky knick-knacks are favourite purchases; also check the text for island specialities. Duty-free Rhodes has some of the biggest bargains.

Non-EU citizens tempted by Greek jewellery, carpets, perfumes and other big ticket items can perhaps justify their indulgences by having the sales tax (VAT) reimbursed—this is 18% of the purchase price (or 13%, on Aegean islands). Make sure the shop has a TAX FREE FOR TOURISTS sticker in the window, spend at least 40,000dr inside, and pick up a tax-free shopping cheque for your purchases. When you leave Greece, you must show your purchases and get the customs official to stamp your cheques (allow an extra hour for this, especially at the airport), and cash them in at the refund point as you leave. If you are flying out of another EU country, hold onto the cheques, get them stamped again by the other EU country's customs and use their refund point. You can also post your tax free cheques back to Greece for refund (10 Nikis St., 10563 Athens, ✆ (01) 325 4995, ✇ (01) 322 4701) but they skim off 20% of the amount on commission.

Sports

watersports

Greece was made for watersports, and by law, all the beaches, no matter how private they might look, are public. All but a fraction meet European guidelines for water cleanliness, although a few could stand to have less litter on the sand. Beaches near built-up areas often have umbrellas and sunbed concessions and snack bars, and if there's a breeze you'll probably find a windsurfer to rent at affordable prices (Léfkas is a favourite windy spot). Bigger beaches have paragliding and jet skis, and waterskiing is available on most islands and large hotel complexes. The Ministry of Tourism has just allocated huge sums to build up marinas on the islands, which may improve chances of finding a small sail or motor boat to hire by the day; at the time of writing they are relatively few.

Scuba diving, once strictly banned to keep divers from snatching antiquities and to protect Greece's much-harassed marine life, is permitted between dawn and sunset in specially defined coastal areas; local diving excursions will take you there. In the Ionian islands, the areas are **Corfu** (around Cape Róda, Paleokastrítsa, and Cape Kountoúri), Meganíssi island by **Léfkas**, off most of **Páxi**, and **Zákynthos** (Láganas bay). For information, contact the Hellenic Federation of Underwater Activities, Post Office of the West Air Terminal, 16604 Elliniko, ✆ (01) 981 9961.

Nudism is forbidden by law in Greece, but tolerated in numerous designated or out-of-the-way areas. On the other hand, topless sunbathing is now legal on the majority of popular beaches as long as they're not smack in the middle of a village; exercise discretion. Even young Greek women are shedding their tops, but nearly always on someone else's island.

Average Sea Temperatures

Jan	Feb	Mar	April	May	June	July	Aug	Sept	Oct	Nov	Dec
59°F	59°F	59°F	61°F	64°F	72°F	75°F	77°F	75°F	72°F	64°F	63°F
15°C	15°C	15°C	16°C	18°C	22°C	24°C	25°C	24°C	22°C	18°C	17°C

land sports

Walking is the favourite activity on every island, but especially on Corfu, with its superb natural scenery and wildflowers; *see* 'special interest holidays', pp.17–9, for guided walking tours. Increasingly locals are arranging treks, and little, often locally produced maps and guides, are a big help for finding the most interesting country paths. Never set out without a hat and water; island shops have begun to sell handy water-bottle shoulder slings. **Tennis** is very popular in Athens with numerous clubs from Glyfáda to Kifissiá, and at all major resort hotels (many are lit up at night so you can beat the heat); often non-residents are allowed to play in the off season. **Golf courses** are rare but there's one on the Ionians: the **Corfu Golf Club**, Rópa Valley, P.O. Box 71, ℗ (0663) 94 220, has 18 holes, par 72, practice range, and similar facilities. Green fees are 7000dr daily in May, Sept and Oct, and less in other months. Many small stables offer horse-riding on the islands. For details, call the **Riding Club of Greece**, Parádissos, ℗ 682 6128 and Riding Club of Athens, Gerakos, ℗ 661 1088.

Telephones

The new improved Organismós Telefikoinonía Elládos, or OTE, has replaced most of its old phone offices with new card phones, which work a treat, although many on the islands, for some reason, are set up for basketball players only. If you can reach the buttons, you can dial abroad direct (dial 00 before the country code). Cards for 100 units are 1500dr. For a decent long-distance chat you may need more, although the 500 unit 6500dr and the 1000 unit 11,500dr *telekártas* are hard to find outside of big resort areas. As a last resort, find a telephone *me métriki* (with a meter), which are often more costly and usually located in kiosks (*períptera*), *kafeneíons*, some travel agents, hotels, and shops. As a general rule, calls are cheaper between 3–5pm and after 9pm, but this may change. **Telegrams** can be sent from one of the surviving OTE offices in big cities or from the post office. When **phoning Greece** from overseas, the country code is 30 and drop the first '0' of the local area code.

Toilets

Greek plumbing has improved dramatically in the past few years, and in the newer hotels you can flush everything away as merrily as you do at home, at least as often as your conscience lets you on arid islands strapped for water. Tavernas, *kafeneíons* and sweet shops almost always have facilities (it's good manners to buy something), and there are often public pay toilets in strategic area of the towns.

In older pensions and tavernas, the plumbing often makes up in inventiveness for what it lacks in efficiency. Do not tempt fate by disobeying the little notices 'the papers they please to throw in the basket'—or it's bound to lead to trouble (a popular new sticker has Poseidon himself bursting out of the toilet bowl and pricking an offender with his trident). Old *kafeneíons* and bus stations tend to have only a ceramic hole squatter. Always have paper of some sort handy.

If you stay in a private room or pension you may have to have the electric water heater turned on for about 20 minutes before you take a shower. In most smaller pensions, water is heated by a solar panel on the roof, so the best time to take a shower is in the late afternoon, or the early evening (before other residents use up the finite supply of hot water). In larger hotels there is often hot water in the mornings and evenings, but not in the afternoons. Actually 'cold' showers in the summer aren't all that bad, because the tap water itself is generally lukewarm, especially after noon. A good many showers are of the hand-held variety, which is potentially dangerous (especially if you have kids) because Greeks don't believe in shower curtains and one thoughtless moment means your towel or toilet paper are soaked.

Greek tap water is perfectly safe to drink, but on some islands it tastes less than delicious. On the other hand, inexpensive plastic bottles of spring water are widely available (and responsible for untold pollution, taking up half the available room in landfill sites).

Tourist Information

If the National Tourist Organization of Greece (in Greek the initials are **EOT**) can't answer your questions about Greece, at least they can refer you to someone who can. They have set up a rather good internet site on the Ionians at *http://www.areianet.gr/infoxenios/english/ionian/ionian.htm* with practical information and advice.

There are several other general sites dedicated to the Ionian islands:
http://www2.shef.ac.uk/info_studies/studwork/agos/ionian/ionian.html
http://odysseas.com/ (followed by name of the island) for pictures and basic info.

Australia and New Zealand

51 Pitt Street, Sydney, NSW 2000, ℗ 9241 1663/4, ✆ 9235 2174.

Canada

1300 Bay Street, Toronto, Ontario, M5R3K8, ℗ (416) 968 2220, ✆ 968 6533.

1233 De La Montagne, Montreal, Quebec, H3G1Z2 ℗ (514) 871 1535, ✆ 871 1498.

Great Britain and Ireland

4 Conduit Street, London W1R 0DJ, ℗ (0171) 734 5997/499 4976, ✆ 287 1369.

Netherlands

Leidsestraat 13, NS 1017 Amsterdam ℗ 625 4212/3/4, ✆ 620 7031.

USA

Head Office: Olympic Tower, 645 Fifth Avenue, 5th Floor, New York, NY 10022, ℗ (212) 421 5777; ✆ 826 6940, *gnto@orama.com*

168 N. Michigan Avenue, Chicago, Illinois. 60601, ℗ (312) 782 1084, ✆ 782 1091.

611 West Sixth Street, Suite 2198, LA, Calif. 90017, ℗ (213) 626 6696, ✆ 489 9744.

in Greece

The most popular islands have EOT offices, while the others often have some form of local tourist office; if not, most have tourist police (usually located in an office in the regular police station, although nine times out of ten they're the only people on the island who don't speak any foreign language). If nothing else, they have listings of rooms on the island. **Legal Assistance for Tourists** is available free, but in July and Aug only: in Athens at 43-45 Valtetsiou St, ℗ (01) 330 0673, ✆ (01) 330 1137; in Pátras, at 213B Kointhou St, ℗ (061) 272481.

Travelling with Children

Greece is a great country for children, who are not barely tolerated, but generally enjoyed and encouraged. Depending on their age, they go free or receive discounts on ships and buses. However, if they're babies, don't count on island pharmacies stocking your brand of milk powder or baby foods—they may have some, but it's safest to bring your own supply. Disposable nappies, especially Pampers, are widely available, even on small islands.

Travelling with a tot is like having a special passport. Greeks adore them and spoil them rotten, so don't be surprised if your infant is passed round like a parcel. Greek children usually have an afternoon nap (as do their parents) so it's quite normal for Greeks to eat *en famille* until the small hours. Finding a babysitter is rarely a problem: some of the larger hotels even offer special supervised kiddie campgrounds and activity areas for some real time off.

Superstitions are still given more credit than you might expect; you'll see babies with amulets pinned to their clothes or wearing blue beads to ward off the evil eye before their baptism. Beware of commenting on a Greek child's intelligence, beauty or whatever, as this may call down the jealous interest of the old gods and some of the nastier saints. The response in the old days was to spit in the admired child's face, but these days, superstitious grannies are usually content with a ritual 'phtew-phtew-phtew' dry spit, to protect the child from harm.

Where to Stay

Hotels

All hotels in Greece are classed into six categories: Luxury, A, B, C, D and E. This grading system bears little relationship to the quality of service, charm, views, etc., but everything to do with how the building is constructed, size of bedrooms, lifts, and so on; i.e. if the hotel has a marble-clad bathroom it gets a higher rating.

Pensions, most without restaurants, are a confusing subdivision in Greek hotel classifications, especially as many call themselves hotels. They are family-run and more modest (an A class pension is roughly equivalent to a C or D class hotel and is priced accordingly). A few islands still have their government-built hotels from the 1960s, the Xenias, many of which resemble barracks, the fashion in those junta-ruled days.

On the Internet, *http://www.greekhotel.com* lists, with musical accompaniment, 8000 hotels and villas in Greece, with forms for more information about prices and availability and booking.

prices

Prices are set and strictly controlled by the tourist police. Off season (i.e. mid-September–mid July) you can generally get a discount, sometimes as much as 40%. Other charges include an 8% government tax, a 4.5% community bed tax, a 12% stamp tax, an optional 10% surcharge for stays of only one or two days, an air-conditioning surcharge, as well as a 20% surcharge for an extra bed. All these prices are listed on the door of every room and authorized and checked at regular intervals. If your hotelier fails to abide by the posted prices, or if you have any other reason to believe all is not on the level, take your complaint to the tourist police.

1999 Approximate Hotel Rates (drachma) for High Season
(mid-July–mid-Sept)

	L	A	B	C	D
Single with bath	20–70,000	15–40,000	15–23,000	9–20,000	4–7000
Double with bath	30–200,000	25–50,000	20–35,000	11–28,000	6–14,000

Prices for E hotels are about 20% less than D rates.
Out of season rates are often 30–40% lower.

During the summer, hotels with restaurants may require guests to take their meals in the hotel, either full pension or half pension, and there is no refund for an uneaten dinner. Twelve noon is the official check-out time, although on the islands it is usually geared to the arrival of the next boat. Most Luxury and class A, if not B, hotels situated far from the town or port supply buses or cars to pick up guests. Hotels down to class B all have private en-suite bathrooms. In C most do, as do most Ds; E will have a shower down the hall. In these hotels don't always expect to find a towel or soap, although the bedding is clean.

In the 'Where to Stay' sections of this book, accommodation is listed according to the following price categories:

luxury	29,000 to astronomical
expensive	12,000–30,000
moderate	6000–13,000
inexpensive	4000–7000

Prices quoted in the book are approximate and for **double rooms**.

booking a hotel

The importance of reserving a room in advance, especially during July and August, cannot be over-emphasized. Reservations can be made through the individual hotel, through travel agents, through the Hellenic Chamber of Hotels by writing, at least two months in advance, to 24 Stadíou St, 105 61 Athens, ✆ (01) 322 5449, or in person in Athens, at the Hotels Desk in the National Bank of Greece building, 2 Karageorgi Servias, ✆ 323 7193, open Mon–Thurs 8.30–2, Fri 8.30–1.30, and Sat 9–12.30.

Rooms and Studios

These are for the most part cheaper than hotels and sometimes more pleasant. Although you can still find a few rooms (ΔOMATIA, *domátia*) in private houses, on the whole rooms to rent are found off a family's living quarters, sometimes upstairs or in a separate annexe; an increasing number have en suite baths. One advantage rooms hold over hotels is that nearly all will provide a place to handwash your clothes and a line to hang them on. Another is the widespread availability of basic kitchen facilities (sink, table and chairs, at least a couple of gas rings, fridge, utensils and dishes) which immediately turns a room into a **studio**; these obviously cost a bit more, but out of season the difference is often negligible. Depending on facilities, a double room in high season will cost between 4000–8000dr with bath, a studio from 6000–12,000. Until June and after August prices are always negotiable. Owners will nearly always drop the price per day the longer you stay.

Prices also depend a lot on how much competition exists between owners on each island. On some it's good-natured dog eat dog; when you step off the ferry you will be courted with all kinds of interesting proposals, photos of the rooms and even guidebook reviews of their establishments. On others, room and hotel owners have co-operated to organize accommodation booths by the port to sort out customers; if the room is not within walking distance, they'll collect you in a car or minivan. If you still can't find a room, most travel agencies will be able to dig one up (although these always cost more).

Youth Hostels

Some of these are official and require a membership card from the Association of Youth Hostels, or alternatively an International Membership Card (about 2600dr) from the Greek Association of Youth Hostels, 4 Dragatsaníou Street, Athens, © 323 4107; other hostels are informal, have no irksome regulations, and admit anyone. Most charge extra for a shower, sometimes for sheets. Expect to pay 2000dr a night, depending on the quality of facilities and services offered. The official ones have a curfew, which in Greece means you miss the fun.

Camping Out

The climate of summertime Greece is perfect for sleeping out of doors, especially close to the sea, where the breeze keeps the the worst of the mosquitoes at bay. Unauthorized camping is illegal (the law was enacted to displace gypsy camps, and is still used for this purpose) although each village on each island enforces the ban as it sees fit. Some couldn't care less if you put up a tent at the edge of their beach; in others the police may pull up your tent pegs and fine you. All you can do is ask around to see what other tourists or friendly locals advise. Naturally, the more remote the beach, the less likely you are to be disturbed. Most islands have at least one privately operated camping ground, though most have only minimal facilities. Islands with no campsites at all usually have a beach where free camping is tolerated. If the police are in some places lackadaisical about enforcing the camping regulations, they come down hard on anyone lighting any kind of fire in a forest, and may very well put you in jail for two months; every year fires damage huge swathes of land.

Camping prices are not fixed by law but these are the approximate guidelines, per day: adult, 1200dr; child (4–12), 600dr; caravan,1800dr; small/large tent, 700dr/1400dr; car, 650dr; sleeping bag, 350dr.

Self-catering Holidays

On most islands it is possible to rent cottages or villas, generally for a week or more at a time. Villas can often be reserved from abroad: contact a travel agent or the National Tourist Organisation (EOT) for names and addresses of rental agents, or see the list below. In the off season villas may be found on the spot with a little enquiry, which, depending on the facilities, can work out quite reasonably per person. Generally, the longer you stay, the more economical it becomes. If you book from abroad, packages generally include flights, transfers by coach, ferry, hydrofoil or domestic planes.

in the UK

Best of Greece, 23–24 Margaret St, London, W1N 8LE, ✆ (0171) 331 7070. Luxury villas.

Corfu à la Carte, 8 Deanwood House, Stockross, Newbury, Berks, RG16 8JP, ✆ (01635) 30621. Range of beach and rural cottages on Corfu and Páxos.

CV Travel, 43 Cadogan Street, London SW3 2PR, ✆ (0171) 581 0851. Upmarket villas at fair prices on Corfu and Páxos. The villas have 6-day-a-week maid service; cooks provided on request. The friendly staff are very knowledgeable and really care about the islands; they support local charities and one employee also runs the **Kérkyra Bird and Wildlife Sanctuary,** set up to treat injured birds.

Direct Greece, Oxford House, 182 Upper Richmond Rd, Putney, London, SW15 2SH, ✆ (0181) 785 4000. Villas and flats on Corfu, Lefkás and Zákynthos plus low season specials. Reps are extremely helpful and knowledgeable; most have lived in Greece for a long time.

Filoxenia Ltd, Sourdock Hill, Barkisland, Halifax, West Yorkshire, HX4 0AG, ✆ (01422) 371796, ✉ 310340. *Haute couture* holidays to Athens and a select range of islands from tiny Elafónissos to quiet parts of Corfu. Suzi Stembridge and family have scoured Greece for unusual holiday places and pass on their favourites to fellow Grecophiles. Houses, villas, tavernas, pensions, fly-drive. Also **Opus 23** for travellers with disabilities.

Greek Islands Club, 66 High Street,Walton-on-Thames, KT12 1BU, ✆ (01932) 220477, ✉ 229346; USA and Canada ✆ (800) 394 5577; *http.//*

www.vch.co.uk/villas/, info@vch.co.uk. Well-run, established specialists of the Ionian Islands, (including Kýthera), with helpful yet unobtrusive reps, and a very wide choice of personalized activity holidays (*see* p.17).

Greek Sun Holidays, 1 Bank Street, Sevenoaks, Kent, TN13 1UW, ✆ (01732) 740317. Helpful and family-run, offering Athens and a range of unusual islands. Tailor-made holidays and two-centre breaks.

Ilios Island Holidays, 18 Market Square, Horsham, West Sussex, RH12 1EU, ✆ (01403) 259788. Self-catering on the Ionians.

Island Wandering, 51A London Road, Hurst Green, Sussex, TN19 7QP, ✆ (01580) 860733, ✉ (01580) 860282. Island-hopping without tears, with hotels or studios on most of the Ionians, pre-booked before you go or with a wandering voucher system.

Kosmar Villa Holidays plc, 358 Bowes Road, Arnos Grove, London, N11 1AN, ✆ (0181) 368 6833. Self-catering villas, studios and apartments on Corfu. Two-centre holidays, flights from Glasgow and Newcastle and good-value family savers.

Manos Holidays, 168–172 Old Street, London, EC1V 9BP, ✆ (0171) 216 8000. Good value holidays to the major resorts and lesser-known islands, island-hopping and two-centres. Ideal for children; they also have low-season specials and singles deals.

Sunvil, Sunvil House, Upper Square, Isleworth, TW7 7BJ ✆ (0181) 568 4499, very friendly, well-run company offering good value self-catering and hotel accommodation on the Ionian islands.

in the USA/Canada

Amphitrion Holidays, 1206 21st St, NWm Suite 100A, Washington DC, 20036, ✆ (800)424 2471, ✉ (202) 872 8210. Houses, villas and apartments.

Apollo Tours, 1051 N. Waukegan Rd, Clenview, IL 60025, ✆ (800) 228 4367, ✉ (847) 724 3277. Upmarket villas and apartments.

CTI Carriers, 65 Overlea Blvd, Suite 201, Toronto, Ontario, M4H 1P1, ✆ (800) 363 8181, ✉ (429) 7159. One of the biggest Canadian operators with attractive villas.

European Escapes, LLC, 483 Second Avenue, San Francisco, CA 94118, Toll-free ✆ (888) EUROLUX, ✉ (415) 386 0477, *EuroEscape@aol.com, http://members.aol.com/euroluxury/.* Luxury villas.

Greek Island Connection, 889 Ninth Ave, New York, NY, 10019, ✆ (212) 581 4784, ✉ (212) 581 5890, *grislcon@gte.net.* Customized villas and condos.

Omega Tours, 3220 West Broadway, Vancouver, British Colmbia, ✆ (800) 663 2669, ✉ (604) 738 7101. Villas and apartments.

Triaena Tours, 850 Seventh Ave, Suite 605, New York, NY, 10019, ✆ (800) 223 1273, ✆ (212) 582 8815. Long-established operator.

Zeus Tours, 209 W. 40th St, New York, NY 10018, ✆ (800) 447 5667, ✆ (212) 764 7912, *www.zeustours.com.*

Women Travellers

Greece is a choice destination for women travellers but going it alone can be viewed as an oddity. Be prepared for a fusillade of questions. Greeks tend to do everything in groups or pairs and can't understand people who want to go solo.

The good news for women, however, is the dying out of that old pest, the *kamáki* (harpoon). These 'harpoons'—Romeos in tight trousers and gold jewellery who used to roar about on motorbikes, hang out in the bars and cafés, strut about jangling their keys, and hunt in pairs or packs—would try to 'spear' as many women as possible, notching up points for different nationalities. A few professional *kamákia* still haunt piano bars in the big resorts, gathering as many hearts, gold chains and parting gifts as they can; they winter all over the world with members of their harem. Thank young Greek women for the decline in *kamáki* swagger. Watching the example set by foreign tourists as well as the torrid soaps and dross that dominate Greek TV, they have decided they've had enough of 'traditional values'. Gone are the days when families used the evening promenade or *vólta* as a bridal market for their carefully sheltered unmarried daughters; now the girls hold jobs, go out drinking with their friends, and move in with their lovers. They laughed at the old *kamákia* so much that ridicule, like bug spray, has killed them dead.

Working

Casual summer jobs on the islands, legal for EU citizens, on the black for others, tend to be bar or restaurant work in a resort (although with the influx of impecunious Albanians low-paying jobs are becoming harder to find) or alternatively as a travel rep/greeter/co-ordinator with island travel offices that deal with holiday companies. Expect wages to pay your expenses but that's about it. One of the seven English/American schools in Athens always seem to be in need of qualified teachers, or, if you have a university degree or TEFL qualification, you may find a job teaching English in a *frontistírion* or private language school (although this is getting to be harder with new laws that give Greeks or people of Greek origin priority). You can get around this by giving private lessons on your own with a bit of advertizing; the market for learning English seems wide open, and you can make quite a decent living. The *Athens News*, the country's English daily, and *The Hellenic Times*, a rather nationalistic weekly paper, often have classified advertisements for domestic, tutorial, and secretarial jobs. Working legally requires an often unpleasant descent into Greek bureaucracy (the local police will tell you what you must do); if you mean to stay over three months, *see* p.17.

History

Each of the various corners of what is now Greece has its own story to tell, and the Ionian islands, located closer to Italy than to Athens, have one of the most colourful. Westerners of various stripes have ruled here far longer than they controlled any other part of Greece, yet at the same time the islands served as a kind of safety deposit box of Hellenism for hundreds of years while the Greek mainland and other islands were occupied by the Turks. At the beginning of the 19th century, the Ionians became the first part of what is now modern Greece to know self-rule since ancient times, a short-lived experience, but a heady one that inspired patriots on the mainland to fight for independence in the 1820s.

Ancient Greeks and Romans

Pirates, conquerors, and earthquakes have conspired with time to leave very few traces of antiquity on the Ionians. The islands were probably settled in the Stone Age by people from Illyria (present-day Albania) among others, although the archaeological evidence on Corfu suggests the first inhabitants there were somehow culturally related to the original Apulian civilization in Italy. But Corfu always remained somewhat apart from its neighbours: the main islands to the south were working in metal by 3000 BC, and actively participated in the Mycenaean golden age of the mainland (rich Mycenaean tombs have been found on Kefaloniá, Lefkás, and Zákynthos, and there was a Mycenaean colony on Kýthera) while Corfu remained backward and apart, lost in legend. Homer was the first to mention the Ionians: Ithaca and

The name Ionian dates back at least to the 6th century BC, but confusingly, has nothing to do with ancient Ionia in Asia Minor, which was named after Apollo's son Ion, the mythical founder of the Ionian race. It was Aeschylus who explained the difference: the Ionian sea and islands were named after the beautiful priestess Io, who caught the philandering eye of Zeus. When Zeus' wife Hera was about to catch the couple in flagrante delicto, the god changed the girl into a white cow, but Hera was not to be fooled. She asked Zeus to give her the cow as a present, and ordered the sleepless hundred-eyed monster Argus to watch over her. When Hermes, working for Zeus, charmed Argus to sleep and killed him, Io the cow escaped, only to be pursued by a terrible stinging gad-fly sent by Hera. The first place Io fled to took her name, the Ionian Sea, before she ended her bovine swimming marathon in Egypt, where Zeus restored the girl to her rightful form. As for the unfortunate Argus, Hera collected his hundred eyes and stuck them on the peacock's tail.

Kefaloniá are generally believed to have been the heart of the kingdom of Odysseus, while Lefkás and Zákynthos may have been part of his domains as well. Corfu, however, was Scheria, the kingdom of the gentle, enigmatic Phaeacians and their princess Nausicaa, who rescued Odysseus and brought him to her father's palace, where he told the tale of his wanderings in the *Odyssey*.

Around the same time as Homer, in the 8th century BC, the Ionian islands were being absorbed into the mainstream of Greek history. Overpopulated and in search of new trade opportunities, the Greek city states of the mainland and Aegean islands began to colonize the western Mediterranean, in particular Magna Grecia (Sicily and southern Italy). Bands of colonists would set out with all their political and religious institutions intact, to overpower and expel the natives, or force them into the interior. The most famous of the colonies on the Ionians was Corcyra (near modern Corfu Town), founded in 734 BC by Corinth. Corinth at the time was one of the leading trading cities in Greece, and its original intention in founding Corcyra, as well as smaller colonies on the Ionian shore and on Lefkás, was to set up ports of call to the richer prizes in Italy. But it wasn't long before Corcyra, thanks to its strategic position and own ambitions, was founding colonies of its own, often as a rival to mother Corinth.

In the end, the rivalry between Corfu and Corinth grew so bitter that it sparked the Peloponnesian war (431–404 BC). Corfu defeated mother Corinth at sea in the first naval battle ever, pitting Greek against Greek, and, if that weren't enough, the Corfiots upset the traditional Corinth-Spartan axis to become an ally of Athens, tipping what was already a very delicate balance of power in Greece. Corfu, as well as Kefaloniá, Zákynthos and Kýthera, contributed ships to the massive Athenian expedition against Syracuse, Sicily. Syracuse was the New York of its day and the greatest ally of Corinth and, in what proved to be the turning point in the war, Athens and her allies went down in catastrophic defeat.

The Peloponnesian war counted the golden age of ancient Greece among its casualties, and the islands went through a confused period as Athens and Sparta declined through exhaustion and the Macedonians, under Philip and his son Alexander the Great, rose to become the power in Greece. But the Macedonians were more interested in conquests in Persia and the east, and neglected the western front, where the growing menace of Illyrian pirates in the 3rd century BC forced Corcyra to appeal for outside help. The Greeks who arrived were defeated at Páxi, but the new rising power in the west—Rome—sent 200 ships to Corcyra and defeated the Illyrians in 229 BC. Impressed by the victory, Corcyra placed herself under Roman protection; eventually Rome incorporated all the Ionian islands into the province of Achaia. It was under their tutelage that the Ionians witnessed their second famous sea battle, at Actium, when the future emperor Augustus' navy defeated the combined fleet of Antony and Cleopatra.

Byzantines and Normans (5th century–1204)

After the fall of the Roman Empire, control of the islands as well as the rest of Greece shifted to an even more distant ruler: Byzantium. The emperors prized the islands as a strategic bridge between Constantinople and the Greek possessions in Sicily, southern Italy and Ravenna. Yet from the beginning the Byzantine fleet was stretched too thin to maintain a constant and credible defence of the Ionian sea: Huns, Vandals, Ostrogoths, Slavs and Bulgars overran and held the Ionians and other Greek islands on a regular basis. Constantinople would rally to gain them back, but life on the islands was precarious at best, with survival the paramount concern.

In the 11th century, Greek possessions in southern Italy were hotly contested by one of the most formidable of the 'barbarian' nations: the Lombards, who occupied northern Italy with the exception of Venice, Constantinople's great ally and business partner. The Lombards, meaning to turn the tide once and for all against the Greeks, hired the Normans, the best warriors of the day, as mercenaries. They didn't bargain on the talent and ambitions of the Norman leaders, the numerous Hauteville brothers, who, inspired by their relative William the Conqueror, carved out a realm of their own when they conquered Apulia and Sicily.

Southern Italy, however, was hardly big enough for the greatest of the Hautevilles, Robert Guiscard (*see* p.165), who set his sights on Constantinople itself. Guiscard began his campaign by seizing Corfu in 1081 and then the other Ionian islands, to use as bases to plunder mainland Greece. The Byzantines eventually dislodged them, defeating the Normans in a great sea battle off the coast of Corfu with the help of their Venetian allies. The Normans withdrew, and in return for their assistance the Venetians, who had ambitions of their own, obtained from Constantinople the right to trade freely anywhere along the coast of Greece. The Normans returned to the islands in the 1140s, and were again forcibly removed by the Venetians—in return for more trading privileges from the Byzantines.

This latter Norman invasion, however, left behind a certain Matteo Orsini, a member of a branch of the famous Roman family that had settled in Apulia. Without too much difficulty, Matteo claimed the southern islands—Ithaca, Kefaloniá, and Zákynthos—as his County Palatine of Kefaloniá. He kept it for the fifty years that remained to him through shrewd diplomacy, and his ability to placate his neighbours and change allegiance when need be.

Venetians, and Angevins (1204–1386)

As the 12th century progressed, the mother-daughter relationship between Constantinople and Venice soured. The Venetians never knew from one year to the next if their trade concessions would be renewed by the emperors, or if all their merchants would be summarily arrested and executed, while on the other side, the Byzantines increasingly looked upon the Venetians as arrogant money-grubbers and

Catholic schismatics, and decided to take them down a peg by playing them against the Genoese, their arch-rivals in east–west Mediterranean trade.

The Venetians saw their chance for revenge in the early days of the 13th century when they received the commission to ferry the soldiers of the Fourth Crusade to Egypt. When the Crusaders couldn't come up with the hefty fare charged by the Venetians, the old and crafty Doge Enrico Dandolo offered to transport them anyway in exchange for certain favours, not to Egypt (one of Venice's major trading partners) but to Christian Constantinople, on the pretence of installing a pretender on the Byzantine throne. The Greeks resisted, and in 1204 Constantinople, at the time the wealthiest city in the world, was captured and pillaged by the Crusaders, who then set up a Latin emperor on the throne.

As part of their share of the spoils, the Venetians claimed the Greek islands, including the Ionians. Matteo Orsini, well ensconced in Kefaloniá, avoided trouble by agreeing that the Venetians were his overlords, while Corfu at the time was ruled by a Genoese pirate king, Leone Vetrano. Vetrano enjoyed widespread support from his subjects, who admired his spunk and hated the Venetians for their role in the capture of Constantinople; it took four attempts before the Venetians succeeded in grabbing Corfu and crucifying Vetrano in 1207.

The prize was no sooner gained when it was lost again, in 1212, when Corfu, Paxí and Lefkáda aligned themselves with the Despotate of Epirus, which then occupied part of Albania and the west coast of Greece. Michael Angelos Comnenus, a relative of the last emperor, had set up the Despotate of Epirus as a centre of Greek Orthodox resistance to the Latin threat; recognizing the strategic import of the islands, Michael and his successors bent over backwards to win their loyalty and granted the islanders huge tax concessions. The Orsini, seeing Venice's discomfit, changed the allegiance of the County Palatine to the Despotate as well, and even picked up Lefkáda, by marriage.

The success of the Despotate of Epirus provoked attacks from the rival Greek state of Nicaea and also from the wealthy Norman Kingdom of Sicily. Trouble flared up in 1258 when Manfred, illegitimate son of western emperor Frederick II and heir of the Norman kings of Sicily, captured Corfu. The Despot Michael II temporarily solved the problem by wedding his daughter to Manfred and letting him keep Corfu uncontested as the dowry. Manfred, however, had too many enemies in Italy, among them Charles I of Anjou, brother of King Louis of France, who with the pope's support appropriated Sicily; Manfred returned to defend his claim and was killed in hand-to-hand combat.

In 1267, Charles I of Anjou, now King of Naples and Sicily, inherited Manfred's Ionian islands and intended to use them as his base for the reconquest of Constantinople, which had already drifted back into the hands of the Byzantines from Nicaea. But the Angevins were foiled by their own greed and intolerance, which provoked the mass revolt of the Sicilian Vespers in 1282. The Catalans, who took Sicily from the Angevins, attacked Corfu and the other islands on several occasions, but on the Ionians the Angevins held tight under their vassals. Their rule—indirect over the County Palatine of Kefaloniá through the Orsini and Tocco families, and direct through a viceroy over the northern islands—set the basis for feudalism, which was to have a longer and stronger life on the Ionians than anywhere else in Greece.

Venetians, Again (1386–1797)

After defeating archrival Genoa in 1379, Venice became the supreme sea power in the Mediterranean while the Angevins, for their part, declined through a series of messy dynastic struggles. In 1386, the Corfiots saw the writing on the wall and at the suggestion of the Venetians, sent a special delegation to Venice to offer their island to the Republic. The Venetians, having learned by bitter experience on Crete and the Cycladic islands how *not* to govern Greeks, treated Corfu from the start with a much greater degree of tolerance, especially towards the prickly issues of religion and education. They inherited the feudal society of the Angevins, and not seeing any reason to change things, confirmed many Angevin barons in their fiefs.

After the fall of Constantinople in 1453, the Ottomans increased pressure on the Ionians. Operating in the mean-spirited world of Italian politics, the Venetians showed their disdain of the Angevins by refusing to help them defend the County Palatine of Kefaloniá when the Turks attacked in 1483, letting all the southern islands fall. In 1499, a combined Venetian-Spanish force dislodged them, and put all seven Ionians under the control of Venice. After that, no expense was spared for their defence —including payments and tributes to the Sultan to guarantee his good will. Each island was granted its own trading armada. Corfu, the capital of the Ionians' government, was 'one of the Chief keys of Christendom', the seat of Venice's supreme military commander and governor in the east, the Provveditore Generale del Levante, a position created in 1488. Corfu's role in the Mediterranean has been compared to that of Pearl Harbor in the Pacific: the permanent fleet of Venetian galleys based there was always ready to strike at a moment's notice.

Politically, the administration of the Ionians evolved along the same lines as the oligarchic government in Venice. Besides the Provveditore Generale, Venice would send a judge (Baillie) and two Councillors to each island, to keep an eye on Venice's interests. Noble titles were granted or sold to a designated number of wealthy, prominent citizens to form local oligarchies, creating a class society unique in Greece. The family names of all these new counts were inscribed in a *Libro d'Oro*, similar to the registry of the nobility back in Venice; Corfu, which had the biggest bigwigs, had the names of 112 families. Members formed the General Assembly, which elected a council of 150, which in turn was in charge of selecting various members to fill minor administrative posts. When many of these noble families from Corfu were completely wiped out during the Turkish siege of 1537, a new allotment of burghers and wealthy merchants was elevated to fill the slots in the *Libro d'Oro*.

As Venice's other possessions in Greece (most dramatically Crete, which fell in 1669 after a 20-year siege) were conquered by the Ottomans, the Ionians became essential to the Republic's trade in the east: Zákynthos and Corfu were their main ports of call, where Venetian warehouses kept goods waiting to be shipped from east to west. The islands' olive oil, wine and currants, but also silk and cotton, enriched Venice's coffers; the Venetians had had the foresight to offer a bounty for every olive tree planted, an act which Corfu and Paxí in particular have profited from down to this very day. Shipping, however, began to decline in the 17th century because of Venetian inconstancy; unable to clearly choose sides between the Christians and Turks and even the Catholics and Protestants meant that Venice had few sure allies and could no longer defend the island armadas, leaving their commerce to other nations; England, for instance, established an important currant trading concern on Zákynthos.

Social disintegration on the Ionians was soon to follow, as a direct result of the archaic feudal system. Barred from trade, noblemen were limited to working in legal or administrative jobs. By the 18th century, these bored and often broke grandees formed one of the most litigious societies in Europe; law suits were passed down through the generations—one suit on Kefaloniá disputing a few acres of land lasted over 150 years. The nobles, because they were forced by law to live in the cities, neglected their estates to the extent that the peasants on the Ionian islands lived little better than serfs and were notably worse off than their peers on the mainland. As time went on, much of the islands' natural wealth was frittered away in luxuries, while the Venetian administration and judges grew notoriously corrupt; the Provveditore Generales refused to go anywhere without four liveried servants, and insisted on private chamber music every evening with supper; their secretaries made fortunes through blackmail and the use of secret denunciations. A privileged few, however, enjoyed a life of a sophistication that often astounded visitors from abroad: sons were sent off to the University of Padua for schooling, and the glitter in the opera theatres and mannerisms at the balls were as fancy as any society in Western Europe.

The Ionian islands adopted the Venetian dialect of Italian as their legal language, but never forced anyone to learn it, so most of the islanders continued to speak Greek just as they continued to attend the Orthodox church. As the rest of Greece was swallowed up by the Turks, the Ionians, which in 1716 became Venice's very last overseas possession, also became the last bastion of Hellenism in Greece: artists, scholars and patriots from all over Greece took refuge on the islands.

A French and Russian Interval (1797–1815)

By the 1790s, however, civilization on the Ionian islands had almost ground to a halt. Back at home, Venice was burning the candle at both ends, and had little time for, or interest in, the Ionians, especially once they became a drain on the Republic's budget. Education, never a strong point, totally ceased to exist; there were no libraries, no schools, no presses, no books to buy; soldiers had to moonlight to survive, the navy had to resort to commerce to feed its sailors; priests excommunicated entire villages until they paid their fees; officials purchased their titles and used their positions to collect as many kickbacks as possible and maintain long lists of dead men on their payrolls. One exception to the sorry state of affairs was the last Provveditore Generale, Widmann, a rare man of honour who pledged his own fortune to islands when he found the treasury empty.

In 1796, Napoleon conquered Venice without a fight and, recognizing at once the strategic importance of the Ionian islands, sent a French fleet over with a Venetian convoy, flying the Venetian flag. Widmann, who could scarcely rustle up enough men to fight, had no idea of the French arrival until it was a *fait accompli,* an act later ratified in the Treaty of Campo Formio. At first the French were welcome, especially on Zákynthos, where the aristocracy was so corrupt that the islanders had already formed their own Jacobin society. The French imported their Revolution wholesale, planting Liberty trees wherever they went, but their total disregard for local feelings, customs and religion alienated even the most oppressed Greek peasants. To the islanders, the French, like the Venetians, only seemed interested in raising as many taxes as possible.

During the French occupation, both France and Britain courted the wily and cruel Ali Pasha, the tyrant of Epirus just over on the mainland. Ali Pasha was won over by the British, convinced that he would be given Léfkada in exchange for his aid against the French, and he sent troops in 1799 to join a combined Russo-Turkish fleet under Admiral Ousakov. Once they captured the islands, however, the British counsel in Ali Pasha's capital Ioanina warned London that it would be a disaster to give away Léfkada and turn the Ionian islanders against the British, so it was secretly agreed that Ali Pasha would have to wait for his reward.

The victorious Russians, immediately more amenable to the Greeks because of their shared Orthodoxy, created the independent Septinsular Republic under their protection—shielding the islands not only from the French but from the designs of Ali Pasha. The Septinsular Republic was exactly the opposite of the government imposed by the Napoleon's revolutionaries; the aristocracy was given total control, leading to a near civil war with the merchants and peasants before the experiment ended in 1807, when Tsar Alexander ceded the islands back to Napoleon in the Treaty of Tilsit. For all its flaws, the Septinsular Republic made a strong impression on the locals: it was the first time in almost four centuries that the Greeks themselves had been allowed a measure of self-rule, and the experience helped to inspire the War of Independence in 1821.

The French, during their second tenure, were responsible for resurrecting the Ionian islands' school system and their printing presses, but they never managed to gain local support; on Corfu especially the people could not forgive them for failing to respect their patron saint Ag. Spirídon, who soon enough punished the French for their disdain with the Battle of Waterloo. One last legacy of the French on the Ionians was the rise of freemasonry: although introduced by the Venetians, the Corfiot lodge first became very influential under the French (the first French Grand Master was Matthieu Lesseps, the father of the builder of the Suez Canal). In 1812, when Freemasonry fell out of Napoleonic favour, the next Grand Master, Count Dionysos Roma of Zákynthos, founded a new lodge, the Serene Grand Orient of Greece under the Duke of Sussex. This Ionian lodge, which still adheres to the English rite, became a vehicle for Greek independence, closely involved with the revolutionary *Philikí Hetaireía* (Friendly Society); the great general Kolokotrónis was a member, among others.

The British Protectorate (1815–1864)

After Napoleon's defeat in 1814, the fate of the islands was up in the air. Their old ruler Venice was now occupied by Austria, which put forth a claim, while the most influential local politician, Count John Capodistrias of Corfu, wanted to recreate the autonomous Septinsular Republic under the Russians. Capodistrias was realist enough to understand that the Austrians and British would never allow it, but instead of the Austrians he put his vote in for a British protectorate. The British were already popular on the islands—the people of Zákynthos had sent Nelson a sword with a diamond hilt after his victory at Aboukir—and British troops had successfully restored civil order after the French departure. The British navy also seemed to be the ideal military protector for Ionian commerce.

Britain didn't say no, although Capodistrias had to manoeuvre smartly to get assurances of some level of local autonomy. The new quasi-independent state was launched in 1815 as the Septinsular Republic of the United States of the Ionian Islands. It was doomed from the start; as one British High Commissioner would later put it, the new entity was 'a sort of middle state between a colony and a perfectly independent country, without possessing the advantages of either'.

Any Greek dreams of autonomy were quickly squelched by the first High Commissioner, Sir Thomas Maitland, a firm believer in British superiority. Nicknamed 'King Tom' by the British, and 'the Abortion' by the Greeks, Maitland forced a constitution down the islanders' throat, giving himself dictatorial powers and denying any political role for Corfu's educated and middle classes; the Ionians weren't even given favourable trade status with Britain. Maitland deeply offended Greeks around the world by giving the city of Párga, an important port on the mainland, to Ali Pasha, obeying an obscure clause in the 1815 treaty that everyone else had forgotten. The High Commissioner then made himself even more disliked by forcing neutrality on the Ionian islands when the War of Greek Independence broke out in 1821, causing much ill will when he disarmed the population and imprisoned, and even executed, members of the secret patriotic Society of Friends. One notable thing Maitland didn't do was change the language of the Ionian courts, which carried on in the Venetian dialect of Italian; although he permitted the establishment of the *Gazette* (which for decades was the only newspaper on the islands), it too was written in Italian, the better to keep the Greek-speaking majority (and the British too) in ignorance.

Although universally despised, King Tom did prove to be the first able and honest administrator the islands ever had: he rebuilt their economy by freeing the peasants from their negligent landlords, took control of the judicial system from the hands of the upper classes, and abolished bribes. For the first time, the islands could afford to build much needed roads, aqueducts, and other public works. When Maitland died of apoplexy in 1824, he left behind a full treasury—another Ionian first.

The second High Commissioner, Sir Frederick Adam, went about emptying it. 'The Greeks said that while Corfu kept the Lord High Commissioner, Cephalonia paid his tailor and Zante his coachman,' wrote Charles Napier, then in charge of administrating Kefaloniá. Despite his vanity and spendthrift ways, Adam and his Corfiot wife presided over a sparkling Anglo-Ionian cultural circle, with the poet Dionysos Solomos in the centre. Other commissioners were more palatable, and some were even well liked, especially Sir Howard Douglas (1835–41), who insisted that his officials learn modern Greek. Douglas, gravely upset that the islanders didn't appear to be benefiting in the least from British rule, established the National Ionian Bank and sponsored state loans to olive- and currant-growers in the great post-Napoleonic slump.

The next High Commissioners, Mr Mackenzie (1841–42) and Lord Seaton (1843–48), were also well-meaning, especially Seaton, ex-governor general of Canada and a handsome, courteous man of considerable charm who was deeply interested in the islands. But feelings were beginning to swing. In spite of Maitland's policy of neutrality, patriotic islanders had demanded or conspired for union with Greece ever since the mainland achieved independence in 1827, with Capodistrias as the first president. However, the turmoil of the first years (Capodistrias was assassinated, and his brother, who took his place, was also deeply unpopular) made British rule seem like an attractive alternative. The international solution to the Greek crises, imposing Otto of Bavaria as the king of the country, brought stability and increased calls for union; the real turning point, however, came in 1848, the great year of European revolutions, when Otto was compelled to grant Greece a more liberal constitution.

High Commissioner Seaton immediately responded by granting an even more liberal constitution to the Ionian State, including free elections and freedom of the press. This backfired at once, as the pro-Greek press immediately attacked the British as foreign oppressors, and pro-British elements attacked Seaton for letting the pro-Greek faction have a say and a chance to vote in their candidates. But Seaton, who personally believed that the Ionians should unite with Greece, refused to repeal his constitution, saying Maitland's had been a mockery, and London had to quickly recall and replace him with a new High Commissioner, Sir Henry Ward (1849–55), who scrapped Seaton's constitution and ruled by edict after suppressing violent anti-British uprisings in Kefaloniá.

In 1858, the next High Commissioner, Sir John Young, had the decidedly unpleasant task of entertaining Gladstone, sent as a special commissioner to 'learn what obstructed good government on the Ionian State'. Gladstone, although he failed to understand why the islanders could ever want to leave Britain to join Greece, was openly positioning himself for Young's job and actually held it for two weeks before events called him home to become Prime Minister. The last High Commissioner, Sir Henry Stow, appointed in 1861 was a despot who managed to alienate all the Greeks, but events in Greece and Europe were about to deprive him of a job.

In 1862 the expulsion of the deeply unpopular Otto of Bavaria from the Greek throne led to an international search amongst the crowned heads for a new candidate. The Greeks demanded Prince Alfred, Duke of Edinburgh; Britain, knowing most of Europe would insist on someone from a smaller country, offered to find the Greeks a suitable substitute, and sweetened the arrangement by ceding the Ionian islands—by this time, possessing Cyprus as well as Malta in the Mediterranean, Britain felt able to afford what was an unprecedented act of generosity by an empire. The replacement candidate they found for the Greek throne, Prince George of Denmark, was approved by the Great Powers, and on 6 June 1864 he arrived on Corfu to receive his coronation gift of seven islands, celebrated with a great Te Deum in the church of Ag. Spyridon. For the Greeks, however, the cession of the islands was tainted by Austria's insistence that the British first blow up all the fortresses they had made the islanders pay for and build.

Part of Greece

Union with Greece translated into some revolutionary changes in Ionian society. It immediately benefited women; until 1864, property on the islands was by law passed down on the male side only. Unlike Britain, Greece never recognized any of privileges of the aristocracy, and its exclusiveness gradually waned. Many of the

Ionian counts never adapted to modern life, but frittered away their existence as before, on law suits and gambling. The last time anyone bothered to publish a Golden Book was in the 1920s.

One of Mussolini's imperialistic fantasies was to retake Venice's old colonies and set up a new Ionian State under Italian protection—a wish that seemed to come true when Italy occupied the islands in the Second World War. As many of the Greeks knew the Italians from long experience and even spoke the language, the occupation, as occupations go, was fairly comfortable until 1943, when Mussolini was repudiated by the Badoglio government. In the confusion that followed on Kefaloniá, thousands of Italian troops were captured and slaughtered by the Germans (*see* p.149). Aerial bombings during the war inflicted terrible damage, especially in Corfu Town.

After the war, the health of the islanders notably improved thanks to DDT and the elimination of malaria, the cause of much of the lethargy so frowningly noted by generations of British travellers. The other events that literally rocked the islands were of a tragic nature: a first earthquake in 1948 severely damaged Lefkáda Town, while a second, in 1956, was one of the worst ever recorded in Europe: the aftershocks lasted a week and killed 600 people, flattening nearly every building on Ithaca, Zákynthos and Kefaloniá, including the beautiful Venetian towns that had been their pride and glory. This accelerated immigration, and recovery on the Ionians only really began in the late 1960s, with Greece's new vocation for tourism.

Topics

The Ionian School

Of all the regional schools of Italian art, perhaps the most obscure is the little one founded on the Venetian-governed Ionian islands, where the strict ideals, inviolability, and consciously naive spirit of Byzantine painting were sorely tried by the Western Renaissance. None of the Ionian masters ever receives an entry in an art encyclopedia, and perhaps the only place to see any of the school's paintings outside of the Ionian islands is in the museum connected to the church of San Giorgio dei Greci in Venice, once the parish for a Greek colony of 15,000 souls.

Most of the members of the Ionian school weren't even native to the Ionians, but were refugees or sons of refugees from the mainland or Crete, who found a last convivial Greek environment after their homes had been occupied by the Turks. What many discovered, however, is that, under the Angevins and Venetians, tastes on the Ionians had changed towards a more western-oriented art. To survive, Greek icon painters had to adjust accordingly, some more willingly and skilfully than others.

For many the task was the equivalent of leaping ahead five centuries, if not selling their souls. Greek artists were still painting in a style that Italian painters had abandoned in the late 12th century, obeying the remote otherworldly dictums of Byzantine art—the strict iconography and formal symbolism that never make a play for the heartstrings, but reside on a purely spiritual and intellectual plane; the saints are spiritualized forms that speak. Byzantine icons and frescoes never ask us to relive the passion of Christ or coo over Baby Jesus; Byzantine angels never lift their draperies to reveal a little leg; the stiff, wide-eyed *Panagía,* dressed like an Orthodox nun, has none of the fashionable charms of the Madonna. After the Ottoman conquest of Constantinople and mainland Greece, Venetian Crete was long a favourite place of exile for Byzantine painters and intellectuals, and when that, too, fell to the Turks in 1669 the choice lay between the Ionian islands or Italy. Some of the finest Cretan painters, Emanuel Tzánes and Theodoros Poulakis among them, left beautiful icons on the Ionian islands to inspire the locals (some of the finest are in Corfu Town's Monastery of Platýteras).

Although the Ionian school's translation of post-Byzantine art into a provincial Italian school is perhaps more interesting historically than artistically, it is important to remember that a large percentage of its finest works have been destroyed by ignorance or earthquakes. The founder of the school, and its greatest master, was Panagyótis Doxaras (1662–1729), who was born in Kalamáta and migrated as a boy to Zákynthos where he apprenticed himself to an icon-painter. He went on to join future Doge Francesco Morosini in the conquest of the Peloponnese, fighting with such distinction in the Mani that he was knighted by Venice. Doxaras later served the Republic as a diplomat, using his time in Italy to study art; he translated the writings of Leonardo da Vinci and Renaissance theorist Leon Battista Alberti into Greek, and set up an academy in Zákynthos, where he was the first teacher of art. Unfortunately his greatest works have been lost: the ceiling of the Faneroméni church on Zákynthos collapsed in the earthquake of 1953 and the ceiling of Corfu's church, Ag. Spyrídon, was removed to be copied hamhandedly. His greatest surviving works are the icons in the church of Ag. Dimítrios in Lefkáda Town.

Most of his followers were anonymous, but a few names stand out. Panagyótis taught and frequently painted with, his son Nikólas Doxaras; in the next generation, the leading painter was Nikólas' apprentice, a priest named Nikolas Koutouzis (1741–1811), who let Byzantine restraint go out the window in favour of a dramatic Baroque style that was already passé elsewhere in Europe. Koutouzis caused a scandal on Zákynthos when he inserted his self-portrait in religious scenes—a common enough occurrence in western art, but unheard of in Byzantine painting. His followers, most notably another priest named Kandounis, produced even more extreme paintings or pure rosy-cheeked fluff that often shocks Greeks from the Aegean, where, for better or worse, the long occupation of the Turks squashed any similar attempts at innovation.

The Environment: Endangered Animals and Plain Old Pests

When Western Europe was busy discovering the beauties of nature in the Romantic era, Greece was fighting for survival; when the rest of the west was gaining its current environmental awareness in the 1960s and 70s, the Greeks were throwing up helter-skelter resorts on their beaches, making Athens the citadel of apartment block sprawl it is today, merrily chucking plastic bags of garbage in the sea and killing off the monk seals to the point of extinction because they ate too many fish.

Ever so slowly, the average Greek is waking up to the fact that nature can only take so much before she turns on her persecutors. A small but dedicated band of ecologists has been sounding the alarm for decades, but most Greeks saw their country as something to exploit: if the law forbids building on forested land, the Greek solution was—and sadly still is—to burn the forest. But these past excessess are beginning to hurt, not just the environment but where it counts, in the wallet.

Tourism has been responsible for much of the damage, but also for many of the sea-changes in attitude. The great influx of people is in part responsible for the severe depletion of fishing stocks. Laws limiting industrial fishing and dynamiting are constantly flouted—demand for fish has drained the Aegean's key resource by nearly 60% in recent years, making what used to be the cheapest staple food in Greece the most expensive. There is often talk about a fishing moratorium of a year or two to give the Mediterranean a break, but the economic consequences are simply too overwhelming for the idea to go past the talk stage. On the positive side, tourist concerns about clean beaches (and Greece now proudly claims the cleanest in Europe) have resulted in proper sewage systems on most islands and a noticeable decline in litter and junk, although there is still work to do here. The Greeks may return their beer bottles but they recycle absolutely nothing: not glass, not paper, not plastic.

The Ionians began to make environmental headlines in the early 1980s, when efforts to save the Mediterranean green loggerhead turtle centred on its nesting grounds, which just happened to be the most popular beaches on Zákynthos (see pp.206–7). Although this began as a bitter war between hoteliers and environmentalists, a compromise was eventually reached, and now the turtles themselves have become one of the island's selling points. Other, less publicized, turtles still nest on the still peaceful beaches of Kefaloniá.

Many other birds use the islands, especially Corfu with its lake and saltpans, as stepping stones on their migratory paths—numerous song birds, swallows, storks, pelicans, herons, bee-eaters, warblers and egrets all pass at one time of the year or another (March to May and late August to October are the best times to spot them) and there are a wide variety of indigenous birds to keep them company. Eagles, vultures and kestrels float over the mountains and cliffs, including the massive Griffon vulture and rare lammergeier, with wingspans of nearly 10 feet. Closer to the ground, Greece's extraordinary variety of wildflowers—some 6000 native species—draws an equally colourful array of butterflies. All suffer in the annual forest conflagrations, many of which (in spite of loud accusations directed at the CIA, Turks and other bogeys) are set by local arsonists, who chaff at the laws forbidding construction on wooded land; in the summer of '97, when the Minister of Agriculture Stefanos Tsoumakas suggested giving in and legalizing buildings erected on burned land since 1975, there was an encouraging outcry from voters.

As for creatures unfortunately *not* on the endangered list, the wily mosquito tops the list for pure incivility. Most shops stock the usual defences: lotions, sprays and insect coils, or, best of all, pick up one of those inexpensive electric mosquito repellents that plug into a wall socket. Greek skeeters don't spread malaria, but bites from their sand-fly cousins can occasionally cause a nasty parasite infection. Wasps have a habit of appearing out of nowhere to nibble that honey-oozing baklava you've just ordered (especially on the lush Ionian islands). Pests also lurk in the sea: harmless pale brown jellyfish (*méduses*) may drift in anywhere depending on winds and currents, but the oval transparent models (*tsoúchtres*) are stinging devils that can leave scars on tender parts of your anatomy if you brush against them; pharmacies sell soothing unguents. Pincushiony sea urchins live by rocky beaches, and if you're too cool to wear rubber swimming shoes and you step on one, it hurts like hell. The spines may break and embed themselves even deeper if you try to force them out; the Greeks recommend olive oil, a big pin and a lot of patience. Less common but more dangerous, the *drákena*, dragon (or weever) fish, with a poisonous spine, hides in the sand waiting for its lunch. If you step on one (rare, but it happens), you'll feel a mix of pain and numbness and should go the doctor for an injection.

Greece's shy scorpions hide out in between the rocks in rural areas; unless you're especially sensitive, their sting is no more or less painful than a bee's. Avoid the back legs of mules, unless you've been properly introduced. The really lethal creatures are rare: there are several species of small viper that live in the nooks and crannies of stone walls, where it is well camouflaged, which only comes out occasionally to sun itself. Vipers will flee if possible, but if they feel cornered they will make a hissing sound like radio static before attacking. Since the time of Homer, mountain sheepdogs have been a more immediate danger in outer rural areas; by stooping as if to pick up a stone to throw, you might keep a dog at bay.

On *Kéfi*, Music and Dancing

In the homogenized European Union of the 1990s, the Spaniards and the Greeks are among the very few peoples who still dance to their own music with any kind of spontaneity, and it's no coincidence that both have untranslatable words to describe the 'spirit' or 'mood' that separates going through the motions and true dancing. In Spain, the word is *duende*, which, with the hard-driving rhythms of flamenco, has an ecstatic quality; in Greek, the word is *kéfi*, which comes closer to 'soul'. For a Greek to give his all, he must have *kéfi*; to dance without it could be considered dishonest. The smart young men in black trousers and red sashes who dance for you at a 'Greek Night' taverna excursion don't have it; two craggy old fishermen, in a smoky *kafeneíon* in Crete, who crank up an old gramophone and dance for their own pleasure, do. It has no age limit: teenagers at discos pounding out all the international hits of the moment are really only waiting for 1 or 2am, when the clubs switch over to Greek music and the real dancing and *kéfi* can start. You can feel the *kéfi* at Easter when an entire village joins hands to dance an elegant *kalamatianó*, an act as simple and natural as it is moving, an enhanced celebration of community that the rest of us are lucky to ever experience.

Greek music has been influenced by Italy (most notably on the Ionian islands), Turkey and the Middle East, and the Balkans, all of whom were once influenced by the Byzantines, who heard it from ancient Greeks, who heard it from the Phrygians, and so on. Traditional island songs, *nisiótika*, are played on bagpipes (*tsamboúna*), clarinet (*klaríno*), and various stringed instruments—the *laoúto* (a large mandolin, used for backing, traditionally picked with an eagle's quill), the *lýra*, a three-string fiddle, held upright on the knee, played on Crete and the southern Dodecanese, the *violí* (violin), the *kítara* (guitar) and the double-stringed hammer dulcimer (*sandoúri*), once limited to Greek Anatolia and now heard most often on the eastern islands. The best time to hear *nisiótika* is during a summer saint's day feast (*panegýri*) or at a wedding; cassettes are increasingly available, but few are good.

Contemporary composers like Mikis Theodorákis often put modern poetry to music, providing splendid renderings of the lyrics of George Seferis, Odysseas Elytis and Yánnis Rítsos; sung by the deep-voiced Maria Farandouri, they are spine-tingling, even if you don't understand a word. Even current Greek pop has surprisingly poetic moments. It owes much of its origins to *rembétika*, the Greek equivalent of the blues, brought over and developed by the more 'sophisticated' Asia Minor Greeks in the 1920s' population exchange, who in their longing and homesickness haunted the hashish dens of Athens and Piraeus. *Rembétika* introduced the *bouzoúki*, the long-necked metallic string instrument that dominates Greek music today, to the extent that nightclubs are called *bouzoúkia*—rougher ones are known as *skilákia*—'dog' shops, where popular singers croon throbbing, lovelorn, often wildly melodramatic music with a Middle Eastern syncopation that offers Greeks some of the catharsis that ancient tragedies gave their ancestors. Although expensive, a night out at one of these nightclubs is an experience not to be missed. Turn up after midnight, buy a bottle of white wine and fruit, and emote. As the evening wears on, members of the audience may take over the microphone, or the singer may be covered with flowers, or even make the enthusiasts forget the law against *spásimo*, or plate-breaking. If enough *kéfi*, or soul, is flowing, you may see middle-aged bank managers dance with wine glasses or bottles on their heads. When the matrons begin to belly-dance on the table, it's time to leave.

Summer festivals and village weddings are the places to see traditional dancing. Every island has its own dances or slight variations, some preserved, some quickly being forgotten. Beginning Greek dancers would do better starting with a *syrtó*, with a slow and somewhat shuffling pace throughout, or perhaps the *kalamatianó*, a 12-step *syrtó*, *the* national dance for many people; everyone joins in, holding hands at shoulder-level, while men and women take turns leading and improvising steps. Nearly as common is the dignified *tsamikó*, where the leader and the next dancer in line hold the ends of a handkerchief; if the leader is especially acrobatic, the handkerchief seems to be the only thing that keeps him from flying away altogether. Women are the centre of attention in the *tsíphte téli*, a free-spirited, sensuous belly dance from Asia Minor for the loose-limbed, swivel-hipped and well-oiled, but just as often men (usually old and fat) steal the show.

Other dances are normally but not exclusively performed by men. The *zeybékiko* is a serious, deliberate, highly charged solo (or sometimes duo) dance with outstretched arms, evoking the swooping flight of the eagle; a companion will go down on one knee to encourage the dancer, hiss like a snake and clap out the rhythm. An introspective dance from the soul, the performer will always keep his eyes lowered, almost in a hypnotic state; because it's private, you must never applaud. Another intense dance, the *hasápiko*, or butchers' dance, is perhaps better known as the Zorba dance in the West. The *syrtáki* is more exuberant, traditionally performed by two men or three men, often to the *rembétika* tune; the leader signals the steps and it require some practice but is well worth learning—as Alan

Bates discovered, when he finally began to fathom *kéfi* from Anthony Quinn at the end of the film *Zorba the Greek*.

An Orthodox Life

With the exception of a few thousand Catholics in the Cyclades and Protestants in Athens, all Greeks belong to the Orthodox, or Eastern church; indeed, being Orthodox and speaking Greek are the criteria in defining a Greek, whether born in Athens, Alexandria or Australia. Orthodoxy is so fundamental that even the greatest sceptics can hardly conceive of marrying outside the church, or neglecting to have their children baptized, even though Papandréou's government legalized civil marriages in the early 1980s.

One reason for this deep national feeling is that, unlike everything else in Greece, Orthodoxy has scarcely changed since the founding of the church by Emperor Constantine in the 4th century. As Constantinople took the place of Rome as the political and religious capital, the Greeks believe their church to be the only true successor to the original church of Rome. Therefore, a true Greek is called a *Romiós* or Roman, and the Greek language is sometimes called *Roméika*. The Orthodox church is considered perfect and eternal and beyond all worldly change; if it weren't, its adherents could not expect to be saved. One advantage is that the Greeks have been spared the changes that have rocked the West, from Vatican II and discussions over women in the clergy and married priests to political questions of abortion, birth control and so on. Much emphasis is put on ceremony and ritual, the spiritual and aesthetic, and yet at the same time service can be powerfully moving, especially at Easter.

This determination never to change explains the violence of Iconoclasm, the one time someone tried to tinker with the rules. Back in the early 8th century, Byzantine Emperor Leo III, shamed by what his Muslim neighbours labelled idolatry, deemed the images of divine beings to be sacrilegious. The Iconoclasm opened up a first major rift with Rome, and it worsened in 800 when the patriarch of Rome, aka the Pope, crowned Charlemagne as emperor, usurping the position of the Emperor of Constantinople. Further divisions arose over the celibacy of the clergy (Orthodox priests may marry before they are ordained) and the use of the phrase *filioque*, 'and the son', in the Holy Creed. This phrase was the straw that broke the camel's back, causing the final, fatal schism in 1054 when the Papal legate Cardinal Humbert excommunicated the Patriarch of Constantinople and the Patriarch excommunicated the Pope. Ever since then the Orthodox hierarchy has kept a patriarchal throne vacant, ready for the day when the Pope returns to his senses.

After the fall of the Byzantine Empire (that 'thousand-year-long mass for the dead' as one Greek writer recently put it), the Turks not only tolerated the Orthodox church, but had the political astuteness to impart considerable powers to the

Patriarch. The church helped to preserve Greek tradition, education and identity through the dark age of Ottoman rule; on the other hand it left Greece a deeply conservative country and often abused its power, especially on a local scale. According to an old saying, priests, headmen and Turks were the three curses of Greece and the poor priests (who are usually quite amiable fellows) have not yet exonerated themselves from the list they now share with the king and the cuckold.

The fantastic quantity of churches and chapels on most islands has little to do with the priests, however. Nearly all were built by families or individuals, especially by sailors, seeking the protection of a patron saint or to keep a vow or to thank a saint for service rendered. All but the tiniest have an *iconóstasis*, or altar screen, made of wood or stone to separate the *heirón* or sanctuary, where only the ordained are allowed, from the rest of the church. Most of the chapels are locked up thanks to light-fingered tourists; if you track down the caretaker, leave a few hundred drachmae for upkeep.

The vast majority of all these chapels have only one service a year, if that, on the name day of the patron saint (name days are celebrated in Greece rather than birthdays: 'Many years!' (*Chrónia pollá!*) is the proper way to greet someone on their name day). This annual celebration is called a *yiortí*, or more frequently *panegýri*, and, if it happens in the summer, it's cause for feasts and dancing the night before or after the church service. If feasible, *panegýria* take place directly in the churchyard; if not, in neighbouring wooded areas, tavernas, town squares or even specially built halls. The food will be basic but plentiful; for a set price you receive more than your share of stewed goat. *Panegýria* (festivals) are also places for traditional music and dancing. Apart from Easter, the Assumption of the Virgin (15 August) is the largest *panegýri* in Greece. The faithful sail to Tínos, the Lourdes of Greece, and to a dozen centres connected with Mary, making mid-August a very uncomfortable time to island-hop, especially in the Cyclades—ships are packed to the brim, the *meltémi* huffs and puffs, and Greek matrons, the most ardent pilgrims of all, are also the worst sailors.

Orthodox weddings are a lovely if long-winded ritual. The bride and groom stand solemnly before the chanting priest, while family and friends in attendance seem to do everything but follow the proceedings. White crowns, bound together by a white ribbon, are placed on the heads of bride and groom, and the *koumbáros*, or best man, exchanges them back and forth. The newlyweds are then led around the altar three times, while the guests bombard the happy couple with fertility-bringing rice and flower petals. After congratulating the bride and groom, guests are given a small *boboniéra* of candied almonds. This is followed by the marriage feast and dancing, which in the past could last up to five days.

Baptisms are cause for similar celebration; they often don't take place until a child is a year or two old. Curiously, until the great day when the godfather announces the child's name (usually that of a grandparent) the child is always called by a little pet name, the better to avert the evil eye and fool supernatural ill-wishers. For extra protection from the forces of evil, babies often wear a *filaktó*, or amulet, the omnipresent blue glass eye bead. If you visit a baby at home you may be sprinkled first with Holy Water, and chances are there's a bit of beneficial garlic squeezed somewhere under the cradle. Compliments should be kept to an absolute minimum: the gods do get jealous. All is well again once the priest completely immerses the baby in the Holy Water three times (unlike Achilles, there are no vulnerable spots on modern Greeks).

Funerals in Greece, for reasons of climate, are carried out usually within 24 hours, and are announced by the tolling of church bells. The dead are buried for three to seven years (longer if the family can pay) after which time the bones are exhumed and placed in the family box to make room for the next resident. *Aforismós*, or Orthodox exhumation, is believed to prevent the body decaying after death—the main source of Greek vampire stories. Memorials for the dead take place three, nine and forty days after death, and on the first anniversary. They are sometimes repeated annually. Sweet buns and sugared wheat and raisin *koúliva* are given out after the ceremony. But for all the trappings of Christianity, the spirit of Charos, the ferryman of death and personification of inexorable nature, is never far away, as beautifully expressed in perhaps the most famous of myrologies, or dirges, still sung in some places:

> *Why are the mountains dark and why so woe-begone?*
> *Is the wind at war there, or does the rain storm scourge them?*
> *It is not the wind at war there, it is not the rain that scourges,*
> *It is only Charos passing across them with the dead;*
> *He drives the youths before him, the old folk drag behind,*
> *And he bears the tender little ones in a line at his saddle-bow.*
> *The old men beg a grace, the young kneel to implore him,*
> *'Good Charos, halt in the village, or halt by some cool fountain,*
> *That the old men may drink water, the young men play at the stone-throwing,*
> *And that the little children may go and gather flowers.'*
> *'In never a village will I halt, nor yet by a cool fountain,*
> *The mothers would come for water, and recognize their children,*
> *The married folk would know each other, and I should never part them.'*

The *Períptero* and the Plane Tree

In Greece you'll see it everywhere, the greatest of modern Greek inventions, the indispensable *períptero*. It is the best-equipped kiosk in the world, where people gather to chat, make phonecalls, or grab a few minutes' shade under the little projecting roof. The *períptero* is a substitute bar, selling everything from water to ice-cream to cold beer; an emergency pharmacy stocked with aspirin, mosquito-killers, condoms and Band Aids; a convenient newsagent for publications, from *Ta Néa* to *Die Zeit*; a tourist shop offering maps, guides, postcards and stamps; a toy shop for balloons and plastic swords; a general store for shoelaces, cigarettes, batteries and rolls of film; recently one in Póros produced an instant breakfast. In Athens they're at most traffic lights. On the islands they are a more common sight than a donkey. You'll wonder how you ever survived before *perípteros* and the treasures they contain.

The other great meeting centre of Greek life is the mighty plane tree, or *plátanos*, for centuries the focal point of village life, where politics and philosophy have been argued since time immemorial. Since Hippocrates the Greeks have believed that plane shade is wholesome and beneficial (unlike the enervating shadow cast by the fig) and one of the most extraordinary sights in the islands is 'Hippocrates' plane tree' on Kos, propped up on scaffolding and as protected as a national monument. In Greek the expression *cheréte mou ton plátano* loosely translates as 'go tell it to the marines', presumably because the tree has heard all that nonsense before. The *plátanos* represents the village's identity; the tree is a source of life, for it only grows near abundant fresh water, its deep roots a symbol of stability, continuity and protection—a huge majestic umbrella, as even the rain cannot penetrate its sturdy leaves. Sit under its spreading branches and sip a coffee as the morning unfolds before you; the temptation to linger there for the day is irresistible.

Lamp Chops and Sweat Coffee

For a country cursed with a mindlessly pedantic system of public education, where rote memorization is the only key to academic success, the Greeks speak astonishingly good English. The Greek dislike of, not to mention their thorough incompetence at, dubbing the likes of *Miami Vice* and *Santa Monica* may have something to do with it, as well as the dogged efforts of thousands of *frontistérion* (private school) teachers, whose task is to get their pupils through their proficiency exams in spite of Greek public education.

All of the above is enough to make the devoted observer of Greek ways suspect that the English mistakes on taverna menus are no accident, but rather part of some crafty plot worthy of Odysseus to keep tourists out of the locals' own secret haunts by making taverna menus such compelling reading that by the time you've spotted the Lamp Chops, Eye Eggs (i.e. sunnyside up), or Sandwitches you're laughing too hard to go anywhere else. Will you have the Rabeet Soupee, Brawn Beans, Stuffed Vine Lives, String Deans, Sours Various, You Court with Gurig and Gogumbers, Eggfish, Chief's Salad or Beet Poots to start? For main course, the Harmbougger sounds distinctly threatening; perhaps it's best to stick with dishes you know the Greeks do well: Scabby Shrimps, Staffed Tomatoes, Reformed Schnitzel, Sguids in Spies, See Food Various, Bowels in Spit, Chicken Pain (i.e. breaded), Souvlaki

Privates, Grumps Salad, T-Buogne Rum Stake, Veal Gogglets and Shrimp Shave, or vegetable dishes such as Zucchini Bulls, Cheek Pees, Jacked Potatoes, or perhaps Wild Herds or Grass Hill (both turned out to be *chórta*, a small mound of boiled greens). You can smack your lips over a Rude Sausage or Rude Meat Pie; ponder where your parents went wrong over a Freud Juice or Freud Salad; enjoy a delicious (and perfectly correct) Fish in Lesbian Sauce; cannibals can find solace at a place where 'We Serve Hot Tasty Friendly Family!' Then it's off to the Snake Bar for a Sweat Coffee, Spite, Kaputsino, or perhaps a Ouisgi, before driving off in your Fully Incurable Rent-a-Care from the Vague Travel Agency of Piraeus.

A Traditional Greek Island Calendar

If the Greek islands were the cutting edge of European culture from 2000–500 BC, the past thousand years or so have shoved them into such an out-of-the-way corner that in recent times they have proved to be goldmines of old beliefs and traditions, some going back to deepest antiquity—though they may not be for much longer, in the face of rural depopulation, mass tourism and television. Nevertheless, if you were to spend a year in an island village, you would find that St Basil, the Greek Santa Claus, still comes from Caesarea on **New Year's Eve** with gifts (rather than on Christmas Day) and gold coins are still baked in pies called *vassilopíta* that bring good luck to the finder; in the morning children sing *kalenda*, or carols, in honour of Basil. Since ancient times **January** has also been closely associated with the Fates; everyone gambles, and readers of palms, coffee grounds, and tarot cards are in demand. Everywhere pomegranates, symbols of abundance and fertility, are smashed on thresholds, a stone is cast to give the household health and 'hard heads' against headaches. On 6 January, **Epiphany** (Theofánia, or Ta Fóta, the feast of lights, Christ's baptism), houses are sprinkled with holy water, and ashes from the hearth kept ablaze since Christmas to ward off werewolves and goblins (the *kallikántzaroi*) are scattered for good luck; in many places the priest will toss a crucifix in the sea, and men dive after it, hoping to be the lucky finder.

February has a reputation for lameness and wetness; one of its names, Flevarius, suggests the opening of veins (*fleva*) of water; a dry February means Greece is in for a drought. The first finches are a harbinger of spring. Olive groves are ploughed in **March**, a very variable month with strange nicknames—the Five-Minded, the Grumbler, the Flayer and *Paloukokáftis*, 'the Burning Pale'. Little bracelets of red and white thread called a *Mertoátano* are tied on children's wrists to protect them from the sun; on Kárpathos they say they tie up 'fatness, beauty, whims and the March sun'. The first swallows come back on Annunciation Day.

April, especially in the poorer, more arid parts of Greece, used to be called the Goggler; food supplies put away in the autumn would run out, leaving everyone 'goggle-eyed'—hungry. Conveniently, most people are fasting anyway, for Lent, although often enough these days fasting means going without alcohol or cigarettes rather than meat, although as Easter week draws near people tend to become more solemn and serious. Wildflowers are gathered to decorate each church's **Good Friday** *Epitáphios*, or bier of Christ; the flowers or candles used in the service are in great demand for their special power against the evil eye. On Holy Saturday morning on Corfu, women smash old crockery and plates off their balconies, a symbolic stoning of Judas. Easter eggs are dyed red, doors are painted with blood from the Easter lamb, and everyone gathers in or just outside church after midnight when the priests announces the Resurrection (*Christós Anésti! Christ has risen!*), and general pandemonium breaks out as bells ring, fireworks explode, and candles are lit and passed from person to person, and greetings and kisses are exchanged. Families return home with lighted candles, mark the sign of the cross on the doorpost, and tuck into a traditional bowl of *magirítsa,* a soup made of minced lamb's tripe and dill that tastes better than it sounds and soothes the stomach after the long Lenten fast. On Easter Day everyone spends the day feasting on spit-roast lamb with all the trimmings, drinking, singing and dancing into the night.

May is the month of flowers, when dead souls live, according to popular belief, granted a brief return to earth between Easter and Whitsun. In ancient times temples and statues would be purified then, and to this day it's a month for mischief and sorcery. On 1 May it's important to get up early and eat garlic before the first donkey brays or first cuckoo sings to avoid being 'stuffed'—losing the appetite, or being made somehow asinine. Everyone, even the urbane Athenians, goes to the countryside to 'fetch the May' and make garlands to bring spring's blessing to the house; hung over the door, they will stay there until November 1, when they are burned. Ascension Day is traditionally time for the first swim of the year, to 'go to the 40 waves', and if you find a stone with 'sea fluff' on it to take home and put under your bed, all the better. In **June** wheat and barley are harvested (often a corner of the field is left 'because the hare must eat, too'), cherries, apricots and peaches are picked and the first tomatoes, aubergines, beans and pulses are ripe. Bonfires are lit for St John's Eve and the young people take turns leaping over the flames. As the year changes with the summer solstice, so does luck. A widespread custom is the *kledónas* 'prophecy': water is silently drawn by young girls named Maria to fill an urn, where everyone deposits a personal item and makes a wish, usually in verse. The water is left open to the stars and on St John's Day, as the wishes are recited or sung, a Maria pulls the items out of the urn; the owner of each item as it is drawn forth gets the wish being sung at the moment, usually leading to a good deal of hilarity.

Hot **July** is the month for threshing and gathering herbs; the first melons, watermelons, figs and grapes are ripe. On 17 July, songs summon Ag. Marína to cure the bites and stings of snakes, scorpions and insects; on 20 July it's the turn of Prophet

Elijah, the saint of mountaintop chapels who inherited Zeus' meteorological tasks, controlling the rain, winds and sun. **August** is known as the Vintner, for the grape harvests begin, or the Fig-gatherer or the Table-bearer for the abundant fruits that are ripe. 'August, my beautiful month, come twice a year,' is an old saying. It is especially sacred to the Virgin, who has feast days on the 15, 23 and 31 (her birthday) and it's the best month to eat mackerel as well as fruit and vegetables. However, the first six days, the *Drymes*, are unlucky, associated with nymphs, who make hair fall out if it's washed or combed. The pious fast two weeks before the Assumption of the Virgin on 15 August, celebrated everywhere in Greece; on the Ionian islands the place to be is the village of Markópoulo on Kefaloniá where little snakes mysteriously appear and disappear. **September** is the month of wine-making. In Byzantine times 1 September was New Year's Day (and still is in the Orthodox ecclesiastical calendar), the day when Archangel Michael gets out his book and notes all the souls he will take during the coming year. Sowing begins after 14 September, but take care not to cross a woman en route to the fields.

October usually has the first rains but generally fine weather; Greek Indian summer is the 'little summer of Ag. Dimítros'. Cranes fly south to Africa, chrysan-themums adorn the tables, priests bless and open the first wine barrel. **November**, 'the showery', signals the beginning of the olive harvests. Flocks are brought down from the mountain pastures, and in some places icons are placed around the newly sown fields. Pancakes are made on 30 November for St Andrew, who is mysteri-ously known as *Trypanoteganitís*, the 'frying pan piercer'; a good housewife will use all her frying pans that day to keep them from getting holes. **December** is called 'good morning, good evening' for its short days. Eating sweet things on 4 December, St Barbara's Day, was believed to ward off smallpox, and women hide their brooms and refrain from cooking beans. Barbara's Day generally elides with that of St Nikólaos on the 6th, the protector of sailors, when boats are decorated and icons paraded around the shore. Christmas Eve marks the beginning of the twelve-day holiday period when the demonic *kallikántzaroi* and werewolves are afoot but can be kept at bay by not letting the hearth fire go out, so everyone chooses the fattest 'Christ log' they can. Pigs are slaughtered, and in the villages pork is the traditional Christmas meal. Among the many cakes are sweets made with flaky filo pastry to represent Christ's swaddling clothes. On Kímolos the oxen can magically speak at midnight but, like lots of people, all they do is complain about their fodder.

A Quick Who's Who in Greek Mythology

Like all good polytheists, the ancient Greeks filled their pantheon with a colourful assortment of divinities, divinities perhaps more anthropomorphic than most, full of fathomless contradictions, subtleties, and regional nuances. Nearly every island has stories about their doings; some have become part of the familiar baggage of western civilization, others read today like strange collective dreams, or nightmares. But as classical Greek society grew more advanced and rational-minded, these gods were rounded up and made to live on the sanitized heights of Mount Olympos as idols of state religion, defined (and already ridiculed) in Homer. The meatier matters of birth, sex, death and hopes for an afterlife—i.e. the real religion—went underground in the mysteries and chthonic cults, surviving in such places as Eleusis (Elefsína) near Athens.

The big cheese on Olympos was **Zeus** (Jupiter, to the Romans), a native of Crete, the great Indo-European sky god, lord of the thunderbolt with a libido to match, whose unenviable task was to keep the other gods in line. He was married to his sister **Hera** (Juno), the goddess of marriage, whose special role in myth is that of the wronged, jealous wife, and who periodically returned to her special island of Sámos to renew her virginity. Zeus' two younger brothers were given their own realms: **Poseidon** (Neptune) ruled the sea with his wife Amphytron (they had special sanctuaries on Póros and Tínos, and the famous 'Heliotrope' on Sýros), while **Hades** (Pluto) ruled the underworld and dead and rarely left his dismal realm. Their sister was **Demeter** (Ceres), goddess of corn and growing things, who was worshipped in the mysteries of Eleusis. **Aphrodite** (Venus), the goddess of love, is nearly as old as these gods, born when Zeus overthrew their father Cronus (Saturn) by castrating him and tossed the bloody member in the sea foam. She first landed at Kýthera, which had a famous temple to her, but later she seems to have preferred Cyprus.

The second generation of Olympians were the offspring of Zeus: **Athena**, the urbane virgin goddess of wisdom, born full grown straight out of Zeus' brain and always associated with Athens, her special city; **Ares** (Mars), the whining bully god of war, disliked by the Greeks and associated with barbarian Thrace; **Hermes** (Mercury), the messenger, occasional trickster, and god of commerce was a god from the northern Peloponnese; **Hephaistos** (Vulcan), the god of fire and the forge and metal-working, married to Aphrodite and worshipped on Límnos; **Apollo**, the god of light, music, reason, poetry, and prophesy, often identified with the sun, and his twin sister **Artemis** (Diana) the tomboy virgin moon goddess of the hunt, both born and worshipped on the little Cycladic island of Délos. Their cross-dressing half-brother **Dionysos** (Bacchus), the god of wine, orgies and theatre, was the favourite on Náxos. In addition to the twelve Olympians, the Greeks had an assorted array of other gods, nymphs, satyrs, and heroes, the greatest of which was **Herakles** (Hercules), the mighty hero who earned himself a place on Olympos, and gods such as **Helios** (Sol), the unassuming sun god, whose special island has always been Rhodes.

ACROPOLIS, ATHENS

Athens and Piraeus

*Love for Athens, a city once famous, wrote these words, a love
that plays with shadows, that gives a little comfort to burning
desire... Though I live in Athens I see Athens nowhere: only sad,
empty, and blessed dust.*

Michael Akominátos, 12th century

Travellers to the Ionians often find themselves in Athens, and
although it has perked up considerably since the days of Michael
Akominátos it's rarely love at first sight. Look closely, however,
behind the ugly architecture and congestion, and you may be won
over by this urban crazy quilt—small oases of green parks hidden
amidst the hustle and bustle; tiny family-run tavernas tucked away in
the most unexpected places; the feverish pace of its nightlife and
summer festivals of wine and song; and best of all, the Athenians
themselves, whose friendliness belies the reputation of most city
dwellers. Another plus: Athens is the least expensive capital in the
European Union.

Getting Around

by bus

The free map of Athens distributed by EOT (*see* below) marks
the main city bus (the blue ones) and trolley routes. Purchase
tickets (75dr) before boarding, and punch in the machine;
if you're caught without a ticket the fine is 2000dr. Note that
all trolleys except 1, 10 and 12 pass in front of the National Archaeology
Museum; for the Acropolis and Thesion, catch bus no.230 from Sýntagma
Square's post office. For info, call © 185 between 7am and 9pm.

by metro

The metro is an important means of getting across Athens, especially from
Piraeus. It runs as far as Kifissiá, stopping at Thissío (Theseum),
Monastiráki (flea market, near Pláka), Omónia (Athens' Times Square), and
Plateía Viktorías (near Areos Park). The network is being extended 20km
with major excavations throughout the city; work is supposed to be fin-
ished in 2000, and might be, if the quibbling stops.

by taxi

Compared to other Western cities, Athenian taxis are cheap, but a pain in
the butt. Because fares are so low, the only way cabbies can make a decent
living is by sharing, which makes hailing a cab a sport not for the faint-

hearted; the usual procedure is to stand by the street, flag down any passing cab and, if they slow down and cock an ear, shout out your general destination. If the taxi is going that way, the driver will stop, if not, not. If there's more than two of you, flagging a cab is hopeless, and you might as well walk to the nearest taxi stand or call a radio taxi. Check the meter when you board (although some taxis now have two meters) and pay from there, with a small surcharge, but more often than not the cabbie will try to nail you to the full fare on the meter. The only thing to do is start writing down the taxi's licence number and threatening to go to the police, which usually settles the issue on the spot.

The meter starts at 200dr, and the 60dr per kilometre doubles if you leave central Athens. There's a 300dr airport surcharge, a 150dr bus station/port surcharge, 50dr per bag luggage surcharge, and all prices double from midnight to 5am and on major holidays such as Easter. A taxi between Athens and the airport should cost about 1500dr. Piraeus is particularly prone to cowboys preying on unsuspecting tourists heading from and to the ferries; take proper yellow taxis with meters and official licence numbers or be prepared to be ripped off. **Radio taxis** charge a 300dr callout fee. Some numbers to try: ✆ 513 0640; ✆ 922 1755; ✆ 411 5200; ✆ 582 1292.

driving

Just don't. If evil chance finds you behind a wheel, note that parking in the central Athens Green Zone is forbidden outside designated areas. Green Zone borders are the following streets: Sékeri, Botássi, Stoúrnara, Marni, Menándrou, Pireás, Likourgoú, Athinás, Mitropóleos, Filellínon, Amalías and Vassilís Sofías.

Orientation: Athens in a Nutshell

Sýntagma (ΣΨΝΤΑΓΜΑ) (**Constitution**) **Square** is the centre of the city, site of the **Parliament Building** which backs on to the **National Gardens** and **Záppeion Park**, a cool haven of green and shade to escape the summer heat, with ducks to feed and benches to snatch forty winks. Traffic is slowly being syphoned away, so you can hear yourself think at the outdoor tables of the overpriced cafés and the great big McDonald's. The McPresence may be a golden arch-blasphemy for old Athens hands, but it's packed just the same, mostly with Greeks who don't give a hang about culture pollution. At the time of writing Sýntagma Square is further convulsed with the construction of the new $2.8 billion metro; a 3rd-century AD Roman bath and villa with lovely murals, an 11th-century BC grave and the tomb of a little dog were found under all the traffic; archaeological finds from the digs will be displayed in a smart underground concourse.

EAPOLI

Lycavitos Theatre

Lycavitos Hill

KOKALI

Ag.Georgios

Funicular Railway

VASSILISSIS SOFIAS

ARISTIPOU

PAPADIAMANDOPOULOU

BINDAROU

Dexameni

CHARITOS
PATRIARHI IOAKIM

PLOUTARHOU

National Gallery

KOLONAKI

SOFIAS

MIHALAKOPOULOU

Goulandris Museum of Cycladic Art

Benaki Museum

VASSILIS

War Museum

Byzantine Museum

IRODOU ATIKOU

VASSILEOS KONSTANDINOU

PANGRATI

National Gardens

Zappeion

Athens Stadium

N

500 metres
500 yards

From Sýntagma Square it's a short walk down to the **Pláka** (ΠΛΑΚΑ), the medieval centre under the Acropolis, where many of the older houses have been converted into intimate tavernas or bars, each tinkling away with its own bouzouki. This is also a good place to look for mid-priced accommodation, now that cars have been banished. On the very top of Pláka, at the foot of the Acropolis, **Anafiótika** (ΑΝΑΦΙΟΤΙΚΑ) is a charming uncommercialized enclave left by the builders of Otho's palaces, who came from the island of Anáfi and, homesick, tried to re-create their village here.

During the day meander through Athens' nearby flea market district, to the west of **Monastiráki** (ΜΟΝΑΣΤΙΡΑΚΙ) **Square** (and the metro station), where bulging shops sell everything from good quality woollen goods and fake Caterpillar boots to furniture and second-hand fridges. Several streets en route all claim to be the flea market, but are nothing more than tourist trap alley; aim for Avysinias Square. Just north of Monastiráki, across Ermoú, **Psirri** is an inner-city workers' neighbourhood of winding little streets that in the past couple of years has become one of the trendiest spots to eat and play in Athens, where retro is definitely in. A ten-minute walk east from Sýntagma will take you to **Kolonáki Square**, Athens' Knightsbridge in miniature, complete with fancypants shops, upmarket restaurants and plenty of well-heeled 'Kolonáki Greeks'—Athenian Sloane Rangers—to patronize them. Above the square rises **Lykavitós** (ΛΥΚΑΒΕΤΟΣ) hill, illuminated like a fairytale tower at night (a long walk, but there's a funicular every 10 minutes from the corner of Aristippoú and Ploutarchoúis). The summit offers the best panoramic views of Athens and Piraeus, *néfos* permitting, and the chapel of **St George**, a restaurant/bar, a lovely outdoor theatre and a cannon fired on national holidays.

For something different, a 15-minute walk north of Sýntagma past the University (Panepistímou) will bring you to funky **Omónia** (ΟΜΟΝΙΑ) **Square**, the Athenian Times Square, open 24 hours a day and embracing a useful metro stop, as well as fast food, huge news-stands, porn-mongers and screwballs. The **National Archaeology Museum** is further north, and behind it lies **Exárchia**, Athens' Latin Quarter, home of trendies, students and literati. Terra incognita for tourists, Plateía Exárchia is one of the city's liveliest centres after dark, with traditional *ouzeries* and *boîtes* where you're likely to find rave alongside bluesy, smoke-filled *rembétika* clubs. For establishment Athens, Exárchia is synonymous with Anarchia, and home to druggies, disaffected youth and graffiti-sprayers. But it's tame by London or New York standards. Two other areas off the tourist trail and pleasant places to stay are residential **Veikoú** and **Koukáki**, reached from the southern slopes of the Acropolis or Filopáppou Hill, both on the nos.1, 5 and 9 trolley-bus routes. Proper Greek neighbourhoods, the local shops, tavernas and *ouzeries* have few concessions to tourism and excellent, authentic food. Good places to go for a leisurely lunch or to round off an evening.

A 20-minute walk from Sýntagma, along Vass. Sofías, brings you to the Hilton Hotel, a useful landmark. Behind it are the essential Athenian neighbourhoods of **Ilíssia** and **Pangráti**, the best place to get a feel for everyday life in the city. Lose yourself in their back streets and you may find your own little taverna (of which there are plenty), rather than restrict yourself to the tourist haunts in the centre. Across Konstantínos Avenue from Záppeion Park, the landmark is the big white horseshoe of the **Olympic Stadium**, site of the 3rd-century BC original used during the Panathenaea festival, and rebuilt for the first modern Olympics, in 1896. Behind this you'll find **Mets**, an old-fashioned neighbourhood popular with artists and media folk with some fine old houses and small pensions: it's a good place to stay with authentic tavernas and *kafenéions*.

From Záppeion Park buses run frequently down to the coast and suburbs of **Glyfáda**, **Voúla** and **Vouliagménis**. Glyfáda, close to the airport, is a green and pleasant suburb that has grown into a busy resort and rival of fashionable Kolonáki. Smart city dwellers shop at the ritzy boutiques, and berth their gin palaces in the swish marina, ready for weekend jaunts over to Kéa and other nearby islands. At the other end of the scale it's the hub of British package holidays to the so-called Apollo Coast. Here and further down the coast at Voúla are pay beaches run by EOT, usually jammed with well-heeled Athenians. There are all kinds of facilities and the sea is cleaner at some than others—watch out for that sewage outfall—but nothing like the crystal waters of the more remote islands. There's also good swimming beyond Voúla in the rocky coves at Vouliagménis, a smart place for a fish lunch and haven for Greek yachties. En route, **Kavoúri** has excellent fish restaurants, ideal for a romantic dinner overlooking the sea. Beyond Vouliagménis, the road continues along the coast to **Várkiza**, another beach playground, and winds to stunning **Cape Soúnion** and its **Temple of Poseidon** (440 BC), famous for its magnificent position and sunsets and where there's always at least one tourist searching for the column where Byron carved his name.

Major Museums and Sites in Athens

The Acropolis

Ⓒ 321 0219; open summer Mon–Fri 8–6.30, Sat and Sun 8–2.30; winter Mon–Fri 8–4.30, Sat and Sun 8.30–2.30; adm exp.

Acropolis in Greek means 'top of the town', and many Greek cities have similar naturally fortified citadels crowned with temples, but Athens has *the* Acropolis, the ultimate, standing proud above the city from a hundred different viewpoints. First inhabited at the end of the Neolithic Age, it had a Cyclopean wall and the palace of Athens' Mycenaean king, although this was later replaced by a temple of Poseidon and Athena, after the two divinities took part in a contest to decide who would be the patron of the city. With his trident Poseidon struck the spring Klepsydra out of the rock of the Acropolis, while Athena invented the olive tree, which the Athenians judged the better trick. In later years the tyrant Pisistratos ordered a great gate to be constructed in the Mycenaean wall, but Delphi cursed it and the Athenians dismantled it. In 480 BC the temple's cult statue of Athena was hurriedly bundled off to Salamis, just before the Persians burnt and smashed the Acropolis. Themistocles built a new rampart out of stones of the old Parthenon, and under Pericles the Acropolis as we see it today took shape.

The path to the Acropolis follows the Panathenaic Way, laid out at the consecration of the Panathenaic Festival in 566 BC. The Acropolis entrance is defended by the **Beulé Gate** (named after Ernest Beulé, the archaeologist who found it); the monumental stairways were built by the Romans and the two lions are from Venice. Themistocles' reconstructed Panathenaic ramp leads to the equally reconstructed **Propylaia**, the massive gateway built by Pericles' architect Mnesikles to replace Pisistratos' cursed gate. The ancient Greeks considered the Propylaia the architectural equal of the Parthenon itself, although it was never actually completed because of the Peloponnesian War. On either side of the Propylaia's entrance are two wings; the north held a picture gallery (Pinakothéke) while the smaller one to the south consisted of only one room of an unusual shape, because the priests of the neighbouring Nike temple didn't want the wing in their precinct. The original entrance had five doors, the central one pierced by the Panathenaic Way.

Temple of Athena Nike

The Ionic Temple of Athena Nike, or *Wingless Victory*, was built by the architect Kallikrates in 478 BC of Pentelic marble. It housed the cult statue of Athena, a copy of a much older wooden statue; its lack of wings, unlike later victory statues, gave the temple its second name. In 1687 the Turks destroyed the temple to build a tower. It was rebuilt in 1835 and again in 1936, when the bastion beneath it threatened to crumble away. Cement casts replace the north and western friezes which were taken to England by Lord Elgin. From the temple of Athena Nike the whole Saronic Gulf could be seen in pre-*néfos* days, and it was here that King Aegeus watched for the return of his son Theseus from his Cretan adventure with the Minotaur. Theseus was to have signalled his victory with a white sail but forgot; at the sight of the black sail of death, Aegeus threw himself off the precipice in despair and, although he was miles from the water at the time, gave his name to the Aegean Sea.

The Parthenon

The Parthenon, the glory of the Acropolis and probably the most famous building in the world, is a Doric temple constructed between 447 and 432 BC under the direction of Phidias, the greatest artist and sculptor of the Periclean age. Originally called the Great Temple, brightly painted and shimmering with gold, it took the name Parthenon (Chamber of Virgins) a hundred years after its completion. Constructed entirely of Pentelic marble, it held Phidias' famous chryselephantine (ivory and gold) statue of Athena, who stood over 36ft high. The builders of the Parthenon wrote the book on mathematical perfection, subtlety, grace and *entasis*, the art of curving a form to create the visual illusion of perfection. Look closely, and you'll see that there's not a straight line to be seen: the foundation is curved slightly to prevent an illusion of drooping caused by straight horizontals. The columns bend a few centimetres inward, and those on the corners are wider to complete the illusion of perfect form. The outer colonnade consists of 46 columns and above them are the remnants of the Doric frieze left behind by the beaverish Lord Elgin: the east side portrayed the battle of giants and gods, the south the Lapiths and Centaurs (mostly in the British Museum today), on the west are the Greeks and the Amazons, and on the north the battle of Troy. Little remains of the pediment sculptures of the gods. Above the interior colonnade, the masterful Ionic frieze designed by Phidias himself shows the quadrennial Panathenaic Procession in which the cult statue of Athena in the Erechtheion was brought a golden crown and a new sacred garment, or *peplos*.

The Parthenon, used as a church and then a mosque, was intact until 1687, when a Venetian bomb hit the Turks' powder stores and blew the roof off; an earthquake in 1894 was another serious blow. Entrance within the Parthenon has been forbidden, to save on wear and tear. Preserving the building, as well as undoing the damage of previous restorations, has been the subject of intense study over the past 15 years, when the alarming effects of the *néfos* on the marble could no longer be ignored: while discovering how to use hot, pressurized carbon dioxide to re-harden stone surfaces, Greek scientists have learned about ancient building techniques, and after all these years are picking up the pieces to reconstruct as much of the temple as possible, stringing column drums on new non-rusting titanium rods.

The Erechtheion

The last great monument on the Acropolis is the Erechtheion, a peculiar Ionic temple that owes its idiosyncrasies to the various cult items and the much older sanctuary it was built to encompass. Beneath the temple stood the Mycenaean House of Erechtheus, mentioned by Homer, and the primitive cult sanctuary of Athena; on one side of this grew the Sacred Olive Tree created on the spot by Athena, while under the north porch was the mark left by Poseidon's trident when he brought forth his spring. The tomb of the snake man Kekrops, the legendary founder of Athens, is in the Porch of the Caryatids, where Erechtheus died at the hand of either Zeus or Poseidon. Within the temple stood the ancient primitive cult statue of Athena Polias, endowed with the biggest juju of them all, solemnly dressed in the sacred *peplos* and crown. After the Persian fires, the sanctuary was quickly restored, but the marble temple planned by Pericles was not begun until 421 BC. Converted into a church in the 7th century, the Turks made it a harem and used the sacred place of the trident marks as a toilet.

Basically the Erechtheion is a rectangular temple with three porches. Inside were two cellas, or chambers: the East Cella dedicated to Athena Polias, the smaller to Poseidon-Erechtheus. Six tall Ionic columns mark the north porch where the floor and roof were cut away to reveal Poseidon's trident marks, as it was sacrilegious to hide such divine work from the view of the gods. The famous maidens or caryatids gracefully supporting the roof on their heads are another Ionian motif. Lord Elgin nicked parts of this temple as well, including one of the six caryatids (now in the British Museum); the other girls, said to weep every night for their missing sister, have also come in from the *néfos* and have been replaced by casts.

The Acropolis Museum

This was built to house sculptures and reliefs from the temples, in particular the Erechtheion's caryatids, the statues of Kores, or Maidens offered to Athena, and the 6th-century BC Calf Bearer (*Moschoforos*). Anti-*néfos* filters have been installed to show the British parliament that Greece is ready to care for the Elgin marbles properly, if they should ever vote to give them back. Below the Acropolis to the west is the bald **Areópagos**, or hill of the war god Ares, with a marble portal to mark the seat of the High Council, who figured so predominantly in Aeschylus' play *The Eumenides* where mercy defeated vengeance for the first time in history during the trial of the matricide Orestes. Although Pericles removed much of the original power of the High Council, under the control of the ex-archons it continued to advise on the Athenian constitution for hundreds of years.

Beyond it, tucked in the side of Philopápou hill, is the **Pnyx**, where the General Assembly of Athens met and heard the speeches of Pericles and Demosthenes. On assembly days citizens were literally rounded up to fill the minimum attendance quota of 5000, but they were paid for their services to the state. Later the assembly was transferred to the theatre of Dionysos. On the summit of the big hill is the **Philopáppos Monument** (AD 114) built in honour of Caius Julius Antiochos Philopáppos, a Syrian Prince and friend of Athens. Come up here for the romantic sunsets and views of the Acropolis; just below is the Dora Stratou Theatre, where Athens' folk dance troupe performs nightly.

The Theatres

Two theatres are tucked into the south flank of the Acropolis. The older, in fact the oldest in the world if you don't count the 'theatre' at Knóssos, is the **Theatre of**

Dionysos (*open daily 8.30–2.30, adm*). Built in the 6th century BC when Thespis created the first true drama, it was continually modified up to the time of Nero. Here 17,000 could watch the annual Greater Dionysia, held in honour of Dionysos, the god of wine and patron divinity of the theatre; the dramatic competitions were awarded prizes, many of which went to the works of Aeschylus, Sophocles, Aristophanes and Euripides. The stage that remains is from the 4th century BC, while the area before the stage, or *proskenion*, is decorated with 1st-century AD scenes based on the life of Dionysos. A couple of streets east in Pláka, the **Monument of Lysikrates** was built by an 'angel' who funded the play that won top prize in 334 BC. It later passed into the hands of Capuchin friars, who hosted Lord Byron; another Lord, Elgin, wanted to take the monument to London but was thwarted this time by the friars.

The second theatre, the **Odeon of Herodes Atticus** (AD 161) was originally covered with a roof when it was built by the Rockefeller of his day, Herodes Atticus (whose life reads like something out of the *Arabian Nights*: he inherited his extraordinary wealth from his father, who found a vast golden treasure outside Rome). The Odeon hosts the annual mid-May and September **Festival of Athens**, where modern European and ancient Greek cultures meet in theatre, ballet, and classical music concerts performed by companies from all over the world.

The Heart of Ancient Athens: the Agora, Theseum & Stoa of Attalos

① 321 0185; open 8.30–2.45, closed Mon; adm.

The Agora was not only the market but the centre of Athenian civic and social life. Here citizens spent as much time as possible, where they discussed the issues of the day and were buttonholed by Socrates. After the Persians destroyed all the buildings of the Agora in 480 BC, it was rebuilt on a much grander style; since then many landmarks have suffered, mostly from angry Romans, firebug barbarians or Athenians in need of cheap building stone. Only the foundations remain of the council house or **Bouleuterion** and the neighbouring Temple of the Mother of the Gods, the **Metroön**, built by the Athenians as reparation for the slaying of a priest from her cult. The round **Tholos** or administration centre is where the *prytanes* worked, and, as some had to be on call day and night like modern police, kitchens and sleeping quarters were included. To the right of the Tholos is the **horos**, or boundary stone; a path from here leads to the foundations of the prison where Socrates spent his last days and drank the fatal hemlock. Opposite the Metroön, only a wall remains of the **Sanctuary of the Eponymous Heroes of Athens**, the ten who gave their names to Kleisthenes' ten tribes. The **altar of Zeus Agoraios** received the oaths of the new archons, a practice initiated by Solon.

The 4th-century **Temple of Apollo** was dedicated to the mythical grandfather of the Ionians, who believed themselves descended from Apollo's son Ion; the huge cult statue of Apollo it once held is now in the Agora museum. Almost nothing remains of the **Stoa Basileios** (or of Zeus Eleutherios), the court of the annual archon, where trials concerning the security of the state were held. By the Stoa of Zeus stood the **Altar of the Twelve Gods**, from which all distances in Attica were measured. Alongside it ran the sacred **Panathenaic Way**, the ceremonial path that ascended to the Acropolis, where devotees celebrated the union of Attica; some signs of its Roman rebuilding may be seen by the Church of the Holy Apostles. South of the Altar of Twelve Gods stood a Doric **Temple to Ares** (5th century BC). The **Three Giants** nearby were originally part of the **Odeon of Agrippa** (15 BC); parts of the orchestra remain intact after the roof collapsed in 190 AD. Both the site and giants were reused in the façade of a 5th-century AD gymnasium, that a century later became the University of Athens, at least until Justinian closed it down. Near the **Middle Stoa** (2nd century BC) are ruins of a **Roman temple** and the ancient shops and booths. On the other side of the Middle Stoa was the people's court, or **Heliaia**, organized by Solon in the 6th century BC to hear political questions; it remained active well into Roman times.

Between the **South and East Stoas** (2nd century BC) is the 11th-century **Church of the Holy Apostles** (Ag. Apóstoli), built on the site where St Paul addressed the Athenians; it was restored, along with its fine paintings, in 1952. Across the Panathenaic Way run the remains of **Valerian's Wall** thrown up in AD 257 against the barbarians, its stone cannibalized from Agora buildings wrecked by the Romans. Between Valerian's Wall and the Stoa of Attalos are higgledy-piggledy ruins of the **Library of Pantainos**, built by Flavius Pantainos in AD 100 and destroyed 167 years later. Artefacts found in the Agora are housed in the **museum** in the **Stoa of Attalos**, the 2nd-century BC portico built by one of Athen's benefactors, King Attalos II of Pergamon, and reconstructed by a later benefactor, John D. Rockefeller of Cleveland, Ohio. Adjacent to the agora, the mid 5th-century BC **Theseum** is nothing less than the best-preserved Greek temple in existence. Doric in order and dedicated to Hephaistos, the god of metals and smiths, it may well have been designed by the architect of the temple at Sounion. It is constructed almost entirely of Pentelic marble and decorated with *metopes* depicting the lives of Heracles and Theseus (for whom the temple was misnamed in later centuries). Converted into a church in the 5th century, it was the burial place for English Protestants until 1834, when the government declared it a national monument.

National Archaeology Museum

Patissíon and Tossítsa Streets, © 821 7717, open Mon 12.30–6.45; Tues–Fri 8–6.45, Sat and Sun 8.30–2.45; adm exp.

This is the big one, and deserves much more space than permitted here. It contains some of the most spectacular and beautiful works of the ancient Greek world—the Minoan frescoes from Santoríni, gold from Mycenae (including the famous 'mask of Agamemnon'), statues, reliefs, tomb stelae, and ceramics and vases from every period. The Cycladic collection includes one of the first known musicians, the 2500 BC sculpture of a harpist that has become the virtual symbol of the Cyclades. The star of the sculpture rooms is a virile bronze of Poseidon (5th century BC) about to launch his trident, found off the coast of Evia in 1928; around him are some outstanding archaic Kouros statues and the Stele of Hegeso, an Athenian beauty, enveloped by the delicate folds of her robe, seated on a throne. The museum has a shop on the lower level, with reproductions of exhibits by expert craftsmen, so accurate that each piece is issued with a certificate declaring it an authentic fake so you can take it out of the country.

Other Museums and Sites in Athens

Benáki Museum: On the corner of Vassilís Sofías and Koumbári Street, ℗ 361 1617, c*losed indefinitely for renovation; shop open.* Byzantine and Islamic treasures from 6th–17th centuries, two icons painted by El Greco, folk art, and a superb collection of costumes and artefacts from the Ionian islands to Cyprus.

Goulandris Museum of Cycladic and Ancient Greek Art: 4 Neofýotou Doúka (just of Vass. Sofías), ℗ 722 8321, *open 10–4, Sat 10–3, closed Tues and Sun.* The Goulandris' collection of Cycladic figurines and other art going back to 3000 BC, as well as ancient art from other parts of Greece, may be second to the collection in the National Museum, but it's better documented and intelligently displayed.

Greek Folk Art Museum: 17 Kydathinaíon St, Pláka, ℗ 322 9031, *open 10–2, closed Mon; adm.* Exquisite Greek folk art, embroideries, wood carvings, jewellery, and nearby, in a renovated mosque, a superb collection of ceramics.

Jewish Museum: 36 Amálias, ℗ 323 1577, *open Mon–Fri 9–2.30 and Sun 10–2.30, closed Sat.* Most of Greece's Jewish population arrived in the 16th century, escaping the Spanish Inquisition, and most of their descendants were killed in the Second World War; documents and artefacts chronicle the time in between.

National Gallery: 50 Vass. Konstantínou, across from the Athens Hilton, ℗ 723 5937, *open 9–3, Sun and holidays 10–2, closed Tues; adm.* The National Gallery concentrates on painting and sculpture by modern Greek artists.

National Historical Museum: 13 Stadiou Street, ℗ 323 7617, *open 9–1.30, closed Mon; adm.* In the imposing neoclassical Old Parliament of Greece, guarded by a bronze equestrian Theodóros Kolokotrónis, hero of the War of Independence, are exhibits on Greek history, concentrating on the War of Independence.

Roman Forum: Located between the Agora and the Acropolis, at Pelopia and Eolou Sts, ℗ 324 5220, *open 8.30–3, closed Mon; adm.* At the end of the Hellenistic age, the Romans built their own marketplace, or Forum, feeling uncomfortable in the Greek Agora, especially after they wasted it. The Forum contains the celebrated 1st-century BC **Tower of the Winds**, or Clock of Andronikos, which was operated by a hydraulic mechanism, so the Athenians could know the time, day or night. Note the frieze of the eight winds that decorates its eight sides, although it has lost its ancient bronze Triton weathervane. The Forum also contains the **Gate of Athena Archegetis**, built by money sent over by Julius and Augustus Caesar; there is also a court and ruined stoae, and the Fehiye Camii, the Victory or Corn Market Mosque.

Temple of Olympian Zeus: Vass. Ólgas and Amalías, ✆ *922 6330, open 8.30–3, closed Mon; adm.* Fifteen columns recall what Livy called 'the only temple on earth of a size adequate to the greatness of the god'. The foundations were laid by the tyrant Pisistratos, but work ground to a halt with the fall of his dynasty, only to be continued in 175 BC by a Roman architect, Cossutius. It was half finished when Cossutius' patron, Antiochos IV of Syria, kicked the bucket, leaving the Emperor Hadrian to complete it in AD 131. Nearby are the ruins of ancient houses and a bath and at the far end stands **Hadrian's Arch**, in Pentelic marble, erected by the Athenians to thank the emperor for his help; the complimentary inscription reads on the Acropolis side: 'This is Athens, the ancient city of Theseus', while the other side reads: 'This is the city of Hadrian, not of Theseus'. The Athenians traditionally come here to celebrate the Easter Resurrection.

Byzantine Churches and Monasteries

Agii Theódori: This 11th-century church in Klafthmónos Square at the end of Dragatsaníou St is notable for its beautiful door; the bell tower is more recent.

Kapnikaréa: A few blocks from Agii Theódori, on Ermoú Street, is the tiny Kapnikaréa (the chapel of the University of Athens), built in the late 11th century in the shape of a Greek cross, its central cupola supported by four columns.

Panagía Gorgoepikoos: 'Our Lady who Grants Requests Quickly', the loveliest church in Athens is in Mitropóleos Square. Known as the little cathedral, it was built in the 12th century almost entirely of ancient marbles: note the ancient calendar of state festivals and the signs of the zodiac. The adjacent 'big' **Cathedral** or Metropolitan was built in 1840–55 with the same collage technique, using bits and pieces from 72 destroyed churches. The Glucksberg Kings of Greece were crowned here between 1863 and 1964, and it contains the tomb of the unofficial saint of the Greek revolution, Gregory V, the Patriarch of Constantinople, hanged in 1821.

Athens ✆ (01–) **Where to Stay in Athens**

Athens is a big noisy city, especially so at night when you want to sleep—unless you do as the Greeks do and take a long afternoon siesta. If you can't find a room, try the Hotel Association's booking desk in Sýntagma Square, in the National Bank building (*open Mon–Thurs 8.30–2, Fri 8.30–1, Sat 9–1, ✆ 323 7193*).

The beautiful **Grande Bretagne**, Sýntagma Square, ✆ 333 0000, ✉ 322 8034 (*lux*) was built in 1862 for members of the Greek royal family who couldn't squeeze into the palace (the current Parliament building) up the square. It is the only 'grand' hotel in Greece worthy of the description, with a vast marble lobby and elegant rooms (now air-conditioned and appointed with modern conveniences). Down from the Grande Bretagne on Sýntagma Square the **Meridian Athens**, 2 Vass Geórgiou, ✆ 325 5301, ✉ 323 5856 (*lux*) is a modern favourite with a very respectable restaurant.

On a less exalted level, but with a far more fetching view, is the **Royal Olympic Hotel** at 28 Diákou, ✆ 922 6411, ✉ 923 3317 (*lux*), facing the Temple of Olympian Zeus and Mount Lykavitós. There are a number of family-sized suites, and if you have the misfortune to get a room without a view, there's a wonderful panorama from the rooftop bar. In Kolonáki, **St George Lycabettus**, 2 Kleoménous (Plateía Dexaménis) ✆ 729 0711, ✉ 729 0439 (*lux*) has an intimate, family-run atmosphere, pool, and views of the Parthenon or out to sea.

Close to Pláka, the **Electra Palace** at 18 Nikodímou, ✆ 324 1401, ✉ 324 1875 (*A*) has views of the Acropolis and a wonderful rooftop swimming pool in a garden setting. More reasonable, just off Sýntagma Square, the **Astor**, 16 Karagiórgi Servías, ✆ 325 5555, ✉ 325 5115 (*A*) has a rooftop garden restaurant. The **Parthenon**, 6 Makrí St, ✆ 923 4594, ✉ 923 5797 (*A*) is not far from the Acropolis, and has a pretty outdoor breakfast area. **Titania**, 52 Panepistímou, ✆ 330 0111, ✉ 330 0700 (*B*) has a rooftop terrace planted with old olive trees, and gorgeous views over the Acropolis and Lykavittós. The **Athenian Inn**, 22 Cháritos in swanky Kolonáki, ✆ 723 8097, ✉ 724 2268 (*C*) was the favourite of Lawrence Durrell.

Adam's, 6 Herefóntos, ✆ 322 5381 (*C*) is in a quiet but central location on the edge of the Pláka; rooms are traditional, comfortable, and good value. Also in Pláka, the 19th-century **Akropolis House**, 6–8 Kodroú, ✆ 322 3244, ✉ 324 4143, has modernized rooms but in a traditional style, with antique furnishings, frescoes and a family welcome. **Pension Adonis**, 3 Kódrou, ✆ 324 9737, a gem, clean and well-run by the Greek who managed the Annapolis Hilton. All rooms have balconies, and there are lovely breakfasts, a roof garden, and bar with views (rates include breakfast). **Museum**, 16 Bouboulínas, ✆ 360 5611, ✉ 380 0507 (*C*), right at the back of the Archaeology Museum, has similar rooms, but the prices are a bit higher. **Tembi**, 29 Eólou, ✆ 321 3175, @ 325 4179 (*D*), near Monastiráki, is nothing special, but is cheaper, with kind owners, and washing facilities. **Hermes**, 19 Apollónos, ✆ 323 5514, @ 323 2073, near Sýntagma (*C*) is comfortable and friendly, with a small bar and roof garden with Acropolis views. **Hera**, 9 Falírou at Veikoú, ✆ 923 6683, @ 924 7334 (*C*) is modern but tasteful with a garden on the ground and roof.

Out in posh Kifissiá, **Katerina**, 3 Mykónou, ✆ 801 9826 (*C*) is one of the least expensive and friendliest places. In Chalándri, a bit closer to Athens, the **Akropol**, 71 Pentélis Ave, ✆ 682 6650, @ 684 5057 (*C*) is very nice with a garden, popular with business people, American tourists and anyone who wants to stay above the *néfos* line. **Art Gallery** at Eréchthiou 5, Veíkoú, ✆ 923 8376, @ 923 3025 (*E*) is a pleasant place at the lower end of this category, though Pláka is a 20-minute walk.

inexpensive

The first six on this list are in Pláka: **Phaedra**, 16 Cherefóndos St, ✆ 323 8461 (*D*) just off Filellínon St, has free hot showers, an unreconstructed pre-war interior, and pleasant staff. **John's Place**, 5 Patróou St, ✆ 322 9719 (near Metropóleos St) (*E*) is simple and cheap, with bathrooms down the hall. **Kouros**, 11 Kódrou St (just off Kidathinéou St), ✆ 322 7431 (*E*), an old house in a quietish backwater near the Greek Folk Art Museum, opposite the small park area on Kidathinaíon. The **Student Inn**, 16 Kidathinéon, ✆ 324 4808, is ideal for the rowdy younger crowd (1.30am curfew). Very near Monastiráki, the **Pella Inn**, Ermou 104, ✆ 321 2229, is simple but welcoming. **Aphrodite**, Apollonos 21, ✆ 322 3357, @ 322 6047, has little character, but good rooms on a quiet street. In Exárchia, book early for **Dryades**, E. Benáki 105 and Anaxartísias, ✆ 382 7191, @ 380 5193 (*D*); the top three rooms have lovely views (the same owner also runs the even cheaper **Orion**, (*D*) adjacent). **Marble House**, 35 A. Zínni, in Koukáki, ✆ 923 4058 (*E*) is a comfortable Greek-French-run pension. The **Student's Hostel** at 75 Damaréos St, Pangráti, ✆ 751 9530, @ 751 0616, is central and not a member of YHA. Athens' nearest **camp-sites** are at Dafní Monastery, and down on the coast at Voúla.

hotels near the airport

If you have an early or delayed flight, or just a day in Athens, there are a few hotels by the airport. They do tend to be desperately noisy—some are practically on the runway. **Emmantina**, 33 Vass. Georgíou, Glyfáda, ✆ 898 0683, @ 894 8110 (*A; exp*) is one of the better ones, with a pool on the roof and an airport shuttle bus. Convenient, moderate choices in Glyfáda include: the **Blue Sky**, 26 Eleftherías, ✆ 894 7722, @ 894 3445; **Avra**, 5 Gr. Lambraki, ✆ 894 7185 @ 898 1161; and **Beau Rivage**, 87

Vass. Geórgiou, ✆ 894 9292. **Kreoli**, 17 Vass. Georgíou, ✆ 894 4301, ✆ 894 8986 (*B*) is basic, but friendly and family-run, with a pool and breakfast room. Front room and ear plugs essential, air-conditioning extra.

Eating Out in Athens

Athenians rarely dine out before 10 or 11pm, and they want to be entertained afterwards. If it's warm they'll drive to the suburbs or the sea. Glyfáda, near the airport, and outer Piraeus (Kalípoli) are popular on a summer evening: the cool sea breeze is a life-saver after the oppressive heat of Athens. The following places are all Greek, but ethnic food, especially Asian, is just as easy to find.

Pláka

Pláka is the place to head for pleasant restaurants and al fresco dining in the evening—the tinkling glasses, music, chatter and laughter ricochet off the medieval walls. **Platanos**, 4 Diogénis, ✆ 322 0666, the oldest taverna in Pláka, is near the Tower of the Four Winds and serves good wholesome food in the shade of an enormous plane tree (*around 3000dr*). *Closed Sun.* In the heart of Pláka, in Filomousón Square, where you will land up sooner or later, you can eat well at **Byzantino**, 18 Kidathinéon, ✆ 322 7368, which serves big portions (the fish soup and lamb fricassée are excellent) at its tables under the trees (*3000dr*). It's also one of the few decent places open for Sunday lunch. **Bacchus**, 10–12 Thrasyllou, ✆ 322 0385 has a lovely cloistered outdoor dining area under the Parthenon; try one of the savoury pies (*around 4000dr*). For a cut above taverna fare, dine at **Daphne's**, 4 Lysikrátous (by the Lysikratos monument) ✆ 322 7971, a neoclassical mansion with an elegant dining room with Pompeiian frescoes and beautiful courtyard—a rarity in Athens—serving refined, traditional Greek and international dishes (*around 9000dr a head*). Athens' oldest vegetarian restaurant, **Eden**, is at 12 Lissíou and Mnissikléous, ✆ 324 8858, with vegetarian quiches and soya moussakas (*around 2500dr*). *Closed Tues.*

Under Pláka: Psirri/Monastiráki/Thísio

Among the many new restaurants and *ouzéries* in Psirri, the first remains outstanding for fun: **Taki 13**, at 13 Táki, ✆ 325 4707 has a superb atmosphere: simple food but a great party bar, often featuring live music (jazz/blues Tuesday and Wednesday, Greek on weekends) and sing songs till 1.30 am. Weekend afternoons bring similar outbursts of drinking and singing at the more bohemian **Café Abysinnia**, in Place Abysinnias, in the centre of Monastiráki, ✆ 321 7047; so-so food but excellent atmosphere.

Closed Mon. If you have a hankering for an excellent *souvláki* and *gýros*, get yourself to **Thanassis**, 69 Mitropoléos, in Monastiráki, ✆ 324 4705, open till 2am. **Vrachakia**, Ortynon 7, nearer the Thesion, overlooks the Acropolis and offers a bizarre 1950s ambiance to go with its taverna classics (*5000dr*). In the same area, **Phanari**, Irakleidon 19A, has some of the best and most economical fish dinners in Athens (*from 4000dr*) and tables in the middle of a street that comes alive after dark.

Kolonáki and Around

The legendary **Gerofinikas**, 10 Pindárou, ✆ 362 2719, still has the ancient palm tree that gave it its name, growing right out of the middle of the restaurant; the food is famous, expensive (*around 7000dr a head*) and the whole meal an experience. *Closed holidays*. Behind the Hilton, the Cypriot restaurant **Othello's**, 45 Mikalakopoúlou, ✆ 729 1481, serves delicious, authentic cuisine (*around 4500dr for a meal*). Out towards the US embassy, **Vlassis**, 8 Pasteur St, ✆ 642 5337, is a superb family-run taverna, *the* place to find true Greek cuisine and one of the rare ones with excellent wines and desserts, too (*around 5000dr*). *Book. Closed Sun*. **Salamandra**, Matzarou 3, ✆ 361 7927, has some of the least expensive but tastiest food in Kolonáki, served in a pretty old house (*under 3000dr*). *Closed Sun*.

Around Omónia Square

Sleazy Omónia Square is a great place to try Greek street food. If you're anywhere near the Central Market, don't miss one of the best *mageiria* in Athens: **Diporto**, Theatrou and Sofokléous, an Athens institution, serving simple but delicious dishes and salads with barrelled retsina (*lunch only, around 3000dr*). **Athinaiko**, 2 Themistokléous, east of Omónia, ✆ 383 8485 is a great place to fill up on tasty *mezédes* and swordfish kebabs while watching the passing crowds. On the same street, at No.18, **Andreas**, ✆ 362 1522, offers tasty seafood at reasonable prices, and tables outside. The traditional Greek hangover cure, tripe soup (*patsas*) and meaty Hellenic soul food is dished up in the early hours to trendy drunkards at **Monastiri**, the butchers' restaurant in the central meat market.

Exárchia

In Exárchia, **Kostayiannis**, 37 Zaími, ✆ 821 2496, behind the National Archaeology Museum, has a succulent display of food in the glass cabinets near the entrance preparing you for a memorable culinary evening. Apart from the superb seafood, the 'ready food' is unbeatable—roast pork in wine and herb sauce or the rabbit *stifádo*, accompanied by barrelled retsina. Prices here are very reasonable (*3500dr for a full evening meal*).

To enjoy the after-theatre ambience, don't get there too early. *Closed lunchtimes, Sun, and Aug.* **Galatia**, 50 Valtetsiou, ℂ 380 1930, offers authentic Cypriot fare in relaxed surroundings. For a night out, book a table at **Strephis**, Athineas 5 and Poulcherias 8, ℂ 882 0780, in a historic house at the foot of Stefi hill, where Xanthis, owner and disciple of Theodorakis leads the public in old Greek songs; good, plentiful food (*evenings only; around 4500dr*). Among several tavernas along Methonis street, try **Ama Lachi**, at No.66, ℂ 384 5978, cheap, good and pleasant; there's another clutch of inexpensive places around Plateía Exárchia.

Entertainment and Nightlife

The summer is filled with festivals attracting international stars from around the world; at other times, classical music fans should try to take in a performance at the **Mégaron**, on Vass. Sofías and Kokkáli, ℂ 728 2333, Athens' brand new acoustically wonderful concert hall. Maria Callas got her start at the **Greek National Opera House**, 59–61 Academías St, ℂ 361 2461, which is shared with the national ballet. From May to September there are nightly folk dance performances at the **Dora Stratou Theatre** on Philapapou Hill (ℂ 921 4650. *Rembétika*, the Greek blues, is in full revival in Athens; the real thing may be heard live at **Stoa Athanaton**, Sophokleous 19, ℂ 321 4362 (*closed Sun*) or **Rota**, Ermou 118, ℂ 325 2517 (*closed Mon and Tues*), and often at **Diogenis Palace**, 259 Syngroú (also a useful street for big bouzouki clubs, or if you're looking for a transvestite), ℂ 942 4267. Irakleidon street in Thissio has popular rock bars, such as **Stavlos** and **Berlin**. For jazz, try **French Quarter**, 78 Mavromicháli in Exárchia, ℂ 645 0758 or **Half Note**, Trivonianou 17 in Mets, ℂ 923 3460, which alternates between Greek and foreign artists. In summer, young fashion slaves and beautiful Athenians head out to the bars and clubs in Glyfáda or by the airport: here you'll find **Vareladiko**, 4 Alkondidon St, ℂ 895 2403, the first 'hyper-club' in Greece, with the latest Greek hits; **Romeo**, 1 Ellinkikou, ℂ 894 5345, a *skyladiko* club for a wild Greek night out, and **Amfitheatro**, Vass. Georgiou, ℂ 894 4538, Athens' biggest rave venue. Gay Athens gathers in Makrigiánni, the neighbourhood just south of the Acropolis: **Splash**, **Lamda** and **Granazi**, are popular dancing bars with cover charges, all along Lembessi St, off Syngroú. In the summer, outdoor cinemas are a treat and all the films are in their original language: two of the nicest are in Kolonáki: **Dexameni**, in Dexameni Square halfway up Lykavittós, ℂ 360 2363 and **Athinaia**, 50 Charitos St, ℂ 721 5717.

Piraeus

The port of Athens, Piraeus (ΠΕΙΡΑΙΑΣ)—pronounced pi-ray-A or the old way, Pirevs—was the greatest port of the ancient world and remains today one of the busiest in the Mediterranean. In Greece, a country that derives most of its livelihood from the sea in one way or another, Piraeus is the true capital, while Athens is merely a sprawling suburb where the bureaucrats live. Still, it takes a special visitor to find much charm in the tall grey buildings and dusty hurly-burly in the streets, although Marína Zéa and Mikrolimáni with their yachts, brightly lit tavernas and bars are a handsome sight, as are the neon signs flashing kinetically as you sail from Piraeus in the evening.

Getting Around

In Piraeus this usually means getting out of town as quickly as possible. **Ships** are grouped according to their destination (*see* map) and almost anyone you ask will be able to tell you the precise location of any vessel. The cluster of ticket agents around the port is very competitive, but prices to the islands are fixed, so the only reason to shop around is to see if there is an earlier or faster ship to the island of your choice. The only Ionian island which can be reached from Piraeus is Kýthera: be aware that services are significantly reduced in the off-season. Flying is definitely the eastiest option; see 'Kýthera', p.170, for more details.For complete non-biased ferry schedules call the **Piraeus Port Authority** © 422 6000 (if you can get through: the number is frustratingly always engaged). The Athens tourist office has timetables of all kinds, © 322 3111.

The **metro** is the quickest way into central Athens, while **buses** on the main 'Green' line (no.040) will take you directly to Sýntagma Square/Filellinon St. The express line no.19 bus service to East and West Airport leaves from Karaiskáki Square.

Where to Stay in Piraeus

Hotel accommodation in Piraeus is geared towards businessmen, and less so towards people who have arrived on a late-night ship or plan to depart on an early-morning one. There are plenty of sleazy hotels within a 10-minute walk of the metro station.

expensive

Kastella, 75 Vass. Pávlou, © 411 4735, @ 417 5716 (*B*) is a nice place on the waterfront beyond Mikrolimáni, with a roof garden. Even more swish is the **Cavo d'Oro**, 19 Vass. Pávlou, © 411 3744 (*B*), with a restaurant and disco, and the most expensive of all, **Mistral**, Vass. Pávlou 105, © 412 1425, @ 412 2096 (*B*) comes with a pool, restaurant and air-conditioning.

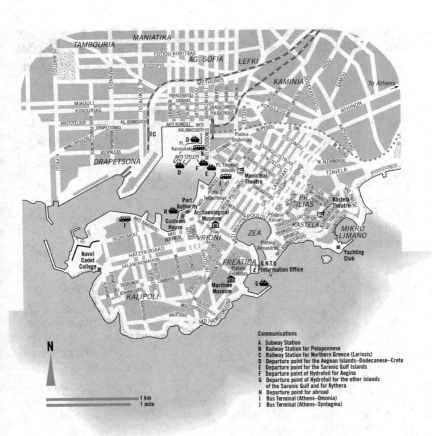

N

| | 1 km |
| | 1 mile |

Communications

A Subway Station
B Railway Station for Peloponnese
C Railway Station for Northern Greece (Larissis)
D Departure point for the Aegean Islands—Dodecanese—Crete
E Departure point for the Saronic Gulf Islands
F Departure point of Hydrofoil for Aegina
G Departure point of Hydrofoil for the other islands
   of the Saronic Gulf and for Kythera
H Departure point for abroad
I Bus Terminal (Athens–Omonia)
J Bus Terminal (Athens–Syntagma)

moderate

If you want to be within walking distance of the docks, the **Triton**,
8 Tsamadou, ✆ 417 3457, 🖷 417 7888 (*B*) is one of the best of the many
in the area. **Lilia**, 131 Zéas, Passalimáni, ✆ 417 9108, 🖷 411 4311 (*C*) is
pleasant and offers free transport to the port.

inexpensive

Known to seasoned travellers as the One Onion, the **Ionian**,
10 Kapodistríou, ✆ 417 0992 (*C*) is getting smellier by the year but is very
convenient for an early ferry or if you've just fallen off one. Others are
Achillion, 63 Notará Street, ✆ 412 4029 (*D*), **Aenos**, near the main harbour, ✆ 417 4879 (*C*), **Santorini**, ✆ 452 2147 (*C*), and **Acropole**,
✆ 417 3313 (*C*), all used to backpackers.

tourist information

The National Tourist Organization (EOT) has thankfully opened a proper tourist information office in the heart of Athens, after 20 years of waiting. It's right near Sýntagma Square at 2 Amerikis Street, ℡ (01) 331 0561 (*open Mon–Fri 9–6.30, Sat 9–2, closed Sun*). EOT also have a branch at the **East Airport**: ℡ (01) 969 9500. On Internet try Welcome to Athens with maps, hotels, and practical info at *http://agn.hol.gr/hellas/attica/athens.htm*.

emergencies

Ambulance: ℡ 178. Doctors on duty: ℡ 105. Fire: ℡ 199. Police: ℡ 100. Pharmacies: ℡ 107.

The Athens tourist police are out at Dimitrakopoúlou 77, Koukáki, ℡ 925 3396, ℡ 924 3406, but they have a magic telephone number—**171**; Agent 171 not only speaks good English, but can tell you everything from ship departures to where to spend the night, 24 hours a day. Piraeus tourist police are in the cruise ship New Passengers Terminal on Aktí Miaoúli, ℡ 429 0665.

left luggage

Pacific LTD, 26 Níkis (just down from Sýntagma Square), ℡ 324 1007, offers a left luggage service; open regular business hours. In Piraeus, the left luggage store next to the HML ticket agency is open 7am–midnight.

lost property

If you leave something on a bus, taxi or metro, try ℡ 642 1616.

shopping

To find bargains, visit the Monastiráki flea market in the morning (don't miss the arcade off Andrianou, selling traditional crafts); to spend lots of money, the latest in Greek designer fashion (Carouzos, Prince Oliver, Parthenis, etc.) is on display in the boutiques along Kolonáki's Tsakalof and Milioni streets. For food, Athens' **Central Market** is on Athinás Street, between Evripidou and Sophokleous; food shops continue all the way to Omónia Square. On a number of islands you can visit workshops where women make carpets, but there's only one place to buy them: **EOMMEX**, 9 Mitropoleos St, ℡ 323 0408. Other fine handicrafts are on sale at the shops run by the **National Welfare Organization**, at 6 Ipatiás and Apóllonos Sts, ℡ 325 0524 and at 135 Vass. Sofiás, ℡ 646 0603.

If you need a good book in English try **Eleftheroudakis**, 4 Níkis, ℡ 322 9388 or **Compendium**, 28 Níkis ℡ 322 1248, both near Sýntagma; also **Pantelides**, 11 Amerikí, ℡ 362 3673, with a wide selection of more academic titles. For used books, try **Koultoura**, 4 Mantazarou, ℡ 380 1348 or **Bibliopolion**, 22 Ifestou St, in Monastiráki. **Metropolis**, 64 Panepistímiou, ℡ 383 0404, has the biggest selection of old, rare and new Greek recordings.

Corfu/Kérkyra (ΚΕΡΚΥΡΑ)

Corfu is a luxuriant Garden of Eden cast up in the northwest corner of Greece, a sweet mockery of the grim, grey mountains of Albania, so close and so unenticing. The Venetian city-capital of the island is one of the loveliest towns in Greece; the beaches that have managed to escape the infectious claw of package tourism are still gorgeous; the gentler mountain slopes, sprinkled with pastel villas and farms, could be in Tuscany. The light is famous for its softness, mellowed by the highest rainfall in Greece.

Corfu's reputation as a distant paradise began with Homer, who called it Scheria, the happy isle of the Phaeacians, beloved of the gods, where the shipwrecked Odysseus was found washed up on a golden beach by the lovely Nausicaa. Shakespeare had it in mind when creating the magical isle of *The Tempest*, even if Prospero offered a different sort of hospitality to his shipwrecked guests. Edward Lear and Gerald and Lawrence Durrell evoked its charms so delightfully that it found a special niche in the English heart—with staggering consequences. During Corfu's first British occupation, it learned to play cricket; during the second (nearly a million British tourists come a year, and 5000 are permanent residents), the island has learned the consequences of run-amok mass tourism speculation, of letting its beauty be cheaply bought and sold. Corfiots have been stunned by the Calibanish behaviour of British lager louts, then stung by the negative reports of their island in the British press. It hardly seemed fair.

The rotten publicity spurred a serious 'culture versus crud' debate on Corfu, and not a moment too soon (in fact way too late for the 10km of coastline either side of Corfu Town, where a depressing jerry-built sprawl litters the road and pebble beaches). A new sewage system has sorted out most of the sea pollution complaints. Stricter zoning and licensing laws are being enforced and a spit and polish of Corfu Town has begun to set the tone for a classier, more genteel Corfu. An Autumn Chamber Music Festival has been added to its successful annual Spring Chamber Music Festival (three quarters of the musicians in the Greek National Orchestra are from Corfu), and the Art Café and the Old and New Fortresses now host innovative art exhibitions, subsidised by the municipality. Count Spíros Flambouriári, member of an old Corfiot family ennobled by the Venetians, has begun an island 'National Trust' to restore its lovely but mouldering country estates, beautifully photographed in his book *Corfu: The Garden Isle*.

These estates of the gentry are scattered in the gorgeous hinterland (especially to the north of Corfu Town), where villages are free of monster concrete hotels, enclaves of expensive villas, and tourist compounds. In some of Corfu's more distant nooks and crannies are lovely beaches that somehow slipped past the cement mixer. Come in the early spring, when the almonds blossom, or around Palm Sunday or the first part of November (coinciding with the colourful celebrations of Ag. Spyrídon), and seek out the old cobbled donkey paths that once provided the main link between villages, and you'll be rewarded with a poignant vision of the old Corfu, strewn with wild flowers (including 43 kinds of orchids), scented with the blossoms of lemons and kumquats, silvery with billowing forests of ancient olives interspersed with towers of straight black cypresses. The olive trees, covering 37,500 acres—half of the island's arable land—still outnumber tourists by three and half million.

History

In ancient times Corfu was called Corcyra, named after a mistress of the sea-god Poseidon. According to tradition, she bore him a son called Phaeax, who became the founder of the gentle and noble Phaeacian race. Archaeological evidence suggests that the Phaeacians were culturally quite distinct from the Mycenaeans, and had much in common, not with any people in Greece, but with cultures in Apulia, in southern Italy. In spite of Homeric tradition, the Phaeacians were technologically backward and may have been rather nasty as well; at least the scanty evidence suggests that the Mycenaeans didn't think Corfu was worth the trouble.

In 734 BC the Corinthians sent a trading colony to the island, to found the city of Corcyra at Paliaopolis, in the modern suburbs of Anemómylos and Análypsos. They booted out some of the natives and cohabited with a group from Eretria on Évia, who were also the first Greeks to establish colonies in Italy, and it wasn't long before Corcyra quickly grew to become the richest of the Ionian islands, establishing a trading empire of its own along the Adriatic coast. They were soon minting their own coins, and had a merchant navy that rivalled Corinth's own; pottery from as far afield as Miletus in Asia Minor has been found at Paliaopolis. Their chief temple housed the sickle that Zeus used to castrate his father Cronos, whose testicles fell to form the two hills around the Old Fortress (*corypho* in Greek means 'peaks', hence 'Corfu'). A prophecy current in Classical Greece foretold that Apollo would one day fetch the sickle to do the same to his father Zeus.

For all their prosperity, the Corcyraeans seem to have been shortchanged on any kind of diplomatic skills. From the beginning their history is cursed with violent political rivalries between their own democrats and oligarchs but most of all with their mother city Corinth. According to Thucydides, the Corcyrans fought the first sea battle in Greek history, defeating the Corinthians in the straits of Corfu in 664 BC. Corinth's tyrant Periander managed to regain control of the independent-minded colony and at one point punished it by seizing 300 young sons of Corcyrans' best families and sent them to Lydia to be castrated (they were rescued on Sámos, however); by 582 BC Corcyra had regained its independence and rather understandably wanted nothing else to do with Corinth, although the feelings were hardly mutual.

In 435 BC, this Corinth-Corcyra rivalry sparked the Peloponnesian War. Epidamnus (modern Durazzo), a city state founded by Corcyra in 627 BC, was in the throes of a civil war. Corfu supported the oligarchs, and Corinth, as Epidamnus' grandmother, supported the democrats and invited any democratically minded Greek to join in the fray. Corcyra took grave offence and sent 80 ships to defeat Corinth and its allies, a battle that made it the greatest power in the Ionian sea. Furious, Corinth began rebuilding its navy; both sides sent envoys to Athens to plead for the city's support. Pericles advised Athens to enter a defensive alliance with Corcyra, and when the long-planned sea battle between Corcyra and Corinth and its allies took place near the islands of Sybota (433 BC) Corcyra was on the verge of defeat when twenty Athenian ships sailed in and clobbered the Corinthians.

After the Battle of Sybota the Peloponnesian War was inevitable. This forced Sparta, Corinth's ally, either to submit to this expansion of Athenian influence and control of western trade routes through the Ionian islands, or to attack. They attacked. Athens, with its maritime empire and its new base on Corfu, was feeling strong enough to take on Sparta and drag the rest of Greece along in a war that lasted 27 years. Corcyra, for its part, fought its own bloody internal war on the fringes of the dispute: its democrats supported Athens while the oligarchs sided with Sparta. Both Athens and Sparta sent troops to the island and the fighting in Corcyra town, where the Athenians and democrats prevailed, was horrific as described by Thucydides: 'There were fathers who killed sons; men were dragged from the temples and butchered on the very altars; some were even walled up in the temple and died there.'

Corcyra was so weakened by the fights that by the fourth century BC it was preyed on by its old archrival Syracuse, and then by King Pyrrhus of Epirus, and in 229 BC by the Illyrians. When the island placed itself under the protection of Rome, it prospered as a trading and naval base. In the first century BC, Corcyra was loyal to Mark Antony—he left his wife Octavia here before sailing off with Cleopatra, and, as a reprisal after his defeat, Octavian's army under Agrippa destroyed every civic monument on the island as punishment. Yet whatever the turmoil, ancient Corcyra never lost its reputation for fertility and beauty; Emperor Nero paid it a special visit in AD 67 to start his theatrical tour of Greece, dancing and singing at the temple of Zeus Kassius in modern Kassiópi.

Corfu/Kérkyra

N

10km
5 miles

The remnants of the population who survived the ravages of the Goths in AD 550 decided to rebuild their town on the more easily defended site of the Old Fortress and the two hills, or petrified testicles, of Cape Sidáro, although the move failed to thwart the Slavs, Bulgars and Normans. In 1148, when Norman raids from Corfu, led by the great Sicilian-Norman Admiral George of Antioch, menaced the Byzantine Empire itself, Emperor Emmanuel Comnenus sent a special fleet to dislodge them. His Venetian allies stepped in again to help, and the siege ended when

Emmanuel came to lead the attack in person. By craftily seeding subversion among the Normans themselves, he succeeded in winning back the island. In 1182, Corfu was seized yet again by a Norman admiral, Margatone, working for the king of Sicily, and once again the Byzantines succeeded in winning the island back. In 1192, Richard the Lion Heart landed here in Corfu on his way home from the Crusades, but he had to beat a hasty retreat in disguise when he found out that the island's Byzantine officials were on their way to arrest him, for trying to convince Saladin to Latinize all the churches in Jerusalem.

When the Venetians picked up Corfu after the Fourth Crusade in 1204, they sent members of the nobility to colonize it, dividing Corfu into ten demarchies. This first instance of Venetian rule was shortlived: in 1214, Michael I, the first Despot of Epirus—that independent Byzantine fiefdom that stretched along the Adriatic from Durazzo to Náfpaktos on the Gulf of Corinth—grabbed Corfu, to the great acclaim of the islanders. Michael was both an excellent statesmen and soldier, and went on to conquer much of Macedonia and Thrace back for the Orthodox before being assassinated in 1215 by one of his slaves. Corfu was content under the Despotate, but the powers in Italy weren't content to let it stay put. While Michael II was fighting the rival Byzantine fief of Nicea, Manfred of Sicily, illegitimate son of Emperor Frederick II, grabbed Corfu and the Sybota islands in 1258 and after a complicated decade of marriages and assassinations Corfu was formally recognized as a possession of Charles of Anjou in the Treaty of Viterbo (1267). The Despotate of Epirus continued to exist, even after the Paleologos family of rival Nicea recaptured Constantinople in 1261 and claimed the imperial throne.

The Angevins ruled Corfu through a Viceroy, Treasurer and Inquisitor, and put the Catholic church in charge of the Orthodox, confiscating monastic landings and in general doing many of the things that made them so unpopular in Sicily. Corfu was divided into four bailiwicks, each with its own court of justice. The revenue earned through the island's salt, wine and olive oil were important to the crown in Naples, and the Angevins further aggravated the islanders' sensibilities by offering incentives to Jews from Italy and the Levant to settle on Corfu for their trading connections, and inviting gypsies to the island for raising horses.

The decline of the Angevins and dynastic changes in France, Provence and Naples left Corfu the subject of chaos and disputes in the 1370s. Without a powerful protector in the offing against growing Serbian ambitions, the Corfiots swallowed their pride and in 1386 sent a delegation of Greeks, Italians, and Jews to Venice to petition the Republic to take control, on the condition that Venice respect the island's privleges and not hand it over to any other power; Venice, at the height of her power after defeating Genoa once and for all, would probably have grabbed it anyway. But everything was done on the up and up; Venice paid 30,000 ducats to the last Angevin pretender and added Corfu to its colonies.

Venetian Corfu

Perhaps because the Corfiots had especially invited Venice, the island received preferential treatment from the start (*see* **History**, p.49). The most important man on Corfu, the Provveditore-General of the Levant, was the supreme military commander of Venice's colonial domains, and his job became increasingly difficult, especially once the Turks occupied Albania, just over the narrow Corfu channel.

In 1537 a serious threat, not only to Corfu but to all of Europe, landed at Igoumenítsa in the form of Suleiman the Magnificent. Suleiman, the greatest of the Turkish sultans, already had most of the rest of Greece in his pocket and was determined to make Corfu his base for attacking Italy and Western Europe. Thanks to a peace treaty with Venice, Suleiman was able to plot his attack in the utmost secrecy. When the Corfiots discovered only a few days in advance what was in store for them, they tore down their houses for stone to repair the fortress and to leave nothing behind for the Turks. The terrible Barbarossa was the first to land and begin the siege of the city, during which he suffered massive losses. Accounts tell of thousands of Corfiots, men, women, and children, who were pitilessly abandoned outside the fortress, caught in the Venetian and Turkish crossfire, and fell prey to Barbarossa's fits of rage at his continual setbacks. Those who managed to survive were carted off to the slave markets of Constantinople when Suleiman, discouraged by his losses and bad weather, ordered the withdrawal of the siege. By then the population of the island was reduced from 40,000 to 19,000; so many of the indigenous nobility were killed that the Signory in Venice ordered the elevation of the local bourgeois to fill the ranks, and many of these stayed on until the last edition of Corfu's Libro d'Oro, in 1925.

Only 21 years after the devastation, Venice, under pressure from the Corfiots, expanded the island's fortifications to include the town. Many houses were left unprotected, however, and when the Turks reappeared in 1571 under Ouloudj Ali, these and the rest of the villages, trees and vineyards on Corfu were decimated. This time the Turks took no prisoners and massacred whoever they caught. A final touch was added two years later by another pirate admiral, Sinan Pasha: of the entire Corfiot population, only a tenth remained on the island after 1573.

After this string of disasters, the Venetians also undertook measures to restore Corfu's economy, most notably by offering a bounty of 42 *tsekínia* for every olive tree planted (today there are an estimated 4.5 million, producing 3 per cent of the world supply). Agents were sent from Venice to make sure it was governed fairly; the Orthodox religion was tolerated and carefully patronized, and the system of secret denunciations used in the Republic was transferred here. In 1576 Venice commissioned the Fortezza Nuova and other fortifications by its expert Sammicheli were considered superb, state-of-the art works in their day, and were defended by 700 cannons. As the eastern Mediterranean fell to the Ottomans, they became a favourite refuge for Greeks who had the wherewithal to escape. Sammicheli's fortresses were given the ultimate test in 1715, when the Venetians retreated from the Peloponnese and the 30,000 Turks staged furious attacks for 42 days—the fortress was on the brink of surrendering when the Turks were repulsed by the stratagems and tremendous personal bravery of a German mercenary soldier, Field Marshal Schulenberg, and a tempest sent by Corfu's guardian, St Spyrídon.

After the fall of Venice to Napoleon, the French occupied Corfu and immediately improved the education system and set up the first public library (1797), but they lost it two years later in a fierce battle against the Russo-Turkish fleet. When Napoleon finally got the island back, he personally designed new fortifications for the town; he loved Corfu, 'more interesting to us than all of Italy put together'. Napoleon's walls were so formidable that the British, when allotted the Ionian islands after Waterloo, did not care to argue the point when the French commander Donzelot refused to give them up. The French government finally had to order Donzelot home, and in 1815, with the signing of Treaty of Vienna, Corfu and the other Ionians became a British Protectorate, with the blessing of Count John Capodistrias, a native of Corfu and, like many of the island's noblemen and scholars, in the employ of the tsars after 1799.

British and Greek Corfu

But while Capodistria had requested 'military protection', the British, who made Corfu their capital, took it upon themselves to run all the affairs of the Ionian State, which they 'legalized' by a constitution imposed under the first High Commissioner, Sir Thomas Maitland. The second son of the Seventh Earl of Lauderdale, Maitland was a rough old soldier and lifelong bachelor who had fought in India and Santo Domingo against Toussaint; in 1806 he was made governor of Ceylon, then in 1813 of Malta. He looked like a bulldog and often acted like one; his brutal and rude behaviour, his contemptuous attitude towards his subjects and his politics earned him the nickname 'the Abortion' from the genteel Corfiots, who were appalled at his swearing and tales of him dropping his trousers and mooning his visitors.

One of Maitland's first acts was to demolish part of the Venetian walls to build new, more powerful ones in their place, calling upon the Ionian government to cough up more than a million gold sovereigns to pay for the improvements. Other public works were more positive and long-lasting—the building of new roads and schools and a university (the 'Ionian Academy', founded by philhellene Lord Guilford), and a permanent water supply to Corfu Town, piped in by aqueduct from Benitses. The locals took up cricket, and ginger beer, and Edward Lear spent months on the island, painting pretty watercolours and writing in his journal: he found the island 'a very small tittle-tattle place'.

In 1858, with the political situation growing increasingly uncomfortable, Gladstone was sent down as a special investigator to propose a solution to the crisis, but, constrained by the international situation (British distrust of King Otto and Greece's support of Russia, Britain's enemy in the Crimean War), he only proposed a reconstruction of the government. The 1862 overthrow of Otto gave Britain a chance to cede the islands gracefully over to Greece, on condition that Greece found an acceptable king. This was Prince William of Denmark, crowned George I, King of the Hellenes; on 21 May 1864 the Ionians were presented as the new king's 'dowry'. The Austrians insisted on one condition to the deal that the Greeks thought eminently unfair: that the British destroy the fortresses of Corfu—not only the walls they themselves had just made the Corfiots build, but also the historic Venetian buildings. A wave of protest from all corners of the Greek world failed to change anyone's minds, and the bulk of the fortifications was blown sky-high.

During the First World War, Corfu was occupied by the French, who in 1916 evacuated 155,000 Serbs to the island after a winter march across Albania, pursued by the Austrians; the Serbian army was reorganized but the march was so gruelling that many ended up in the Serb cemetery on Vido.

In 1923 Mussolini gave the world a preview of his intentions in the 'Corfu Incident': an Italian delegate to the Greek-Albanian border council sponsored by the League of Nations was assassinated on Greek territory, and Mussolini, who may have engineered the murder, held Greece responsible and retalitated by bombing and occupying Corfu Town. The Italians left only under pressure from the League of Nations, after an inquiry found Greece blameless and ordered Mussolini to pay a large indemnity.

An even worse bombardment occurred in 1943, when the Germans blasted the city and its Italian garrison for ten days; a year later, the British and Americans bombed the Germans. By the end of the war, 525 buildings—a whole quarter—of the old city had been destroyed, including 14 of the loveliest churches.

Getting There and Around

By air: Frequent charter flights from London, Manchester, Glasgow and other UK airports; also regular flights from many European cities; three flights a day from Athens, two in the winter. The Olympic Airways office in Corfu Town is at Kapodistríou 20, ℗ (0661) 38 694/5/6. There is no special bus service linking Corfu's airport to the town, but there is a regular bus stop on the main road, several hundred metres away. For general airport info, call ℗ (0661) 30 180/37 398.

By sea: Year-round **ferries** from Brindisi, Bari, Ancona, and possibly other Italian ports such as Trieste and Ortona. Ships stop en route to

Pátras with some lines like Strintzis allowing a free stop-over in Corfu. (You must specify this when you purchase your ticket.) A catamaran links Brindisi to Corfu in 3½ hours (Corfu: Charitos Travel, 35 Arseníou, ✆ (0661) 44 611; Athens: 28 Níkis, Sýntagma, ✆ (01) 322 0503). Services to Croatia have been suspended. Ferries sail regularly all year round from Igoumenítsa to Corfu Town and Lefkími. In season there are connections with Pátras, Ithaca, Kefaloniá and a year-round ferry service to Paxí. Ferry links with the small islands of Eríkousa, Othoní and Mathráki are only twice a week; for details call ✆ (0661) 36 355. **Port authority**, ✆ (0661) 34 036.

By bus: Several buses a day from Athens and Thessaloníki board the ferry at Igoumenítsa, so that your luggage can be checked straight through. The bus depot in Platéia Theotóki–San Rócco Square, ✆ 31 595, has blue KTEL buses to villages just beyond Corfu Town (Kanóni, Pótamos, Konokali, Goúvia, Dassiá, Pérama, Ag. Ioánnis, Benítses, Pélekas, Kastelláni, Kouramádes, Áfra, Achilleíon and Gastoúri). From the depot in Avramíou St, ✆ 39 985/30 627, green buses run to the more distant villages (Ipsos, Pírgi, Glyfáda, Barbáti, Kassiópi, Paliokastrítsa, Sidári, Ag. Stéfanos (west coast), Róda, Kávos, Messóghi, Ag. Górdis, and both resorts named Ag. Geórgios, as well as to Athens (leaving at 9am, journey time 7 hours) and Thessaloníki.

By bicycle: The Dutch Bicycle company, Ag. Ioannis Tríklino, ✆/📠 (0661) 52 407, rents out mountain bikes for exploring Corfu's hidden corners.

By car: Although lately much improved, Corfu's roads are not always well-signposted, and there seem to be more than the usual number of Greek island hazards: dangerous curves and farm vehicles, careless tourists on motorbikes, sudden deteriorations in the pavement. Road maps often confuse donkey tracks with unpaved roads. Petrol stations are generally open Mon–Fri 7am–7pm, Sat 7am–3pm, but can be a bit flexible. Make sure you get a decent map; best at time of writing is 'The Precise All New Road Atlas of Corfu', hand-drawn by S. Jaskulowski.

Tours: Travel agents in Corfu offer one-day Classical tours to the mainland: to Epirus to visit the Oracle of the Dead (consulted by Odysseus after crossing the perilous River Styx), and the ancient cities of Kassopea and Nicopolis, founded by Augustus after the defeat of Mark Antony and Cleopatra in 31 BC. A second tour takes in Dodóni, with its ancient theatre and Ioannína, the modern capital of Epirus, with its island of Ali Pasha and museum. In the past, excursions to Albania have visited the ancient Roman city of Saranda but, owing to the touchy political situation, there is none at present.

Tourist Information

EOT: 7 Rizospaston Voulefton, ✆ (0661) 37 520/37 638 ✉ 30298.
Tourist police: Samartzi Street, near San Rocco Square, ✆ 30 265.
OTE telephones : Mántzaros and Kapodistríou Streets.
Post office: Alexándras Avenue, ✆ 39 265, open 8am–8pm.

Consulates

✆ (0661)	
Great Britain	11 Aléxandras Av, ✆ 30 055/37 995.
Ireland	20a Kapodistríou Street, ✆ 32 469/39 910.
Netherlands	2 Idroménou Street, ✆ 39 900.
Germany	57 Guilford Street, ✆ 31 453.
France	15 Desillas Street, ✆ 30 067.
Denmark	4 E. Antistásseos, ✆ 38 712.
Norway	7 Donzelótou Street, ✆ 32 423.

Festivals

Procession of Ag. Spyrídon in Corfu Town on **Palm Sunday, Easter, 11 August** and **first Sunday in November**. Holy Saturday is celebrated in Corfu Town with a bang—the sound of everyone tossing out their chipped and cracked crockery, a custom organized by the Venetians to replace the old Corfiot custom of celebrating the day by stoning Jews as scapegoats for Judas. **First Friday after Easter**, Paliokastrítsa; **21 May**, Union with Greece; **5–8 July**, at Lefkimi; **10 July**, Ag. Prokópios at Kávos; **14 August**, the Procession of Lights at Mandoúki; **15 August**, Panagías at Kassiópi; The Corfu Festival in **September** brings concerts, ballet, opera and theatre to the island.

Corfu Town (Kérkyra)

Corfu Town, or Kérkyra, with a population of 40,000 is the largest town and capital of the Ionian islands, and one of the most attractive towns in Greece: a unique mélange of Venetian, French First Empire, British Georgian, and traditional and modern Greek that through decades of familiarity has produced a colourful urban ratatouille. It was first laid out by the Venetians in the 15th century, when the medieval town, crowded onto the peninsula of Cape Sidáro (where the old fortress now stands), had no room to expand: 'the houses are numerous and so crammed that their roofs touch one another and the sun is not bothersome,' as one visitor wrote in 1494. The embryo of the new town was Campiello (from *campo*, Venetian for 'square') where narrow three- or four-storey houses loom over the narrow streets, as they do back in the lagoon capital. By the time the new walls were added in the 16th century, the Venetians built at a more leisurely pace in the more open style of the Renaissance, laying out an exquisite series of central streets and small squares; some of the finest Venetian houses, with their arches decorated with masks and half-moon windows over the door, can be seen along the upper Esplanade. The British knocked down most of the old Venetian walls to allow the pent-up town to expand again, and then constructed a set of elegant Georgian public buildings.

Besides Campiello, the old city is divided into a number of small quarters such as Garítsa, the 19th-century residential district to the south. The Old Port, on the east side of the New Fortress, is now used by only one ferry—the excursion to Paxí; all the other ferries and excursion boats come in and out of town through its back door at Mandoúki or New Port, west of the New Fortress.

The New Fortress

The New Fortress, or Néo Froúrio, is the mass of walls that dominates the view if you arrive by sea, built after 1576 by the Venetians following the Ottomans' third attack on Corfu. It bore the brunt of the Turks' siege of 1716, and although most of the walls were dynamited by the British, enough masonry survived for the installation of a Greek naval base. Over the gates are carved Lions of St Mark and inscriptions in various states of erosion. Now open to the public (*daily 10–6, entrance from Solomós Street*), there are excellent views of Corfu Town from the top of its bastions, and two underground tunnels to explore. Corfu's **market** is in the Fortress's moat along G. Markorá Street; if you're self-catering or planning a picnic, try to come early to get the pick of the fresh fish and produce.

Quite a bit further west, on the slopes of Mt Abraham beyond the hospital on Polichroni Konstantá Street, the **Monastery of Platýteras** was built in 1744 by monks from Lefkáda. The French destroyed it in 1798, but it was rebuilt soon afterwards, and given a new bell tower in 1864 to celebrate the union of the Ionian state with Greece. It contains beautiful icons donated by Catherine the Great in honour of Capodistrias (*see* below) who is buried here; also note the silver and gilt columns by the altar, a typical Russian feature. There are also some fine representative icons from the Ionian school, by Koutouzis and Kandounis and especially by Emanuel Tzánes (the *Fountain of Life* and the *Pilgrims*); the imaginative, rich and ornate *Apocalypse* is by another Cretan, Theodoros Poulakis, who died on Corfu in 1692.

To the east of the New Fortress in Spiliá, near New Fortress Square, stands the 1749 Catholic **church of Ténedos**, named after an icon brought to Corfu by the Venetians from the now Turkish island of Ténedos. You can reach the centre of town from the Old Port through the 16th-century Spiliá Gate, incorporated into a later structure, or take the narrow steps up into the medieval Campiello Quarter (*see* below). Corfu's **Ghetto**, once equally old and picturesque, occupies the web south of Plateía Solomoú.

Jewish Corfu

Before the Second World War, this was a large, prosperous and cultivated Greek-speaking community, founded at the end of the 12th century when the island's Angevin rulers invited Jewish merchants to settle on Corfu to take charge of trade. The community quickly rose to such prominence that the delegation sent to Venice to ask the Republic for its protection in 1386 included a Jew named David Somos as well as a Greek and an Italian. The Venetians, although never fanatical or religious enough to be openly intolerant, were very ambivalent about Jews. Although they have to answer for the invention of segregated, walled Jewish neighbourhoods (the original *Ghetto* was the name of a quarter in Venice) and for inventing a special costume—a red hat, or the star of David—for Jews to wear (unless they paid off the authorities), Jews were safer under the Venetians than just about anyone else; their trade networks, their medical skills and knack for languages were of invaluable service to the Republic. So many new arrivals appeared in the early 16th century, fleeing the persecutions in Spain and Portugal, that a second Ghetto was set up near the harbour.

On Corfu, even though they were over-taxed and deprived of their civil rights, Jews were given special status, considered among the island's leading citizens. Although not allowed to own any land, they ran the island's economy, learned Italian, and their rabbis made the very first written translation into demotic Greek (the book of Jonah). But they were compelled to return to the Ghetto by sundown and made to perform the dirty jobs. Over the years Corfu's Ghetto became something of a tourist attraction, based on the common belief that Judas Iscariot was from Corfu; his descendants would be pointed out for tourists to gawk at. By the 18th century, a quarter of the population of Corfu Town was Jewish; the heroic Marshal Von der Schulenburg even suggested to Venice that they invite more Jews to move to the island, for they were the town's bravest defenders against the Turks. The British census in 1860 counted 6000 souls, a whole third of the population of town. Although a few escaped, most of the Jewish population was rounded up by the Germans in June 1944 and held in the Old Fort for three days without food or water, before being forced into ships and vanishing; only 170 out of 1800 people sent to Auschwitz survived to return to Corfu after the war. Although the Greek synagogue and a school remain in the heart of the quarter, along with a few shops and houses in Velissáriou Street (the Italian synagogue was bombed and burned in 1943), the heart and life of a once vibrant community has all but vanished.

The Esplanade (Spianáda) and the Listón

A series of long parallel streets—the main residential district of the Venetians—all lead to the town's centre, the great green space called the Spianáda or Esplanade, one of the largest public squares in Europe. Originally a field left open for defensive purposes, it began to take its present form as a garden and promenade, under the Venetians; at first for the nobility only (hence the name **Listón,** from the Lista d'Oro; it was the only place in all of Greece reserved exclusively for the aristocracy). In the 18th century, travelling actors and acrobats from Italy would set up booths and perform here. Napoleon ordered the building of the arcades on the west edge of the Esplanade, in imitation of the rue de Rivoli, one of his proudest Paris creations. Then, as now, the Listón was a solid row of elegant cafés; at night the monuments and trees are floodlit for dramatic effect.

The northern end of the Esplanade is filled by the Georgian **Palace of St Michael and St George** (1818–23) the oldest official building still standing in Greece and one of the finest. Designed by Sir George Whitmore, the palace was commissioned by Sir Thomas Maitland as the residence of the High Commissioner of the Ionian state and the treasury for the new knightly Order of Saints Michael and George officially inaugurated in 1818 by the Prince Regent. Like Napoleon, who cynically invented the Legion d'Honneur to cater to the human yearning for awards, Maitland founded the Order of Saints Michael and George to flatter natives of the Ionian

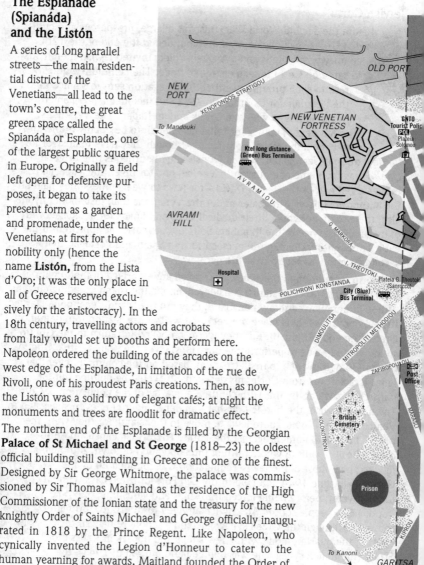

ARSENIOU

CAMPIELLO

PROSFOROU

ARSENIOU

Byzantine
Museum

APOLODOROU

SPILIA

ZAVITSIANOU

GNTO
Tourist Police

POL
Plateia
Solomou

Tourist
Information

PALEOLOGOU

PRYOSALENDIOU

SOLOMOU

AG. THEODORAS

AG. NIKOLAOU

MANESSI

DOUSMANI

AG. ELENIS

EKATERINIS
LEONDOS

G.

METROPOLEOS

TRIMARCHIAS

TELEOUS

THEODOSSIOU

Agia Theodora
Augusta

N. THEOTOKI

PHILARMONIKIS

AG. SPIRIDONOS

Palace of
St Michael and
St George

HISTORICAL
CENTRE

AG. PATERON

Agios
Spyridon

PARGAS

N. THEOTOKI

Cricket
Ground

MANDRAKI

Offshore
Sailing Club

VELISSARIOU

PALEOLOGOU

Plateia
M. Theotoki

SEVASTIANOU

AG. PANDON

VOULGAREOS

THE LISTON

Buses for
Kanoni

Sound and
Light
OLD
VENETIAN
FORTRESS

VOULGAREOS

Town
Hall

WINDMANN

DIMASTRIOU

DOUSMANI

Statue of
Schulenburg

G. MARKORA

THEOTOKI

PANDOVA

MANOU

KAPODISTRIOU

ESPLANADE

Agios
Georgios

Plateia G. Theotoki
(Sarocco)

Municipal
Theatre

DESSILA

N. POLITI

EPARHOU

ARISTOTELOUS

MOUSTOXIDI

Maitland
Rotonda

MANTZAROU

N. ZAMBELI

MAVILI

Corfu Nautical Club

SAMARA

Tourist
Information

RIZOSPASTON VOULEFTON

GUILFORD ST

SOULIOU

DIMODOKOU

G. ASPIOTI

AKADIMIAS

IROPOULOU

ALEXANDRAS

N

Post
Office

I. ROMANOU

VRAILA

POLLA

Tennis
Courts

Archaeological
Museum

300 m
300 yds

MARASLI

G. KALOSGOUROU

DIMOKRATIAS

Corfu Town

Tomb of
Menecrates

MENEKRATOUS

KIPROU

MARASLI

GARITSA

Garitsa
Bay

islands and Malta. Whitmore had to put up with a lot: he dutifully planned a palace to contain both the residence and treasury, and had begun to teach his unskilled labourers how to build, when Maitland informed him that he had to fit in a senate chamber for the Ionian assembly into the palace as well. Somehow Whitmore coped and came out on top. The two grand gates are each dedicated to a saint, and symbols of the seven islands are carved on the cornice over its Maltese marble façade: a rudderless ship for Corfu (symbolic of its independent ways); the hunter Cephalus for Kefaloniá; Zakynthos with his lance for the eponymous island; a trident for Páxi; Odysseus for Ithaca; Bellerophon and Pegasus for Lefkás, and Aphrodite on a dolphin for Kýthera. Originally a statue of Britannia sitting in a boat crowned the top, but it was removed when the Ionians were united with Greece.

In 1864 the palace became the summer residence of the King of Greece. In 1913 it was abandoned, and it suffered exterior damage in the fighting between the Italians and the Greeks in the Second World War, then serious interior damage during the Greek Civil War when the troops of General Zervas were lodged here by the Royal Navy, after they had been overwhelmed by the Communists. In 1953 the state rooms were renovated to their original splendour by the British ambassador in Athens as a memorial to Britain's role in Greece, and now house a magnificent **Museum of Asiatic Art** (*open 8.30–3, closed Mon; adm*), one of the largest and most important privately formed collections in the world, and the only one of its kind in Greece. A gift to Corfu from Greek diplomat Gregórios Mános, with further contributions from Michélis Chadjivasilíou and others, the museum contains 10,000 works (masks, ceramics, metal work, armour and weapons, screens and much more) from all the countries of the Far East, dating back to 1000 BC. At the **Art Café**, in a corner of the Palace, you can linger over coffee and drinks and enjoy one of the permanent and temporary local art exhibitions. Adjacent to the palace is the *loggia* of the **Reading Society** or *Anagnostikí Etería* (*open daily 9–1*), housed in a delightful little *palazzo*, founded in 1836 by a group of young Corfiot idealists freshly returned from their studies in France; the library has a fine collection of books on the Ionian islands. Just in front of the palace is another British legacy—the **cricket ground**, where little boys play football until their older white-clad brothers chase them off the field. In the summer, matches pit the six local teams (which aren't at all bad) against visitors from Britain, the Greek mainland, and Europe.

Numerous monuments embellish the Esplanade. In the centre of the Upper Plateía is the **memorial to Sir Thomas Maitland**, voted by the Ionian senate in 1827 and designed by Sir George Whitmore in the form of an Ionian rotunda, where, ever since the days of the British Protectorate, brass bands have serenaded the summertime crowds; you can often hear them practising in the evening in the old quarters. There is a marble, rather overblown, **statue of Marshal Von der Schulenburg**, the crafty and heroic soldier of fortune from Saxony, who outwitted the Turkish High Admiral in the Great Siege to spoil the last major attempt of the Ottoman Empire to expand in the west. The Venetians were so grateful that they granted Schulenburg the unique privilege of seeing his own statue in his lifetime. The **Guilford Memorial** is of Corfu's favourite Englishman, the Hellenophile Frederick North, Earl of Guilford (1769–1828), founder of the Ionian state university; like Maitland, North had previously served as Governor of Malta and was a lifelong bachelor, but in every other way he was exactly the opposite of his contemporary. The seated statue portrays him dressed in ancient robes, a touch he would have appreciated.

On the southern end of the Esplanade the other bronze Brit in a toga, standing on a column, is Sir Frederick Adam, the second High Commissioner, who commanded the infantry at the Battle of Waterloo, allowing Wellington to advance his Imperial Guard to victory before taking charge of Corfu, and bankrupting it. Here too is a **statue of Count John Capodistrias**, by Prosalendis, a student of Canova; the sculptor shows him looking towards the palace that Maitland built, but raising his hand in protest, or perhaps revulsion.

The First President of Greece

Capodistrias' life epitomizes the turmoil of loyalties, class and national yearnings on the Ionian islands in the post-Venetian era. Some of the bluest blood on the island ran through his veins: his family, originally from Istria, moved to Corfu in the 14th century and their name was inscribed in the island's *Libro d'Oro* from the year 1471. John, born in 1776, attended a Franciscan monastery school at Garítsa and studied medicine at Padua University. He hated the French revolution, and was imprisoned by the French on Corfu in 1798 for failure to pay taxes; he escaped and worked in a Turkish military hospital during the Russian offensive on the Ionian islands. It was while working as a doctor that he became the great favourite of the Venetian-Zantiot minister Count Mocenigo, who governed the Russian protected Septinsular Republic and made Capodistrias his secretary in 1802.

It was during this period that Capodistrias became a firm believer in the national goals of the Ionian state, a belief he soon extended to all of Greece, although he thought it essential that smaller countries, such as Greece, should have a powerful protector. His own aristocratic background and friendship with Mocenigo naturally inclined him towards Orthodox Russia.

Capodistrias was a born leader, and proved it on the field when he led the defence of Lefkáda against Ali Pasha. On Lefkáda he first became acquainted with great chieftains from the mainland, especially Kolokotrónis, who would soon be key players in the Greek War of Independence. When the French reoccupied the Ionian islands, Capodistrias went off in disgust to Russia, where he quickly rose through the ranks to become the chief foreign officer of Czar

Alexander I; at the same time he continued to influence island affairs back home and chose Britain over Austria as the Ionians' new protector, but only because he knew neither would accept the return of the Russians. Choosing Britian was an act he lived to regret, especially after Maitland forced the passage of his autocratic constitution; when Capodistrias returned to Corfu he got an earful from his compatriots and went up to London to protest, in vain, but earning the eternal hatred of Maitland, who from then on seemed to go out of his way to imprison and execute supporters of Greek independence.

In 1827, the Greek War of Independence was going so badly it looked like a lost cause; the Greeks had divided into warring factions and the Turks had reoccupied much of the territory they had conquered. Capodistrias, as the experienced diplomat, was chosen as president to negotiate with the Turks for some kind of autonomy for Greece when the unexpected victory at Navarino turned the tables completely. Capodistrias kept his post of president, but his aristocratic upbringing made it impossible for him to understand the aspirations of the now liberated Greeks, and all of his diplomatic skills were not enough to reconcile the various quarrelling parties. He annoyed many of them by continuing to rely on his Russian connections and when he tried to suppress one powerful faction, the Mavromichele family, they assassinated him, in 1831.

Near the Esplanade, on Moustoxídi, one of the streets traversing Guilford, is a **Serbian War Museum** (*open 9–12; adm free*). This is not at all what immediately springs to mind, but a collection of photographs and memorabilia from the Balkan War of 1915–17 covering Corfu's role in reorganizing the Serbian army after its retreat. In the same area, the church of **Ag. Eleftherias** has a beautiful iconostasis with twelve scenes of the Creation. Some of the loveliest views over Corfu Town are from the hills occupied by the **Old Fortress** (*open 8.30–3, closed Mon; adm*), out on Cape Sidáro, separated from the Esplanade by the moat, or *contra fosse*, dug over a 100-year period by the Venetians. The medieval town of Corfu was located on the two little hills of the cape; scholars have identified the site with the Heraion acropolis mentioned by Thucydides. The walls, built up over the centuries, were badly damaged by the British; others have fallen into decay. Part of the fortress is still used by the Greek army, but you can wander about and explore the Venetian tunnels, battlements, drawbridge, the Venetian well, cannons dating back to 1684 and **St George's**, the church of the British garrison, designed to resemble an ancient temple. Now Orthodox, the little church was used by the refugees from Párga when their city was handed over to Ali Pasha by Maitland in 1815; the icons and relics they brought with them from their own churches remained here until 1913, when Epirus became part of Greece.

Ag. Spyrídon

The church of Corfu's patron saint Ag. Spyrídon—the original Spiros—is in the old town, not far from the Ionian and Popular Bank of Greece. It's easy to find: the campanile soars above town like the mast of a ship, often bedecked with flags and Christmas lights. Ag. Spyrídon started his life in the 4th century as a shepherd who rose to become the Bishop of Tremanti on Cyprus; when he died he was quickly canonized and buried in Constantinople. When Constantinople fell to the Turks, a priest named Georgio Kalochairetis smuggled out his body, along with that of Ag. Theodóra, burying them in sacks of straw of his mules' provender. He took the holy relics to Corfu, married, and passed the remains on to his sons, and then as part of a marriage dowry to the Voulgaris family, all of whom made a living by showing them to pious Corfiots; in 1596 the Voulgaris built this church as a proper home for Spyrídon, and installed his bones in a silver Renaissance reliquary, and administered the church and its revenues until 1925 when the Orthodox church took over.

According to the Corfiots, Spyrídon 'the Miracle-Worker' has brought them safely through many trials, keeping famine, cholera and the Turks away from his beloved island. He gave the Catholics a good scare when they considered placing an altar in his church; the night before its dedication, he blew up a powder magazine in the Old Fortress with a bolt of lightning to show his displeasure. He did, however, peacefully accept the large silver lamp from the Venetians in thanks for his intervention against the Turks in 1716. The ceiling panels, the masterpiece of Panagyótis Doxaras, were unfortunately replaced in the mid 19th century with dismally inferior copies; the originals, stored in a barn, went missing. Even the copies are now blackened by candle smoke, while below the church's gold fittings shimmer through in the flickering light of votive candles. Ag. Spyrídon goes out to take the air four times each year (Orthodox Palm Sunday, Easter Saturday, 11 August and the first Sunday in November) with great pomp, while the faithful gather from all over Corfu and the mainland to queue to kiss the lid. The Venetians never failed to send dignitaries to attend the processions, nor did the British, who assigned four colonels the task of carrying the coffin. The story goes that sick people who lie in the road so that the coffin passes over them will be cured—but only if they have enough faith.

The nearby Ionian Bank houses a **Museum of Paper Money** (*open 9–1, closed Sun; adm free*) with a collection of banknotes from around the world, and Greek notes dating from the nation's birth; upstairs, you can learn how they're printed. Across the square, the 1689 church of the **Holy Virgin Faneroméni** contains some fine icons of the Ionian School; another church on the square, **Ag. Ioannés**, has an icon of Ag. Dimítrios by Emanuel Tzánes and the tombs of all the Russians who died on Corfu during their Protectorate.

The square gives on to the main street Nikifórou Theotóki, one of the prettiest in the town and address of the popular church of **Panagía tou Xenou**, Our Lady of the

Foreigners. E. Voulgáreos Street leads up to the elegant square with Corfu's **Town Hall**, a Venetian confection begun in 1691 as a Loggia dei Nobili, a club for the aristocrats; it was soon converted into a theatre and later did duty as the municipal opera house, until a new one was built in 1903 (only to be destroyed in the Second World War). Grotesque faces grimace all around the building and a bas-relief shows the triumphant Doge Francesco Morosini, conqueror of the Peloponnese; in the basement, there's a trophy to Morosini that was erected, like Schulenburg's in the Esplanade, in his own lifetime.

It shares the square with the 17th-century **Catholic Cathedral of Ag. Iakovos** (St James), the replacement for a far grander one, destroyed in the 1718 siege; it was also nearly destroyed by the German bombing in 1943. Only the façade and bell tower survived intact; the rest has been reconstructed. The parishioners are mostly Corfiots of Maltese descent. The British brought the first Maltese over to build the Palace of St Michael and St George, then encouraged others to settle and raise fruit and vegetables for British tables.

Campiello

The Campiello, between the Old Port and the Esplanade, is the city's oldest quarter, where tall tenements and palazzi jostle along the stairs and twisting lanes, called *kantounia*. Bombs in the last war have left it some rather unexpected open spaces, but managed to miss a number of buildings worth seeking out, beginning with the 1577 **Orthodox Cathedral**, its 18th-century façade rather unfortunately located next to the rudest T-shirt shop in town. It is dedicated to Ag. Theodóra Augústa, daughter of Theofilos the Iconoclast and Empress of Byzantium (829–842), who was canonized for her role in restoring icon worship in the Orthodox Church following the Iconoclasm. Her relics were brought to Corfu along with those of Ag. Spyrídon and lie in a silver casket in the chapel to the right of the altar, although they've been completely overshadowed by the miracles of her fellow saint (even Theodóra's bell tower is lower than Spyrídon's). If the priest in charge likes the look of you, he'll let you kiss her and take home titbits of her slipper; donations more than welcome. The gold-ground icons are lovely, reminscent of 13th-century Italian art.

The **Byzantine Museum of Corfu** (*open 8.45–3, Sun and holidays 9.30–2, closed Mon; adm*) is near here, up the steps from Arseníou Street. The collection is housed in the beautifully restored 15th-century Antivouniótissa, typical of the Ionian style of church, with its single aisle, timber roof and exonarthex, or indoor porch, that runs around three sides of the building. Among the eminent Corfiots buried under the flagstones is Capodistrias's sister, who was a nun here. The church has one of the elaborately decorated ceilings or *ourania* ('heaven') that the Ionians were so fond of, and a stone iconostasis from a later date, and very Italianate 17th-century Old Testament murals on the walls. Icons from all over the island have been brought here; note especially the mid 16th-century *SS Sergius, Bacchus and Justine* by Michael Damaskinós, the 17th-century *St Cyril of Alexandria* by Emanuel Tzànes, the 17th-century four-handed *Ag. Panteléimon* and icons by the 18th-century painter Geórgios Chrysolorás. On the same street is the **Solomós Museum** (*open weekdays 9–1; adm*) with a collection of old photographs and memorabilia associated with the great Zákynthos poet Diónysos Solomós, who lived here in his later years (*see p.204*).

On a narrow stairway off Philharmonikí Street, **Ag. Nikólaos** had the distinction of once serving as the parish church for the King of Serbia. After the defeat of the Serbian army by the Austro-Bulgarians in 1916, the King, his government and some 150,000 troops took refuge on Corfu. A third of them died shortly thereafter from the flu and are buried on **Vído island**. Boats from the Old Port regularly make the trip to Vído; often the key to Corfu, the Venetians fortified it after the Turks built a gun battery on it to attack the Old Fortress in 1537—a strategy successfully repeated by the Russians in 1799. The walls were refortified and later demolished by the British. Today the island is a quiet refuge with footpaths, a little beach, and a memorial to the Serbs.

South of Corfu Town

Garítsa and the Archaeology Museum

South of the Old Fortress, Garítsa Bay is believed to have been the harbour of King Alcinous of the Phaeacians; it became a fashionable residential district in the 19th century, just in time for the neoclassical building craze. On Kolokotróni Street the beautiful, peaceful **British Cemetery** is famous as a natural botanic garden, where rare species of wild flowers bloom, including 25 species of orchid; the graves, many with intriguing headstones, date from the beginning of the British protectorate. Another monument from the period is an obelisk overlooking Garítsa Bay, dedicated to one of the better High Commissioners, Sir Howard Douglas.

The star attraction in Garítsa is the **Archaeology Museum** (*open 8.30–3, closed Mon; adm*), with an excellent collection of finds from the island and nearby mainland. Opened in 1967, the musuem has already been extended but is still too small to display the more recent discoveries.

Among the new exhibits are bronze statuettes from Archaic to Roman times, a horde of silver staters from the 6th century BC, an iron helmet with silver overlay from the 4th century BC, and Cycladic sculptures, discovered in 1992 by a customs officer as the smugglers attempted to spirit them abroad from Igoumenítsa. Upstairs are grave-offerings and archaic statues of the *kore* and *kouros*, figure sculpture inspired by the Egyptians; poses are stiff, formal, and rigid, one foot carefully placed before the other. Unlike Egyptian models, however, Greek statues are marked by their easy, confident Archaic smiles, as if they were all in on a secret joke. There are two statues of Aphrodite, the favourite goddess of the lusty Corinthians; here, too, is the snarling, stylized Lion of Menecrates, found on the tomb of the same name (*see* below) and the relief of a Dionysiac Symposium (*c.* 500 BC), showing the god Dionysos with a youth, lying on a couch, their eyes focused intently on a something that is probably lost forever. A lion sleeps under the couch; a dog comes striding up.

One room is given over to the striking wall-sized Gorgon Pediment (585 BC) once part of the Doric temple of Artemis in Kanóni (see below). The oldest preserved stone pediment in Greece and one of the largest (56ft wide), it shows how advanced the Corinthians were in the early days of monumental sculpture. The grinning Gorgon Medusa, 9ft high, is powerfully drawn, with her tongue sticking out and snakes for her hair, running with one knee on the ground, flanked by her two children, Pegasus the winged horse (only his forefoot, hindquarters and wing survive) and Chrysaor of the golden sword and terrible grin; according to myth they were born from her blood when she was slain by Perseus, although here she looks very alive indeed. Two large leopards on either side suggest that this is actually Artemis herself in her form of 'the Lady of the Wild Animals', a fearsome goddess who demanded an annual holocaust of the creatures she protected, burned alive on the altar; in the far corners of the pediment, much smaller scenes show the Clash of the Titans—Zeus blasting one with a thunderbolt.

The circular, 7th-century BC **Menecrates tomb** was discovered in 1846 in an excellent state of preservation. Its lower sections are still intact in the garden of a building at the junction of Marasslí and Kíprou Streets, three blocks south of the museum: Menecrates was a Consul of Oeanthe in Locris who drowned and was buried in this tumulus; the lion was found nearby, although no one is sure if it was actually associated with the tomb.

Southern Suburbs along the Kanóni Peninsula

City bus no.3 from Corfu Town passes through all of the garden suburbs draped over the little **Kanóni peninsula** that dangles south of Garítsa Bay. Ancient Corcyra originally occupied much of this peninsula, and had two harbours: what is now the Chalikiopóulos lagoon to the west and the ring-shaped 'harbour of King Alcinous' (now filled in) in the northeastern corner of the peninsula, at Anemómylos. Above it, right on top of the centre of ancient Corcyra, Sir Frederick Adam, the second High Commissioner of the Ionian State, built the little Regency villa of **Mon Repos** for his famously moustachioed and well-loved Corfiot wife, just before leaving his post in 1832, accepting a £2000 diamond star as a going away present from the Ionian senate, which he had nearly bankrupted. The Greek royal family later adopted Mon Repos as a summer villa; Philip, Duke of Edinburgh, was born here in 1921. In 1994, the Greek Government allowed the Municipality of Corfu to repossess the estate from ex-King Constantine and the beautiful wooded park is to be developed as an archaeological park. So far a Roman villa and bath have been discovered on the periphery, at Kasfíki, opposite the ruined 5th-century basilica of **Ag. Kérkyra** at Paleópolis (by the crossroads, opposite the gate of Mon Repos).

Little Mon Repos beach—Corfu's town beach—is just below if you need a dip; a few lanes back, don't miss the 11th-century church of **Ag. Iássonos and Sosipater**, the only Byzantine-style church on the whole island; inside are lovely icons and iconostasis and the tombs of the church's namesakes, two disciples of St Paul, who introduced Christianity to Corfu in AD 70. Davianus, the head of the Roman senate on the island, responded by having Sosipater and plenty of poisonous snakes nailed up in a barrel and thrown in the sea. When the barrel washed ashore on Vido islet and opened up, the snakes were found petrified around Sosipater's perfectly intact body. Davianus and the senate then had a change of heart and were baptized by St Jason.

Near the Venetian church, along the wall of Mon Repos, a path leads to the bucolic spring of **Kardáki**, which flows year round from the mouth of a stone-winged lion of St Mark; the ancient Greeks, and later the Venetians used it to supply their ships. The cold water is good, but an inscription above warns: 'Every stranger who wets his lips here to his home will not return.' Below the spring are the ruins of a 6th-century BC Doric temple of Apollo. From here it's an easy walk to the lush and lovely residential area of Análypsos.

Further south, a minor road leads to the Doric **Temple of Artemis** (585 BC), first discovered by the French General Donzelot when he excavated ancient Corcyra's moat as part of the city's southern defences. In 1911–14, Kaiser Wilhelm sponsored the systematic excavation by Dörpfeld that led to the discovery of the Gorgon Pediment in the Archaeology Museum. Corinth was the first city to build temples in stone, but after its devastation by the Romans in 146 BC none have survived: this limestone structure, 138 by 72ft, is the oldest periptal stone temple in Greece, the prototype of the Classical era temple with its columns, pediments and metopes. The large altar and the retaining wall of the Hellenistic stoa remain intact; some of its stones were cannibalized in the 5th century to build the adjacent convent of **Ag. Teodóri**. Kanóni, at the southern tip of the lovely little peninsula, is named for the old cannon once situated on the bluff, where two cafés now overlook the pretty bay, the harbour of ancient Corcyra. Two islets protected it: that of the oft-photographed convent **Panagía Vlacharína**, connected to the shore by a causeway, and **Pondikonísi**, the Isle of the Mouse, with its 13th-century chapel, Ag. Pnévmatos. Pondikonísi was the Phoenician ship that brought Odysseus home to Ithaca, but on its way back to Corfu, the angry Poseidon smote 'with his open palm, and made the ship a rock, fast rooted in the bed of the deep sea', according to the *Odyssey*. An airport runway built on a landfill site now crosses the west end of the shallow lagoon, and a collection of big new hotels has toadstooled nearby, in spite of the noise of planes day and night, which can interrupt a good night's sleep.

Pérama, Gastoúri and the Achilleion

Once past the Kanóni peninsula and linked to it by a pedestrian causeway over the lagoon, **Pérama** claims to be the site of King Alcinous' wonderful garden and is where the Durrell family first lived when they arrived. The pretty village of **Gastoúri** is the dreamy setting for a neoclassical neo-Pompeiian villa called the **Achilleion** (*open for tours daily in summer, 8.45–3.30*), with lovely views in all directions. The villa itself is more of a nightmare, sufficiently kitsch to be used as a location for the James Bond film *For Your Eyes Only*. Built in 1890 by the Empress Elisabeth ('Sissi') of Austria after the tragic death of her only son Rudolphe, the villa was named for Sissi's passion for the hero of Homer's *Iliad*; Sissi fancied herself as the immortal sea goddess Thetis, with Rudolphe as her son Achilles, idealized by a large marble statue she had made of the *Dying Achilles* for the garden. Ten years after Sissi was assassinated in 1898 by an Italian anarchist, Kaiser Wilhelm II bought the Achilleion and made it his summer residence from 1908 to 1914, and, true to character, had the *Dying Achilles* replaced with a huge bronze *Victorious Achilles*, with the inscription 'To the Greatest of the Greeks from the Greatest of the Germans.'

Among the bevy of more delicate statues, note the Grace standing next to Apollo, sculpted by Canova, using Napoleon's sister Pauline Borghese as his model. The small museum contains, among its collection of imperial mementoes, a gold coin that Maximilian, emperor of Mexico, used to bribe his execution squad to shoot at his heart instead of his face, and one of the Kaiser's swivelling saddles, from which he dictated plans for the First World War, and photos of him swanning around on his huge yacht, the *Hohenzollern*, which he used to anchor off the 'Kaiser's Bridge' just south of Pérama. Amid this fetid mix of bad art and power, note, over the gate of Troy in Franz Matsch's stomach-churning painting of the *Triumph of Achilles*, a little swastika.

Shopping

Xenoglosso, Ger. Markóra 45, near San Rocco Square, has a good selection of books in English. Autolycus Gallery, now closed, sells some of its fine collection of antique prints, maps, postcards and watercolours at Mrs Paipeti's antique shop next to the Cavalieri Corfu Hotel.

There are a number of high-fashion shops, although the most famous must be Panton on Panton Street, the main outlet of Corfu designer Lisa Palavicini, whose clothes have been featured in Vogue and are sold in outlets in Athens, London and Jordan.

Shops with a predominantly touristy clientele hardly ever seem to close, but non-tourist shops are closed every evening except Tuesday, Thursday and Friday.

luxury

Just south of the centre, the enormous **Corfu Palace**, Dimokratías Ave, ✆ 39 485, 🖷 31 749, has two swimming pools and all the trimmings from baby-sitting to 24-hour room service. Most rooms have sea views but can cost as much as 50,000dr in high season. There's also a cache of luxurious high-rise palaces in Kanóni: the **Corfu Holidays Palace**, ✆ 36 540, 🖷 36 551, is a hotel and bungalow complex with casino and bowling alley; rooms have either sea or lake views.

expensive

For old-style elegance, no hotel on Corfu can compete with the **Cavalieri Corfu**, located on the end of the Esplanade at 4 Kapodistríou, ✆ 39 336, 🖷 39 283 (*A*) in a renovated French mansion; comfortable, air-conditioned, and with a magnificent roof garden, open for drinks to non-guests and overlooking the town in all directions. In an old building overlooking the Old Port and the New Fort, there's the **Astron Hotel** at 15 Donzelótou, ✆ 39 505, 🖷 33 708 (*B*); the rooms are a bit basic for the price despite good bathrooms and mostly balconies.

moderate

The salmon-coloured **Bella Venezia**, just back from the Esplanade at 4 Napoleon Zambeli, ✆ 44 290, 🖷 20 708 (*B*) is a renovated old building in a relatively quiet, yet central, part of town; pretty garden terrace. If you'd prefer to be on the Esplanade, the **Arcadion** at 44 Kapodistríou, ✆ 37 671 (*C*) has balconies overlooking it. On the waterfront in the Old Port, **Konstantinoupolis**, ✆ 48 716/7, 🖷 48 718 (*C*), is a good choice, originally established in 1862 and very well refurbished in 1997. The **Royal**, in Kanóni, ✆ 37 512 (*C*) enjoys a commanding position and could be a class higher with its three swimming-pools on descending levels, and roof garden with views over Mouse Island and the airport. **Hermes**, 12 Ger. Markóra, ✆ 31 747 (*C*), is a moderate-sized hotel away from the tourist crowds, on the inland side of the New Fortress.

inexpensive

Europa, 10 Gitsiáli, at the New Port, ✆ 39 304 (*D*) is one of the better modern choices. For something even less dear, try the list of rooms to rent from the National Tourist Office, 7 Rizospaston Voulefton, ✆ 37 520/638. Most of these are in the old quarters and cost *5000dr* upwards for a bed in season. The youth hostel, and nearest campsite, are 8km north in Kontókali (*see* below).

Corfu shows its Venetian heritage in the kitchen as well as in its architecture. Look for *sofríto*, a veal stew flavoured with garlic, vinegar and parsley; *bourdétto*, a fish stew, liberally peppered, and *pastitsátha*, a pasta and veal dish; the island's own sweet is *sikomaeda*, or fig pie. Eating out on the genteel Listón, with front-row seats on the crowds, can be expensive unless you stick to pizza. One street back at 66 Kapodistríou, **Rex**, ✆ 39 649, has a good varied menu—try the local speciality *sofríto* and other Corfiot dishes, and pay *2500dr* for a meal. **Yoryias Taverna** on Guilford Street is a popular, traditional taverna. Just opposite, **Porta Remounda** has a well-earned reputation for fish.

On the seafront below the Palace of St Michael and St George, **Faleraki** is tucked away in a historic spot where the steam passengers used to disembark; now an ouzerie/restaurant, it has views of the sea, old walls and the off-shore yacht club. In Kremastí Square, the **Venetian Well**, ✆ 44 761 has a varied and international menu with a wide choice of Greek wines (*3000dr*). **Pizza Pete,** with its lively location on the waterfront on Arseníou, has free entertainment in the form of a chatty mynah bird called Lolo (which means 'crazy', given the right emphasis); a pizza meal will run to 2000dr. The **Averof**, at Alipíou and Prossalendíou, is a long-established favourite of tourists and locals alike and **L. Gigisdakis**, at Solomoú 28, is as authentic an old Greek taverna as you could hope for, with old pots bubbling away in the kitchen and ready oven dishes; try their pickled octopus (*achtapóthi xytháto*); meals around *2500dr*.

By the New Port, in Xen. Stratigoú St, the smart **Orestes** has dining inside and in a pleasant little garden opposite; seafood specialities from *4000dr*. For something much cheaper, **Becchios** in Mandoúki, opposite the ferries to Igoumenítsa, does splendid charcoal-grilled meats; and in the suburb of Potamós two restaurants offer outstanding traditional fare, **Nicholas** and **Menios** (especially noted for fish). The elegant **Xenichtes**, on the road to Paleokastrítsa, ✆ 24 911/22 035, has served excellent Greek food with a sprinkling of dishes from other countries for 20 years; fresh salmon is delivered every morning on the Oslo–Corfu flight (*3500dr*). In Garítsa, near the Church of Ag. Iássonos and Sosipater, **Yannis** is one of the few remaining tavernas where you are still invited to go into the kitchen, lift lids off pots and choose your food.

Futher out in Kanóni, **Restaurant Nausicaa**, Nausicá 11, ✆ 44 354, serves delicious Greek, French and Eastern dishes under the garden trellis (fairly dear, but they take credit cards). Its close neighbour, **Taverna**

Pelargos, looks a bit corny from the outside but serves a vast array of well-prepared Greek dishes: the *stifádo* and *sofríto* are superb.

In Kinopiástes, 3km from Gastoúri, **Taverna Tripa** ('Hole in the Wall'), run by the Anyfantís family since 1947, is something of a Corfu national monument, completely cluttered inside with bottles, knick-knacks, a hurdy gurdy, photos (mostly of the late Spiros Anyfantís with celebrity diners), while up on the ceiling strings of salamis, sausages, peppers and garlic are linked by cobwebs. Greek nights here are renowned, with up to 10 courses served; although it's not cheap, the food and service are excellent and the costumed waiters put on a folk-dancing show to boot. Nearby, on the Achilleion road (about 7km from town) are two tavernas with live music and good, reasonably priced food; the **Barbathomas**, with meat specialities, and **Pontis**, with a big selection of *mezédes*, spit-roasted lamb, charcoal grills and local dishes.

Entertainment and Nightlife

Pick up a copy of the monthly *The Corfiot* for local news and a calendar of events; published primarily for residents, it makes interesting reading. Other media are even better served: Corfu has three cable TV stations and 17 radio stations, and a flip through the FM dial may even dig up an English-speaking DJ. Apart from the disco ghetto north of town and, a bit less brash, in the Kanóni area, most of Corfu's nightlife revolves around the Listón with a smattering of bars playing late night music. For more of a bop, **Karnayio** has dancing until the wee hours and two of the most popular clubs are **Coca Flash** and **Apokalypsis**. There are a number of *bouzouki* joints, most of which can be avoided without fear of missing anything wonderful; the best live Greek music, with dancers and the works, is at the **Loutrovio** restaurant in Kefalomandoukó, on the hill overlooking 'disco strip'. There are two cinemas that show undubbed English language films, but one is under threat of closure. **The Gallery**, on Ag. Spyrídon Street, is a favourite watering hole of Greeks and ex-pats, and **Remezzo** is fun for late night ice-cream.

North of Corfu Town

The roads along the east coast of Corfu are fast-moving and hotel developers have followed them every inch of the way. To the immediate north of Corfu Town begins a 10km stretch of beach, hotel, self-catering, campsite and restaurant sprawl, most intensely at Kontókali, Goúvia, Dassiá, Ipsos and Pírgi; yet if they all missed the boat in architecture and design, there's visual redemption in the dishevelled beauty of the surrounding green hills and olive groves.

Eight kilometres from Corfu Town, the coast road veers sharply right through **Gouviá** (ΓΟΥΒΙΑ), overlooking a lagoon once used by the Venetians as a harbour; in return, the impressive remains of the Venetian **arsenal** overlook Gouviá's popular marina. The pebble beach offers watersports and reasonable swimming, while back on the dual-carriageway of a main road, the recently rehoused **Corfu Shell Museum**, ✆ 99 340 (*open daily 10am–9pm; adm*), with its thousands of beautiful sea treasures seems rather at odds with its new location. Sadly, despite several moves to try to find this charming and unusual museum a good home, its future in Gouviá, or indeed anywhere, is still cloudy. Emerald **Cape Komméno** extends out here, but looks better from a distance and has poor beaches to boot.

A few kilometres further north on the still excruciatingly built-up main road, **Dassiá** (ΔΑΣΙΑ) has a long, narrow sand and shingle beach fringed by olive groves, a favourite for sports from waterskiing to paragliding. Excursion boats run as far as Kassiópi (north) and Benítses (south). A few years ago, if a good night's sleep was a priority, it was best to avoid **Ípsos** (ΥΨΟΣ) and **Pírgi** (ΠΥΡΓΙ), former fishing villages at either end of Corfu's 'Golden Mile' north of Dassiá. Although the plethora of bars and discos no longer reverberate till dawn, you still might want to head for the scenic hinterland or continue up the coast if you want to escape the carousels of inflatable crocodiles and 'I ♥ Corfu' postcards which line the long scimitar of shingle beach, with barely enough room for a good wiggle.

From Ípsos, head inland to **Ano Korakiána** with its olive wood workshop and delightful exhibit of folk sculpture at the **Museum of Aristedes Metalinós** ✆ (0663) 22 317. The road leading up into the Troumpetta range via Sokraki is an awesome series of hairpins and about as green and gorgeous as it gets. From Pírgi, noodle up though Spartílas to Strinílas, for lunch and excellent local wine in the beautifully shaded main square; or browse through olive wood shops, like family-run 'Pantokratora' with its workshop at the entrance to the village.

Corfu ✆ *(0661–)*   ***Where to Stay and Eating Out***

Kontókali ✉ 49100

Corfu's **youth hostel** is here (take bus no.7 from San Rocco Square), ✆ 91 202); an IYHA card is required. The nearest **campsite** to Corfu Town (✆ 91 202) is here as well. **The Viceroy**, on the back street between Kontókali and Gouviá, serves tasty tandooris and a superb chicken korma; prices are a bit high (*around 4000dr a head*) because the spices have to be imported. The **New Locanda** flirts with the cuisines of the world, including many vegetarian dishes. **Gerekos,** in the village, and **Roula's** on the promontory past the Corkyra Beach Hotel are both excellent for fish.

Gouviá ✉ 49100

Debonos, ✆ 33 708 (*A; exp*) has a garden with a pool. *Open Mar–Oct.*
Louvre, ✆ 91 506 (*D; mod*) is adequate but don't expect any master-pieces. **Bella Mama**, on the edge of the strip, is Greek-owned and run in spite of its name, and serves a delicious *sofríto*, lamb *kléftiko*, and other meats and chicken, with a house wine to quaff. **Tartufo** up the hill, is owned by the same family and is similar, but set in a quieter area (*both from 2500–4000dr*). **La Bonita** is a good Italian and **O'Kapetanios** is best for fish.

Dassiá ✉ 49100

Corfu Chandris and **Dassia Chandris**, ✆ 97 100, 🖷 93 458 (*A; exp*) form a huge double resort on the beach; their bungalows and villas in the environs also have use of the pools, tennis, playground, restaurants and a free shuttle service into Corfu Town. The Dassia is currently the most recently renovated, but the Chandris is shortly due an overhaul, so check before booking; ask for a sea view since the so-called mountain view faces right on to the hideous main road. *Open April–Oct.* In the same league, there's the **Corfu Imperial**, overlooking Koméno Bay, ✆ 91 481, 🖷 91 881 (*A; exp*).

Ípsos ✉ 49083

Costas Beach, ✆ 93 205 (*D; mod*) is one possibility. Although no longer allowed to boom all night, there are still plenty of young bars in Ípsos; **Hector's Club** and **B52** are especially popular.

The Northeast Corner: Barbáti to Ag. Spyrídonos

Continuing north, **Barbáti** (ΜΠΑΡΜΠΑΤΗ) has a long stretch of pebbles and every conceivable facility to go with it, but from here on there is a gentle and welcome gear-change; as the coastal road wiggles its way up from the sea, the resorts below become smaller and cosier. No longer spread over vast stretches of coastline with wall-to-wall shops and tavernas, the traditional village charm of these smaller resorts is allowed to peek through. The first, **Nissáki**, is a fishing hamlet which trickles along the main road; below, roads and goat tracks lead to a number of quiet coves, though its tiny eponymous beach has two good tavernas and a good arts and crafts shop ('The Loom') so tends to get pretty full. Even if you don't venture off the main road here, it is worth pausing at Nissáki's fine olive wood shop, opposite the Hotel Ilios. Just on from Nissáki, you can drive (nose-first) to **Kamináki**; a pebbly bay bordered by villas (*many bookable through CV Travel, see p.127*) with the clearest waters, perfect for snorkelling. There are some water sports here, boat hire and two beach tavernas. Still heading north is the delight-fully picturesque and unspoilt bay of **Agní**, with crystal-clear waters and three outstandingly good tavernas. The next little resort off the main road is built around the popular pebble beach of **Kalámi** (ΚΑΛΑΜΙ), one of the biggest self-catering compounds on Corfu, where you can stay overlooking the bay in Lawrence Durrell's famous White House (*see* below). **Kouloúra**, a kilometre or so from the rugged Albanian coast, is a lovely seaside hamlet on a narrow horseshoe bay with a shingle beach, which has not yet succumbed to the developers; the brothers Durrell spent their youth here. Kouloúra was also favoured by Venetians: note the 16th-century **Koúartanou Gennatá**, part villa and part fortified tower, and two 17th-century mansions, **Vassilá** and **Prosalenti**. The next beach north is **Kerásia**, a pretty strand of white pebbles with shade and a taverna, most easily reached by doubling back 2km from beautiful, pricey South Kensington-on-Sea, known locally as **Ag. Stéfanos.**

Kassiópi (ΚΑΣΣΙΟΠΗ), an important Hellenistic town founded by Pyrrhus of Epirus (the famous generalissimo of pseudo-victories), is now the largest and busiest resort on the northeast coast. It flourished under the Romans who surrounded it with great walls and built its famous temple of Zeus. Cassius was visited by count-less sailors voyaging between East and West, and by Cicero, and by Emperor Nero, who stopped to make an offering on his way to the Isthmian Games in Corinth, praying for victory in the lute-playing competition; Tiberius had a villa here. In Christian times the temple was replaced by a church of the Virgin. This was destroyed like so much of Corfu in the Turkish siege of 1537 and replaced with a Venetian church that saw a famous miracle. An innocent young man was con-victed of theft and sentenced to be blinded by the Venetian Bailie; he wandered Corfu in despair until he came to the church and fell asleep. He was awakened by hands resting on his eyes, and when he opened them he saw the Virgin smiling over him. The news of the miracle reached the Bailie, who came to Kassiópi to make amends, and to this day the anniversary of the miracle is celebrated with a special mass every 8 May. A plaque by the door records the Venetian rebuilding of the church in 1538. Kassiópi's Byzantine fortress was the first place in Greece to fall to Robert the Guiscard's Normans, on their compaign to capture Constantinople itself. As every subsequent marauder from the north passed by Kassiópi to reach Corfu Town, the town bore the brunt of their attacks. When, after a long struggle, the Venetians finally took the fortress, they rendered it use-less to avenge themselves. Without any defences the Kassiopiots suffered terribly at the hands of the Turks and the town lost all of its former importance.The ruined fortress still stands above the village, guarding only wild flowers and sheep.

Although still a fishing village with a pretty waterfront, Kassiópi has discovered the profits to be made from the tourist trade and the main shopping street is positively groaning with touristy trinkets; however, on the road skirting town, 'Barbara's' is worth a peek if you're after locally designed and painted ceramics. Four small, well-equipped beaches can be reached by footpath from the headland, and when you're tired of windsurfing or basting yourself on the beach, you can explore the rocky coastline on foot. Two of Corfu's most tastefully developed beaches, **Avláki** and **Koyévinas**, are a quick drive, or 20–30-minute walk, south of Kassiópi; both beautiful white pebble bays, Koyévinas sports a taverna, while Avláki has two, along with boats, pedaloes and windsurfers for hire.

Continuing west beyond the grey sand beach of **Kalamáki** (also with a taverna), a sign for Loútses and Perithía announces the way up the brooding slopes of 900m **Mount Pantokrátor**, Corfu's highest point.

You can take a car as far as **Old Perithía**, one of Corfu's erstwhile secrets: a charming cobblestoned village of stone houses, abandoned by all but three farming families, one of whom now runs the Capricorn Grill, an understated taverna in the hub of the old village. Lost in a mountain hollow, Old Perithía's once lush garden terraces are slowly disintegrating since everyone left for the coast to seek their fortune. The path from here to the summit of Pantokrátor takes about an hour, but rewards you with a wondrous display of flora even into the hot summer months, and a view of emerald Corfu spread at your feet and white-capped Albanian peaks on the mainland, a view enjoyed every day by the single monk and his somewhat less orthodox pylon in the mountaintop monastery. On a clear day you can see the coast of Apulia, in southern Italy; few people realize that Brindisi is actually closer to Corfu than Pátras. The rutted road from Old Perithía by way of Láfki takes in some of Corfu's most enchanting countryside.

Back down on the coast road, **Ag. Spyrídonos** may be the answer if you've been looking for a small sandy beach, a simple taverna or two and a handful of rooms to rent, although Corfiots converge on it on Sundays.

Where to Stay and Eating Out

Nissáki/Kalámi/Ag. Stéfanos ✉ 49100

The **Sol Elite Nissaki Beach Hotel**, © 91 232, 🖷 22 079 (*A; lux–exp*) is the only big hotel on this stretch of coast; despite being a mammoth eyesore, it offers great views, a pool, gym, shops, restaurants and good facilities for kids. This is the perfect area for glimpsing the old Corfu and to rent from an exquisite selection of villas, ranging in size and plushness, and including Lawrence Durrell's White House in Kalámi; book through CV Travel in London, © (0171) 581 0851 (*see* **Practical A–Z**, p.25); in Corfu, © 40 644 or 39 900.

Up on the coast road through Nissáki, **Vitamins** is a smart and friendly taverna with excellent food and a lovely terrace. **Mitsos** on Nissaki beach is always busy for lunch, with good reason. One evening a week, three local musicians play good old-fashioned Greek music at next-door **Nikos** and the **Olive Press** celebrates with the occasional and relatively tasteful Greek Night. For a bit of unparalleled romance on a moonlit evening, take a water-taxi from Kalámi to any one of the three excellent tavernas in Agní.

Kassiópi ✉ 49100

Kassiópi bulges with Italians in August and unless you are pre-booked, forget it. Even at other times, the hotel situation is meagre to say the least.

Oasis, ✆ 81 275 (*D; inexp*), halfway up the main street, is pretty basic but about the only one that caters for the independent traveller. For help finding a studio or flat, try **Cosmic Tourist Centre**, ✆ 81 624, or **The Travel Corner**, ✆ 81 220, ✉ 81 108, or again, pre-book through one of the specialist companies featured on p.17. **Kassiopi Star** and **The Three Brothers** on the waterfront serve Greek and Corfiot specialities (*4000dr*), while **Psilos** is a traditional no-frills taverna. At Imerólia, the nearest beach, the **Imerolia Taverna** has good food and dancing every other night. In the opposite direction, **Cavo Barbaro** is a good choice on Avláki beach.

Ag. Spyrídon ✉ 49100

Tucked away in the olive groves, 100m from the sea, **St Spíridon Bay**, ✆ 98 294, ✉ 98 295 (*B; exp–mod*) is an unpretentious bungalow complex.

The North Coast

Almirós, at the quiet east end of Corfu's longest beach, is a warm shallow lagoon with trees and migratory birds. The rest of the coast has been clobbered with the magic wand of package tourism, from **Acharávi** (ΑΧΑΡΑΒΗ), where the beach is framed by pretty scenery, to **Róda** (ΡΟΔΑ), where egg and chips seems to be everyone's special of the day but where there's enough sand to escape the worst of the crowds by walking a bit in either direction. **Astrakéri**, on the west end, has a downbeat feel but is the one place along here where you might find a room.

Inland from Acharávi, **Ag. Pantelèimonos** has a huge ruined tower mansion called **Polylas**, complete with prisons used during the Venetian occupation; another Venetian manor lies further up in **Episkepsís**. Inland from Róda, **Plátonas** is in the heart of Corfu's kumquat country. Introduced from the Far East half a century ago, kumquats look like baby oranges but are too sour for many tastes; the annual harvest of 35 tonnes produced by 70 farmers are distilled into kumquat liqueur (using both blossoms and fruit) and preserved as kumquat jams and conserves. Inland from Astrakerí, **Karoussádes** is a pretty agricultural village with the 16th-century Theotóki mansion as its landmark.

Sidári (ΣΙΔΑΡΙ) has rolled over and surrendered itself wholesale to package tourism and mosquitoes. If you're passing through, the **Canal d'Amour** is a peculiar rock formation said to be two lovers—swim between them and you are guaranteed eternal love, which is more than promised by the local disco. If you have your own transport, less crowded beaches await west of Sidári below the village of **Perouládes**; the wind-sculpted tawny cliffs are high enough to cast the sandy beach in shade in the early afternoon.

✆ *(0663–)*   **Where to Stay and Eating Out**

Róda/Astrakéri ✉ 49081

In season nearly every room in Róda is block-booked; but outside the high summer months try **Villa Portoni**, ✆ (0661) 31 498, in Athens, ✆ (01) 901 6115, for simple flats in a quiet location, with a pool.

Once the only taverna in town, **Kind Hearted Place** (at the eastern end of the waterfront) has been offering a good, if limited, Greek menu since the early '60s; a small back terrace overlooks the water. **Astrakéri Beach Hotel**, ✆ 31 238 (*C; inexp*), on the gently shelving sands, is surrounded by lush lawns and two minutes from a couple of good value fish tavernas; all rooms have sea view balconies but, at the time of writing, are badly in need of renovation. **Sandra** is a very basic pension 100m from the sea, also in Astrakéri, ✆ 31 120 (*E; inexp*). **Roda Camping**, ✆ 93 120, may have space if all else fails.

Islands near Corfu: Othoní, Eríkousa and Mathráki

Northwest of Sidári three sleepy islets, Othoní (the largest), Eríkousa and Mathráki, comprise the westernmost territory of Greece. Transport to them is not always reliable: there are organized excursions and caiques from Sidári (caiques run most of the year, depending on demand and weather), ferries from Corfu Town, or a summer excursion from Ag. Stéfanos. The population is disproportionately feminine, the wives of husbands who fish or work in the USA. Olives and aromatic table grapes are produced locally, and fresh fish is nearly always available; each island has rooms to rent, but food supplies can be scarce.

Of the three, **Othoní** is the largest and driest (a lack of water is one of the problems), but has the friendliest atmosphere and the most to offer if you like to ramble. There are a handful of shingle beaches and donkey trails up to the pretty, nearly abandoned villages and a well-preserved medieval fort on a pine-covered hill.

Most of the excursions make for **Eríkousa,** which has the best sandy beach and a pair of villages set in the cypresses and olives; **Mathráki,** the smallest island, also has a sandy beach—a nesting place for loggerhead turtles (*see* pp.206–7)—and very limited facilities.

℗ (0663–)   ***Where to Stay and Eating Out***

Othóni/Eríkousa/Mathráki ✉ 49081

Book early for the **Locanda dei Sogni,** on Othóni *℗* 71 640, which offers pretty rooms and good Italian food; ditto for **Hotel Eríkousa,** *℗* 71 555 (*C; mod*) the only hotel on Eríkousa, directly on the beach.

Western Beaches: North to South

This whole northwest corner of Corfu is covered with forests. The main roads have been resurfaced, but once off the beaten track be warned that the roads can bottom out the best shock-absorbers. The main coastal road from Sidári cuts off the corner of the northwest on route to **Ag. Stéfanos** (not to be confused with the Ag. Stéfanos on the east coast), a large and uninspiring bay with brown sand and windsurfing; **Aríllas** just south has a wide, sandy, steep bay with an attractive backdrop of green hills. The village of **Afiónas** is on a headland with magnificent views in either direction, its sandy beach steadily developing. Best of all is **Ag. Geórgios** (Pagói), a long, magnificent stretch of beach under steep cliffs; as yet it is not over-developed but already offers watersports, tavernas and discos; during the day it fills up with trippers from Paleokastrítsa.

One of Corfu's celebrated beauty spots and the major resort in west Corfu, **Paleokastrítsa** (ΠΑΛΑΙΟΚΑΣΤΡΙΤΣΑ) spreads out from a small horseshoe bay, flanked by sandy and pebbly coves, olive and almond groves, mountains and forests. Paleokastrítsa is chock-a-block in the summer with holiday-makers; in the early spring, however, you can believe its claim to have been the fabled home of the King Alcinous and princess Nausicaa. The sea is said to be colder here than anywhere else in Corfu. On a promontory above town, **Zoodóchos Pigí** (or Paleokastrítsa) monastery was built in 1228 on the site of a Byzantine fortress, and tarted up by an abbot with Rococo tastes in the 1700s. Tour groups queue up to buy a candle (the price of admission) as a monk hands out black skirts and shawls to the underclad. Inside, a one-room museum contains some very old icons and an olive press; outside, there's a peach of a view of the sapphire sea below.

The most spectacular view of the magnificent coastline is on the steep climb (or drive) out of Paleokastrítsa through cypress and pine woods north towards the village of **Lákones** and its celebrated Bella Vista Café, affording nothing less than 'the

Most Beautiful View in Europe.' Lákones itself is the hub of one of the loveliest walks on Corfu, especially to Kríni and the formidable **Angelókastro** (you can also walk from Paleokastrítsa). Built in the 13th century by the Byzantine despot of Epirus, Michael Angelos, it is mostly ruined, but makes an impressive sight clinging to the wild red rocks over a 1000ft precipice. Angelókastro played a major role during the various raids on the island, sheltering the surrounding villagers (as well as the Venetian governor, who lived there). However, the Corfiots were rarely content to stay behind the walls of Angelókastro, and often spilled out to attack their attackers.

If you have a car, the mountain roads from Lákones north to Róda through the little villages of **Chorepískopi**, **Valanión** (3km on a by-road) and **Nímfes** offer a bucolic journey through the Corfu of yesteryear.

South of Paleokastrítsa stretches the fertile, startlingly flat **Rópa Valley**, where Homer's description of the island rings home: 'Pear follows pear, apple after apple grows, fig after fig, and grape yields grape again.' Along with orchards, Rópa has the **Corfu Golf Club**, 18 holes designed by Harradine and Pencross Bent, and rated one of the 100 top courses in the world; club hire available (℗ (0661) 94 220). Westwards on the coast, **Ermónes,** with its pebble beaches and hotels, is another candidate for Odysseus' landing point; Nausicaa and her servants would have been washing the palace laundry in a little cascade—near the present Snackbar Nausicaa.

Pélekas, a 17th-century village up on a mountain ridge, was Kaiser Wilhelm II's favourite spot to watch the sunset; bus-loads of people arrive every evening in the summer to do the same, from a tower known as **Kaiser's Throne**. Pélekas was one of Corfu's nudie beaches until a road built from Gialiskári brought in crowds of trippers; now a completely unadorned walk down the steep track takes you to lovely **Mirtiótissa** beach (the other half of the beach, by the monastery, is not nudist). After sunset the village throbs to the sound of disco music. **Glyfáda**, one of the island's best beaches, is a long gentle swathe of golden sand. It fills up during the day with hotel residents and day-trippers, but early evening is perfect for a swim here, with steep cliffs dropping straight down into the blue bay.

Where to Stay and Eating Out

Ag. Geórgios ✉ 49080, ℗ (0663–)

    St George, ℗ 31 147 or 96 213 (*D; inexp*) is convenient for the beach. *Open April–Oct.* **Vrachos** is the best place for freshwater crayfish and lobster. Nearby Afiónas is a good place to rent rooms away from the brouhaha.

    Here at **Dionysos**, delicious *mezédes* complement the spectacular views over Ag. Geórgios bay and **The Three Brothers** is a bar-restaurant with a splendid terrace from which to watch the sunset. A bit further north, on the road to Kavádes from Aríllas, **Mon Amour** is one of the best tavernas on Corfu, specializing in lamb-on-the-spit and other meaty delicacies.

Paleokastrítsa ✉ 49083, ✆ (0663–)

Prices have come down here, but so have standards; most apartments are pre-booked and the choice of hotels is uninspiring. The **Akrotiri Beach**, ✆ 41 275 (*A; exp*), five minutes uphill from the beach, enjoys some of the best views, and there's a seawater pool for those who don't want to commute to the real thing. Bizarrely dark red **Zefyros**, ✆ 41 244 (*D; mod–inexp*) is near the sea and very basic. **Paleokastritsa Camping**, ✆ 41 204, is probably the nicest campsite on Corfu. There are a number of seafood restaurants. **Chez George** commands the prime location and the highest prices; residents and long-term visitors prefer the **Astakos.**

Nímfes ✉ 49080, ✆ (0663–)

Platonas, ✆ 94 396 (*D; mod*) is a pleasant place to escape the crowds on the coast, and there's a taverna, too.

Ermónes/Glyfáda ✉ 49100, ✆ (0661–)

Hermones Beach, ✆ 94 241 (*A; exp*), is a huge bungalow complex, with every facility; the much more intimate **Athena Hermones Golf**, ✆ 94 226 (*C; mod*) is near the course. The **Grand Glyfada Hotel** ✆ 94 201, ✆ 30 184 (*A; exp*) has many watersport activities which dominate the beach.

Southern Corfu

The southern half of the island has attracted the worst excesses of tourism. For years **Benítses** (ΜΠΕΝΙΤΣΕΣ) has been the numero uno offender, a British package resort bubbling with hormones and devouring a little Greek fishing village (with its permission, of course), inhabited since ancient times. More recently, tour operators have pulled out and Benítses is an altogether gentler place again, but the damage is already done. The patches of beach it offers will always be too close to the coastal highway and the rowdies seem to have chased the resort's former enthusiasts away for good. But if you look hard enough, you can still find a few remnants of Benítses' more aesthetic past. The arches and mosaics just behind the harbour belonged to a Roman bathhouse. And you can walk through the old, residential quarter of the village, past the local cemetery through delightful rural scenery towards **Stavrós**, where the Benítses Waterworks was built by Sir Frederick Adam, British High Commissioner from 1824–32. Originally the waterworks supplied all of Corfu Town; now Benítses somehow manages to use it all, even though few people there would be caught dead drinking it. Further south, the nearly continuous resort sprawls past the beaches of **Moraítika** (ΜΟΡΑΙΤΙΚΑ) and **Messónghi** (ΜΕΣΣΟΓΓΗ), a cut above Benítses. If you're down here for the scenery, skip the coast altogether and take the inland route, beginning at Kinopiástes (near Gastoúri), passing by way of Ag. Déka (one of Corfu's prettiest villages), Makráta, Kornáta and Strongilí.

The more inaccessible west coast is also more worthwhile: **Ag. Górdis** (ΑΓ. ΓΟΡΔΗΣ) is one of Corfu's most attractive village-resorts with a lovely, sheltered two-mile-long beach of soft golden sand and minimal waves. Inland, **Sinarádes** is a large and pretty village surrounded by vineyards and home to a fine folk museum. Further south, **Ag. Mathías**, planted 1000ft high on its own mountain, is a serene place to daydream under the plane tree and write up your diary, disturbed only by the occasional roar of hired scooters and jeeps as they zip through the village on a quest for true peace and quiet. The village remains delightfully Greek, and the locals are more concerned about their olive crop than threatened decreases in tourist numbers. There are 24 churches in or near the village, and by asking around you can find your way down the steep slopes to the really peaceful beaches of **Tría Avlákia**, **Paramónas** and **Skithi**, with a few rooms and the odd inexpensive taverna. An octagonal Byzantine castle at **Gardíki**, south of Ag. Mathías, was another work by the despot of Epirus, Michael Angelos II. This is one of the most unspoilt areas of Corfu, and is a good starting point for some excellent walks. A minor road by Gardíki leads in 4km to one of Corfu's few lakes, the lagoony **Límni Korissíon**, which is separated from the sea by a long stretch of huge, wild dunes; in spring and autumn it fills with migratory birds. Take your mosquito defences, however; they grow as big as pterodactyls here and have appetites to match. **Lagoúdia**, two islets off the southwest coast, are the home of a tribe of donkeys; some of their ancestors were eaten by a boatload of Napoleon's troops who were wrecked there for three days.

The scenery from here down to Corfu's tail is flat and agricultural but the beaches are sandy and clean. South of Lake Korissíon a busy family resort has grown up around (another) **Ag. Geórgios**. **Linía**, the northern extension of Ag. Geórgios beach, is more tranquil and backed by dunes; the beach of **Marathiás** is the southern extension of the same strand, with a few tavernas. In the centre of a large fertile plain, **Lefkími**, the largest town in the south, is dusty and uninviting; the nearest beaches, **Mólos** and **Alykés** 2km away on the east coast, are flat and grey, set amid salt pans.

Kávos (ΚΑΒΟΣ) is a one-time fishing village turned all-day-and-night package holiday rave party where things have got so out of hand that locals now refuse to work there. At the southernmost tip of Corfu, the quieter beaches of **Asprókavos** and **Arkoudílas** (near a ruined monastery, reached by a path from Sparterá) have white sand and tavernas; the pretty beach below **Dragotiná** is a long walk from the village but never crowded.

Ag. Górdis ✉ 49084

Yaliskari Palace, ✆ 54 401 (*A; exp*), a vast fancy complex with a pool and tennis courts and sea sports, is 3km from the beach; **Ag. Gordis**, ✆ 53 320 (*A; exp*) is similarly large, ultra-modern, and endowed with facilities, but right on the sand. **Chrysis Folies** (Golden Nests), ✆ 44 750 (*C; mod*) is a medium-sized choice within easy walking distance of the sea beach. **Pink Paradise**, ✆ 53 103 (*E; inexp*) is a resort complex run by Americans.

Ag. Mathías ✉ 49084

Gamillon Oros, ✆ 55 557, serves spit-roast lamb and fresh fish, with live music and dancing most nights; there's even a playground to keep the kids out of your hair.

Benítses ✉ 49084

San Stefano, ✆ 36 036, 📠 72 272 (*A; exp*) is spread across terraces, overlooking the sea; it has the largest swimming-pool on the island, sea sports and other facilities. Benítses is not known for its cuisine, but the **Marabou** bravely presents some tasty local dishes (*2500dr*). **Stefanos Pizzeria** whips up delicious authentic pies.

Moraítika/Messónghi ✉ 49080

Messonghi Beach Hotel and Bungalows ✆ 38 684 (*B; exp–mod*) is a giant, self-contained, family-fun complex. **Korifo Apartments**, in Moraítika, ✆ 75 511, in Athens ✆ (01) 981 8889, 📠 982 2445, for pretty flats, 400m from the sea (*exp*). **Roulis**, Messónghi, ✆ 92 353 (*C; mod*) is small and near the sea, with some sea sports. It's fairly easy to find a room to rent, and there's also a campsite, **Ippokambos**, ✆ 65 364.

The Islands

Ithaca/Itháki (ΙΘΑΚΗ)

Every traveller is a citizen of Ithaca.

sign in the port

Ithaca is one of those places that have become a compelling and universal symbol, although many who have heard of it have no idea where it is, and those who do visit it usually have a hard time reconciling the island's reality with their idea of Odysseus' beloved home. But re-read your Homer before you come, and you'll find that nearly all of his descriptions of Ithaca square with this small, mountainous island—it is indeed 'narrow' and 'rocky' and 'unfit for riding horses'. Some ancient and modern scholars have theorized that Homer's Ithaca was elsewhere—Lefkáda and Kefaloniá are popular contenders. Don't believe them. Itháki, as the locals call their home, the eternal symbol of all homes and journey's end, is the real thing, and 'even if you find it poor,' as Caváfy wrote, 'Ithaca does not deceive. Without Ithaca your journey would have no beauty.'

Ithaca has a jagged, indented coast (as Homer says), with no exceptional beaches, but its harbours make it a big favourite with sailors. Best of all, it has changed little over the years; the atmosphere is relaxed and low-key.

Mythology

Three sons of the king of Kefaloniá—Ithakos, Neritos and Polyktor—were the founding fathers of Ithaca: the first son gave it his name, the second left his name on the island's highest peak, and Polyktor is the name of its northern half. Another king of Kefaloniá, Kefalos, had a son named Arkikious who annexed Ithaca and made it the centre of his realm; his son was Laertes, who participated on the voyage of the Argo and married Anticleia, who gave birth to Odysseus. But a strong ancient tradition says that two crafty shepherds, Autolykus, a son of Hermes, and Sisyphus, used to graze their flocks next to each other, and through all kinds of trickery and wiles would steal one another's sheep. Autolykus thought that if he married his daughter Anticleia to Sisyphus, their child would inherit cunning from both sides of the family and be the ultimate trickster. Sisyphus was equally keen and had his evil way with Anticleia even before their wedding; but during the interval, King Laertes asked to marry her, and did. She was already pregnant by Sisyphus, and Autolykus, the child's grandfather, named him Odysseus, which means 'angry' or 'he who is hated by all', as Homer explains it.

History

Items found on the north half of Ithaca go back to 4000–3000 BC; on Pilikata hill near Stavrós, a road, buildings and walls show that some kind of communal life was established by the early Hellenic era (3000–2000 BC). The inhabitants and passing sailors worshipped at the cave of Loízos, where early cult items were discovered. By Mycenaean times, settlements had relocated further south as Arikious organized a kingdom (c. 1200 BC) that included Kefaloniá, Zákynthos, Lefkáda and a part of the Peloponnesian coast. Ithaca, owing to its central location, was made the capital, and under Odysseus the kingdom reached its prime, sending 12 ships to the Trojan War.

In the last 200 years scholars and archaeologists have combed Ithaca for signs of Odysseus. Schliemann came after his great discovery of Troy, and since Schliemann always got what he sought, he unearthed a large structure he immediately labelled 'Odysseus' Palace'; although it dates from only 700 BC, the name has stuck. Later finds, while failing to produce any concrete evidence of the Crafty One's existence, at least indicate that the ancients considered Ithaca Homer's Ithaca. Inscriptions show that Odysseus was worshipped as a divine hero, ancient coins bore his picture, and pottery decorated with the cockerel, the symbol of Odysseus, has been found on the island.

Odysseus unsuccessfully sought Helen's hand in marriage, then wed Penelope instead and had a son, Telemachus. Having been warned by an oracle that if he went to Troy he would be absent for 20 years and return alone without any booty, Odysseus pretended madness by ploughing the sand and sowing it with salt when the Greek representatives came to fetch him; to test him, the Greeks placed his baby son Telemachus in front of his oxen. Odysseus proved his sanity by diverting their course, and was constrained by his promise as one of Helen's ex-suitors to depart for Troy and bring her back.

After his homecoming in disguise, mass murder of Penelope's suitors, and recognition by his wife, Homer's story ends, but there are two accounts of Odysseus' death: one, that the families of the suitors forced him to live in exile, and that he died at a ripe old age in Italy; another, that Odysseus was not permitted to die until he had at last appeased the anger of his old enemy Poseidon, and the only way to do so was to take an oar and walk until he came to a land where people asked him what he carried. Then, after a sacrifice to the sea god, he sailed home, and was drowned on the way.

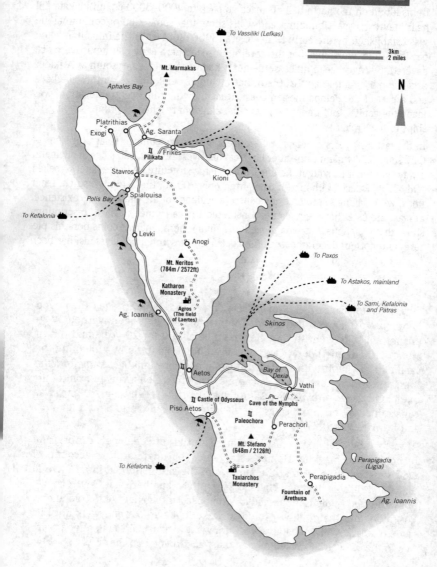

Ithaca/Itháki

To Vassiliki (Lefkas)

3km
2 miles

N

Mt. Marmakas

Aphales Bay

Platrithias
Exogi
Ag. Saranta
Pilikata
Frikes
Stavros
Kioni
Spialouisa

Polis Bay

To Kefalonia

Levki

Anogi

Mt. Neritos
(784m / 2572ft)

Katharon
Monastery

Agros
(The field
of Laertes)

Ag. Ioannis

Aetos

Castle of Odysseus

Piso Aetos

Paleochora

Cave of the Nymphs

Perachori

Mt. Stefano
(648m / 2126ft)

To Kefalonia

Taxiarchos
Monastery

Fountain of
Arethusa

To Paxos

To Astakos, mainland

To Sami, Kefalonia
and Patras

Skinos

Bay of
Dexia

Vathi

Perapigadia
(Ligia)

Perapigadia

Ag. Ioannis

The topography of the island is perhaps even more convincing. In *The Odyssey*, Odysseus describes Ithaca as 'horrid with cliffs, our meagre land/Allows thin herbage for the mountain goat to browse' and later, 'The rugged soil allows no level space/For flying chariots, or the rapid race'; he says his palace is set above 'three seas' and the hill near Stavrós fits the description, overlooking three bays. In 1930 two ancient fortifications were discovered that may have been used for signals and beacons to the palace. Other sites from Homer have been tentatively identified on the island, such as the Fountain of Arethusa, where Odysseus met his faithful swineherd Eumaeus, and the cave where he hid the treasure given him by the Phaeacians. One tradition, found in a manuscript kept on Mount Áthos, claims that Homer himself was born in Ithaca; another says that, although born in Smyrna, he was invited as a young man to stay in Ithaca and that he wasn't blind at all but knew at first hand the places he described.

After the Mycenaeans, Ithaca lost most of its importance and even its name; for a period it was humiliatingly known as 'Little Kefaloniá', and in the 12th century as Val de Comparé, after a shipwrecked sea captain who came ashore just when a baby was born, so he was made its godfather (*koumbaros*). After a violent Turkish raid in 1479, the entire island was simply abandoned, and the Venetians offered generous incentives to any Venetian or mainland Greek who would settle and farm there. The cash crop was velonia—the husks of acorns, ground into a powder used to make dyes fast. Once again Ithaca prospered, but, unlike the other Ionian islands, it had only one noble family (one, however, that claimed lineal descent from Odysseus) and not a full-blown aristocracy.

Under the British, the great philhellene Lord Guilford spent a year here as a young man, and with the support of poet Ugo Foscolo strongly pushed Ithaca as the seat of a university of the Ionian islands, for the sake of its central location and historical resonance, its healthy air and lack of vice; the Ithacans greeted his proposal with enthusiasm and the donation of land and money for the buildings before Sir Thomas Maitland usurped the idea and insisted that the university be located on Corfu. Ironically, union with Greece in 1864 initiated a great migration from the island, many Ithakans going to Romania, Australia and South Africa. Like their countryman Odysseus, the islanders are well known as great sailors, and even those who call Ithaca home spend much of the year away at sea.

Getting There and Around

By sea: In high season, daily **ferry** to Pátras, Kefaloniá (Frikés to Fiskárdo, and Váthi to Sámi and Ag. Efimía), Vassilikí (Lefkáda) and Astakós; also daily caiques between Váthi and Frikés.

Port authority: ✆ 32 209.

By road: One **bus** a day from Kióni to Frikés, Stavrós and Váthi. Off the road, there are some wonderful walks as outlined in an excellent free pamphlet, 'Trails of Ithaca'.

Tourist Police

See regular police at Váthi, ✆ (0674) 32 205.

Festivals

1 May, Taxiárchos; **24 June**, Ag. Ioánnis, at Kióni; **August** wine festival, Peráchori, **5–6 August**, Sotíros at Stavrós; **14 August**, Anogí; **15 August**, Platrithias; **mid-August to mid-September**, theatre and cultural festival held at Váthi; **8 September**, Kathará Monastery.

Váthi (ΒΑΘΥ)

Váthi, 'the deep', built around the end of a long sheltered horseshoe bay, has been the capital of the island since the 16th century. Its beautiful harbour, surrounded by mountains on all sides, embraces a wooded islet called **Lazaretto**, a quarantine station established in 1668 by the Venetians; to prevent the spread of plague, any letters sent between Lazaretto and Ithaca had to be smoked, and all money was soaked in sea water. The station converted in 1864 to a prison before being pummelled by earthquakes; now there's only a chapel. When Byron stayed in Váthi in 1823 he swam out to the Lazaretto every day. The ruins of two forts, **Loútsa** and **Kástro**, built in 1805 by the French, stand at either side of the harbour entrance; there's a small beach by the former.

Although damaged by the 1953 earthquake, Váthi (pop. 1800) was reconstructed as it was with red tile roofs and is considered a 'traditional settlement' of Greece, a designation that ensures that all new buildings must conform to the local style. One building that survived the quake is the neoclassical mansion of the Drakoulis family, who brought the first steamship to Greece, which they named the *Ithaka*. The **Archaeology Museum** (*open 8.30–2.30, closed Mon*) one street back from the Mentor Hotel, is a low modern building housing a collection of vases, offerings, coins and other Mycenaean and classical artefacts; one of the prizes in the library of the neighbouring **Cultural Centre** is a Japanese edition of Homer's works printed in 1600. For a brief insight into local history, the little **Folklore Museum**, near Polyktor Tours, is well worth a visit. The church of the **Taxiárchos** contains an icon of Christ attributed to the young El Greco. Every four years since 1981, Váthi's Centre for Odyssean Studies has hosted an International Congress on the *Odyssey*. But if it's a beach you need, the state of the island's roads should encourage you to make use of the caique services in Váthi port: fine pebble strands are at **Skinós** (by jeep only), **Bímata** (by caique), or **Filiatró** (with its new camp-site) and **Sarakinikó**, named after the Saracen pirates that once plagued the coast. The latter two are both manageable by car; bring your own provisions.

Southern Ithaca: On the Odysseus Trail

Some of the sites traditionally identified with places in the *Odyssey* make pretty walks from Váthi. West of Váthi, it's a 4km walk to the **Cave of the Nymphs** or Marmaróspilia (signposted, but make sure the gate is unlocked before you set out, and bring a torch) where Odysseus is said to have hidden the gifts of King Alcinous. The cave has a hole in the roof—'the entrance of the gods'—which permitted the smoke of the sacrifices to rise to heaven. Stairs lead down through the narrow entrance into a small stalactite chamber. Below, the narrow **Dexiá** inlet is generally believed to be Homer's harbour of Phorcys where the Phaeacians gently put the sleeping Odysseus on shore. You can sleep where Odysseus slept, at Ithaca's first campsite; the narrow beach is equipped with a bar and showers.

South of Váthi, an unpaved road runs 7km to the pretty Maráthias plateau. About 4km along, a donkey path to the left is signposted to the **Fountain of Arethusa** (ΚΡΙΝΙ ΑΡΕΘΟΥΣΑ); it takes about an hour and a half to walk. According to the myth, Arethusa wept so much when her son Corax 'the raven' was killed that she turned into a spring; the water flows (in the summer, dribbles) from under the towering rock Corax (or Coracus) and is good to drink, although beware its reputation for making you as hungry as a bear. Occasionally the odd raven comes circling over, as if to prove the old story. Further south, at **Ellinikó**, Odysseus, disguised as a beggar, first met the faithful swineherd Eumaeus; excavations at Ellinikó duly uncovered some Mycenaean odds and ends. From the Arethusa fountain a rocky scramble descends to the pretty little beach, facing the islet of **Perapigádia** (the Homeric Asteris), where the murderous suitors hid, awaiting Telemachus' return from Pýlos.

The only other real village in the south of Ithaca is **Perachóri** (ΠΕΡΑΧΩΡΙ), occu-pying a 300m-high fertile balcony 2km from Váthi, where most of Ithaca's wine is produced. The village dates from the Venetians, although the first houses were built up in the walled confines of **Paleochóra**, Ithaca's first capital, where you can see the ruins of the fortified houses and churches, one minus its roof but still adorned with fading Byzantine frescoes. In Perachóri the villagers will show you which path to take. Another road—it's for four-wheel-drives only—climbs 3km from Perachóri to the **Monastery of the Taxiárchis** (1645) near the top of Mount Stéfano. Although the earthquakes have blasted it, the views from the monastery and the road are lovely. Perachóri has a restaurant, Kyparisi, and a pair of small high-season tavernas with panoramic views, serving local wine and *tserépato*, meat slowly roasted in a special clay pot.

North of Váthi

Ithaca has an hourglass figure, with a waist, the narrow mountain stretch of **Aetós**, only 500m wide. Overlooking the two bays below is what the locals (as well as Schliemann) have always called the **Castle of Odysseus**, although it's apparently the citadel of the 8th-century BC town of Alalkomenes, which was abandoned in Roman times. Impressive Cyclopean walls and the foundations of a temple remain. Since 1984 the 'Odysseus Project', sponsored by the Archaeological Society of Athens, Washington University and the National Geographic Society, has concentrated its excavations around Aetós' church of Ag. Geórgios, and has shown that the site has been inhabited continuously since the 13th century BC. There's a pebble beach in the bay below to the east and another excellent one at the little bay of **Píso Aetós** in the west, where ferry boats from Sámi (Kefaloniá) call.

Just north of Aetós, near Agrós, is the **Field of Laertes**, supposedly where Odysseus encountered his father after killing the suitors; note the massive 2000-year-old 'Laertes' olive'. From here a road ascends the slopes of 784m **Mount Níritos** (formerly Mount Korifí—Ithaca is slowly reclaiming its Homeric names) to the lofty **Monastery of the Katharón**, 'of the dry weeds', believed to be built on the site of an ancient temple of Athena. One far-fetched story says it was built by the heretical Cathars; another explains that local farmers were burning dry weeds here when they found an icon of the Birth of the Virgin attributed to St Luke, which holds pride of place in the church of the **Panagía Kathariótissas**. When Byron visited in 1823, a special mass was held in his honour. From the lighthouse of a bell tower you can see the Gulf of Pátras on a clear day, and if you want to stay, there may be a few guest rooms in the monastery (© 31 366).

From Moni Katharón, a paved road continues 3km up to **Anógí**, 'at the top of the world', passing many large and unusually shaped boulders, including a very phallic 25ft monolith named Araklís, or Heracles. The village retains some Venetian ruins, including a sturdy grey campanile and a restored 12th-century church dedicated to the **Panagía** with Byzantine frescoes; note the clay amphorae embedded in the walls to improve the church's acoustics. Ask at the *kafeneíon* for the key, or call © 31 306.

The second and easier road from Agrós follows the west coast. At Ag. Ioánnis, just opposite Kefaloniá, is a lovely, seldom-used white beach, Aspros Gialós, with many trees. **Lévki**, the small village to the north, was an important base and port for the resistance movement during the war, and, when it was destroyed by the 1953 earthquake, Britain officially adopted it and helped rebuild it. There are small beaches below and a few rooms to rent.

The two roads meet at **Stavrós**, the most important village in the north, overlooking lovely **Pólis Bay** ('city bay'), its name referring to the long lost Byzantine city of Ierosalem, which sank into it during an earthquake in AD 967; Anna Comena, in her famous chronicle of her father Emperor Alexis Comnenus' reign, wrote that Robert Guiscard (see 'Fiskárdo', p.165) had been told by a soothsayer that he would die after seeing Jerusalem, but he never thought Jerusalem would be the ruins of a town on Ithaca. Some Byzantine tombs have been discovered nearby, at Roussanos. A bust of Odysseus in the centre of Stavrós looks sternly out over the bay. The **Cave of Loízos** to the right of the bay was an ancient cult sanctuary; some believe it was Homer's Cave of the Nymphs. Prehistoric pots, Mycenaean amphorae, bronze tripods from 800–700 BC, ex-votos of nymphs and an inscription dedicated to Odysseus were found here (unfortunately the cave and path to it have collapsed).

Another plausible Odysseus' palace was located at **Pilikáta**, or the Hill of Hermes, just north of Stavrós. The site also fits the Homeric description almost perfectly, in sight of 'three seas' (the bays of Frikés, Pólis and Aphales) and 'three mountains' (Níritos, Marmakás and Exógi or Neion). Although the ruins you see on the site are of a Venetian fort, excavators have found evidence underneath of buildings and roads dating back to Neolithic times. In 1930, within Pilikáta's Cyclopean walls, archaeologists found a pit containing the remains of sacrifices and two ceramic shards engraved in Linear A, believed to date from 2700 BC. In 1989, Professor Paul Fauré attempted a translation of them, based on Linear B and the index of symbols established for Linear A, written in an Indo-European language—a very, very early form of Greek—called Kreutschmer by the linguists: Fauré translates one as: 'Here is what I, Aredatis, give to the queen, the goddess Rhea: 100 goats, 10 sheep, 3 pigs' and the other as: 'The nymph saved me.' The other finds from Pilikáta and the Cave of Louizos are in the small but interesting **Stavrós Archaeological Museum** on the Platrithiás road (*open 9–2, closed Mon*). Unfortunately it lacks the most compelling find ever made on the island: a golden helmet and gold and silver ornaments discovered in a tomb in the 1820s. The head of the British Corscian rangers, who were in charge of Ithaca, melted them down to make a coffee pot and barbecue skewers.

From Stavrós a road leads north to Ithaca's remotest village, called **Exógi** ('beyond the earth'). Set high up on terraces, all but a handful of its inhabitants have left, but there are a few rooms to rent, and beautiful views. Above the village is Ithaca's oddball attraction, three narrow pyramids built in 1933 by a pyramid-fancier named Papadópoulos. He lies buried under one, his mother under another, while the third has a jar with a coin collection. Another 2km up, the disused monastery of Panagía Eleoússa offers extraordinary views over the Ionian islands. Between

Exogí and Platrithiás is an area known as '**Homer's School**'. The ruined 7th-century church of Ag. Athanásios has a wall of great hewn blocks reused from an ancient wall. By the Melanydrus spring, there's a little stepped well that the locals call 'Penelope's Bath'—actually a Mycenaean tomb. This fertile area is one of the most pleasant on the island; it was here that Odysseus was ploughing his field when he was dragged off to Troy by the Achaeans (*see* p.136–7). **Platrithiás** is the biggest of a set of agricultural hamlets; one of them, **Kóllieri**, greets wayfarers with an outdoor 'folklore museum', with stone obelisks made out of millstones.

Frikés and Kióni

North of Stavrós, **Frikés** (ΦΡΙΚΕΣ) is a tiny fishing village and popular stopping-off point for flotilla yachts. It was a favourite pirates' lair into the 19th century. About 100 people live there year-round, and there are two tiny beaches near by, Limenária and Kourvoúlia, and a new hotel, rooms and tavernas. The road continues to **Rachí**, a tiny hamlet of old stone houses, and continues down to **Kióni**, one of Ithaca's prettiest villages built around a tiny harbour, guarded by three ruined windmills. Twice the size of Frikés, it is popular with the yachting set; landlubbers can hire motorboats to the surrounding beaches. Kióni means 'column', and an ancient one still stands on the altar in the church of Ag. Nikólaos. And there are more Cylopean walls nearby, at a site called Roúga.

Itháki ✆ *(0674–)*

Where to Stay and Eating Out

Ithaca as a whole has very little in the way of hotel accommodation; most people sleep on their boats, or rent rooms and villas, particularly in and around Kióni, Frikés and Stavrós. For help with rooms or apartments, contact **Polyctor Tours** in Váthi's Plateía Drakoúli, ✆ 33 120, 🖷 33 130, or book apartments and villas in advance through **Greek Islands Club** (*see* p.17) or **Simply Ionian**. In the tavernas, enquire about Ithaca's red wine, considered the best on all the Ionians, but made only in small quantities and famous for not travelling well at all.

Váthi ✉ 28300

The newest here is **Captain Yiannis Hotel**, ✆ 33 173, 🖷 32 849, an appealing bungalow complex with pool and tennis, across the bay from the hub of the town. **Hotel Mentor**, Georgíou Drakoúli St, ✆ 32 433 (*B; exp*) is modern and central. The **Odysseus**, ✆ 32 381 (*B; mod*) is nice too and a bit cheaper. **Andriana Koulouri Rooms**, on the quay, ✆ 32 387, are quiet and complete with bathrooms. There are campsites at **Dexía Beach**, ✆ 32 855, and **Filiatró Beach**, ✆ 33 243.

There's a good smattering of tavernas around the harbour and back lanes. Near the centre, little **Trexandiri** is inexpensive with good local food, and in Plateía Polytechnieíou the **Grill Restaurant** serves delicious grilled octopus and *kokorétsi*—lamb's innards on a spit. **Palio Karavo**, 800m from town, is a favourite, especially for fish (*2500dr*). Both the Mentor and Odysseus hotels have good restaurants.

Frikés/Kióni ✉ 28301

In Frikés, there's the **Nostos Hotel**, ✆ 31 644 (*C; mod*) and a handful of rooms and apartments to rent; contact Panayiótis Raptópoulos, ✆ 31 629. By the sea, **Taverna Ulysseus** has good fresh fish and other dishes; **Symposium**, also smack on the waterfront, is a complete hoot; the ambitious menu features the likes of 'Odyseas Meat-pie', 'Penelope's Dish', *Saboró* (Eptanesian Spaghetti), 'Brides' Salad (Magical callings of a mythical world)' and carafes of Ithacan wine.

Up in Kióni, the elegant **Kionia Hotel**, ✆ 31 362, is *expensive* and mostly block-booked by Simply Ionian. For the prettiest self-catering properties contact **Greek Islands Club**, ✆ (UK) (01932) 220 477. **Maroudas Apartments** ✆ 31 691, ✉ 31 753 (*mod*) are also pleasant.

Kióni has three tavernas, and a *kafeneío*, cleverly renovated to attract the boaties without losing the approval of locals.

Kálamos (ΚΑΛΑΜΟΣ) and Kástos (ΚΑΣΤΟΣ)

Kálamos and Kástos, two mountains in the sea east of Meganísi, are under the jurisdiction of Lefkáda, but can only be reached on a daily regular basis by way of Mítikas on the mainland; occasionally Kálamos, the larger one, is connected to Sámi, Ithaca, the port Astakós and Meganísi, as well as Nidrí and Vassilikí on Lefkáda. Both are associated with the Delladecima family: the story goes that the family's founder, a Colonel Floriano, was Morosini's right hand man and was responsible for the Venetian capture of Lefkáda in 1684. As a reward the colonel was ennobled and given the tithes of Kálamos and Kástos, so he took the name Count Delladecima, 'the Count of Tithes.'

Kálamos lives primarily by fishing and its small gardens, and most people live in the attractive north coast village of Kálamos, or **Chóra**, where the island's few rooms to rent are concentrated. It has all the essentials of village life, even a pair of tavernas on the town beach, and tolerated rough camping on the far end. Better beaches may be found towards **Episkopí**, but are easiest reached by boat. A donkey path leads up from Chóra to the abandoned walled village of **Kástro**, where everyone used to live.

Only two or three families live on **Kástos**, now unable to care for all the vineyards which once produced a fine wine. There aren't even any regular connections; you'll have to hire a caique from Mítikas, but there's a taverna and maybe a room or two if you're lucky.

Kefaloniá (ΚΕΦΑΛΟΝΙΑ)

'The half-forgotten island of Cephallonia rises improvidently and inadvisedly from the Ionian Sea,' writes Dr Iannis in Louis de Bernières' *Captain Corelli's Mandolin*, the best book to be set on a Greek island in years. Its Jabberwocky silhouette contains 781 square kilometres of ruggedly beautiful mountains, making it the largest of the Ionian islands by a long shot, although it supports a mere 30,000 people, and even many of these live in Athens in the winter. But Kefalonians have always been famous for wandering (one, Constantine Yerákis, went on to make a fortune in the British East India Company and become Regent of Siam), and it's not uncommon to meet someone whose entire family lives in Canada, Australia or the United States. Only in the last few years has tourism begun to slow the diaspora and keep more people put. Kefalonians have been called the Irish of Greece: they are friendly, quick-witted, and good-humoured, but have the reputation of being hard-headed, quarrelsome, cunning, eccentric, tight with their money and the worst blasphemers in Greece, swearing at their patron Ag. Gerásimos one minute and swearing by him the next. Other Greeks say the Kefalonians have drunk a toast with the devil himself.

Although the earthquake in 1953 shattered all but a fraction of Kefaloniá's traditional architecture and all the quaintness and charm that goes with it, the big, sprawling island has lost none of its striking natural beauty. It has fine beaches (one of which, Mýrtos, is perhaps the most dramatic in all of Greece), two of the country's loveliest caves, lofty fir forests, splendid views, and Robóla wine. Because Kefaloniá is so large, it is easy to escape the summertime crowds, although beware that even on the main roads driving distances and times can be exhausting.

History

Fossil and tool finds in Fiskárdo, Sámi and Skála go back to at least 50,000 BC and perhaps earlier, making Fiskárdo man (and woman, one supposes) among the earliest known inhabitants in Greece. Later inhabitants appear to have been culturally related to the Pelasgians in western Sicily and Epirus; their skulls, all banged about, suggest that Kefalonians have always been a feisty lot. The Achaeans introduced Mycenaean culture from the Peloponnese in the 14th century BC; Krani, near Argostóli, was their most important colony. Although the name Kefaloniá does not occur in Homer, scholars believe that the 'glittering Samos' of the *Odyssey* refers not to the Aegean island of that name but to Kefaloniá's town of Sámi. Others

Kefaloniá

8km
5 miles

N

To Lefkas
To Paxos
To Astakos

Ithaca

Fiskardo

Fortress
Assos
Playia
Xarakas
Myrtes
Divarata
Neochori

Atheras
Zola
Kardakata
Ag. Evfimia

Petani
Kontoyenada
Ag. Dimitrios
Farsa
Dilinata

Moni
Panagias
Thenaton
Melissani
Cave
Mt. Vlachata
(1132m)
Karavomylos
Cape
Dixalia
Sami

To Patras

Drogarati Cave
Koulouvrata

Kipourion
Monastery
Tafion
Monastery
LIXOURI
Katovothri
Prangkata
Araktion

Drakondi
Cave
Michalitsata
Lepeda
Makri
Gialos
ARGOSTOLI
Krani
LIVATHO
Ag. Gerasimos
Ag. Georgios
Castle
Megalo
Soros
Tzanata
Poros
To Kilini

Kounopetra
Ag.
Georgios
Xi
Platis
Gialos
Lakidra
Peratata
Ag. Andreas
Convent
Vlachata
Mt. Ainos
(1628m)

VARDIANA
Svoronata
Kourkomelata
Metaxata
Lourdata
Pastra
Fanies

Pessada
Markopoulo
Katelios
Skala

To Kilini
To Zakynthos

Kefaloniá: History   147

believe Homer doesn't mention Kefaloniá because, as part the kingdom of Odysseus, he simply calls it Ithaca. The recent discovery of a major Mycenaean tomb near Póros has given the argument new weight as archaeologists scramble to locate the big jackpot—the Palace of Odysseus.

Historically, the first sure references to Kefaloniá are in Herodotus and Thucydides, who describes its four autonomous city-states: Sámi, Pali, Krani and Pronnoi, allies of Corinth who spent much of their history fighting for their independence from Athens. Pirates from Kefaloniá harassed Roman shipping to such an extent that, as soon as the second Punic war was over in 189 BC, the Romans, under Titus

Quintus Flaminius, turned their sights on the four cities. All realized the inevitable and surrendered without a fight, each sending the Romans four hostages as tokens of their good will, with the exception of Sámi, which changed its mind for no apparent reason, according to Livy, and suffered the consequences—a four-month siege followed by annihilation. The hamlet of Markantónio in northern Kefaloniá is said to be named after Mark Antony, whose uncle Caius Antonius Nepos, exiled here from Rome, ruled the island as its 'king'.

In Byzantine times Kefaloniá prospered, in spite of many attacks by the pirates from Spain and Sicily, and in the 9th century was made the capital of its own *theme*. In 1085, Normans based in Southern Italy unsuccessfully besieged the Byzantine forts of the island and their duke, Robert the Guiscard, died of fever in the village that has taken his name—Fiskárdo (*see* p.165).

If the Kefalonians breathed a sigh of relief then, it was too soon; the Guiscard was still warm in the grave when a colourful adventurer from Apulia, Count Matteo Orsini, took the island, along with Ithaca and Zákynthos which he grouped together under the grand title the County Palatine of Kefaloniá. Through diplomacy, changes of allegiance and adroit marriages, the Orsini, and later the Tocchi who married into the family, ruled as the High and Mighty Counts of Kefaloniá for 150 years, as allies of the Frankish princes of Achaia in the Peloponnese and the Greeks at Epiros, under the Angevin kings of Naples. The County Palatine was famous as a haven of peace and prosperity in the Middle Ages.

In 1483, when Venice, miffed by the Tocchi's alliance with the Angevins in Naples, refused to extend sea protection to Kefaloniá, the Turks captured the island and many of its inhabitants, sending them as slaves to Istanbul to be mated with Ethiopians with the idea of creating a new 'slave race'. But, as on the other Ionian islands, Turkish tenure was brief; in 1504 Venice and Spain under the command of the Gran Capitan, Gonzalo Fernández de Córdoba, besieged and took the fort of Ag. Geórgios and slaughtered the Turkish garrison. Afterwards, the island was under direct Venetian control, when it was noted for its overwhelming number of lawyers; one English traveller in 1822 noted how court cases were like family heirlooms, passed down over the generations. On a more positive side, Kefaloniá has always been famous for its doctors, the traditional occupation of second sons of the landed gentry, who were sent off to the University of Padua and worked in nearly every country on the continent (one of the most famous was Louis XVI's physician, Count Carberry—originally Charvouris). When a family produced a girl, the midwife's prayer was for her to marry a doctor.

During the British Protectorate, the Kefalonians were especially lucky with their appointed governors, or Residents. The first was Colonel Hudson Lowe, who had been Napoleon's gaoler on Elba and St Helena; the second, the Swiss-born Resident De Bousset built new roads, the causeway, and aqueducts to supply water to the city, and tried to introduce the cultivation of the potato in the face of opposition from the local priests, who declared the spud was the fruit that Eve gave to Adam in the Garden of Eden.

The third Resident, Colonel Charles Napier, is still fondly remembered on the island to this day for his honesty, integrity and love for Kefaloniá: he even named his daughter Emily Cephalonia. 'The merry Greeks are worth all the other nations put together,' he wrote. 'I like to see them, to hear them; I like their fun, their good humour, their paddy ways, for they are very like Irishmen. All their bad habits are Venetian; their wit, their eloquence, their good nature are their own.' He built a quay for Argostoli, two lighthouses, a model prison to improve conditions for prisoners and a model farm. He befriended Byron in 1823 during his four-month stay on Kefaloniá working as an agent of the Greek Committee in London. His enthusiasm for the island, and his refusal to be subservient to Sir Frederick Adam, the High Commissioner on Corfu, forced his dismissal. Attempts to lure him back to a similar position in Zákynthos failed, and he went off to conquer Sind instead, although throughout his career in India he always insisted that he loved his first love, Kefaloniá, best of all.

Napier always insisted that the British should let the Ionians choose their own destiny (perhaps because he mistakenly believed they would soon come running back to benevolent Britain). The fact is that the Kefalonians, feeling exploited by the British on Corfu, never stopped demanding union with Greece, demands that only increased once Greece became independent. In 1849, the state of affairs reached such a nadir that 21 nationalist leaders were hanged under High Commissioner Sir Henry Ward.

Ioannis Metaxás, prime minister-dictator of Greece from 1936 to 1941, came from one of Kefaloniá's oldest families, and for all his faults has gone down in history for laconically (and apparently, apocryphally) saying 'No' to Mussolini's ultimatum at the beginning of the Second World War—celebrated nationally on 28 October as *Ochí* ('No') Day. The subsequent occupation of the island by the Italian Acqui Division was on the whole benign; many of the Kefalonians, after all, had Italian blood, and the upper classes still spoke the language. The trouble began in September 1943, after Mussolini was deposed in Italy and the Allies came to terms with the Badoglio government. Rome sent a message to the general of the Acqui Division to hold out against the Germans. A few days later, a message arrived from the Italian command in Athens, which had already fallen under the control of the Nazis, to place himself under German orders.

The general hesitated; he had sufficient troops on Kefaloniá to defy the relatively few Germans on the island, but they had planes and he had none. He hoped that the allied advance in the Aegean would give him the air power to resist, but the advance proved to be temporary. Finally, the Germans lost their tempers and bombarded the Italians in an all-out attack with their Stukas and quickly finished off their artillery; after a week the remaining pockets of Italian resistance surrendered. Officially, 341 officers and 4750 troops (or perhaps twice that many, according to some) died in the subsequent mass execution of the entire Division, ordered, it is said, by Hitler himself. To hide the evidence, their bodies were burned in huge pyres all along the slopes of Mt Aenos, at Karadakata, Kourouklata and Troianata. The Greeks call them the Kefaloniá martyrs.

A decade later nature itself struck Kefaloniá a blow that made all the previous earthquakes on the island seem like cocktail shakers. For five days in August, 1953, 113 tremors reduced the island's 350 towns and villages to dust; the first, deadliest quake had the estimated force of 60 atom bombs. As the dust slowly cleared, money for reconstruction poured in from Europe and the tens of thousands of Kefalonians who live abroad. To this day quite a few of these are doctors and some have become wealthy shipowners, but the island is especially proud of its university professors—it has produced a greater portion of scholars *per capita* than anywhere else in Greece.

Getting There and Around

By air: Daily flights from Athens, several a day in summer, and summer flights three times a week to Zákynthos; frequent charters from British cities. The Olympic Airways office is in Argostóli, at R. Vergotí 1, ℘ (0671) 28 808/881; the airport is 9km south of Argostóli, ℘ (0671) 41510.

By sea: Kefaloniá has six ports. Sámi (℘ (0674) 22 031) has the most connections, with daily **ferry** links to Váthi and Píso Aetós (Ithaca), Vassilikí (Lefkáda), Fiskárdo, Pátras, and several times a week with Corfu, Brindisi, Bari and Ancona. There are numerous ferries a day between Argostóli (℘ (0671) 25 151) and Kilíni (in the Peloponnese); in summer there are daily ferries from Fiskárdo (℘ (0674) 51212) to Frikés (Ithaca) and Nídri and Vasilikí in Lefkáda. Sámi has connections to Váthi (Ithaca) and Astakós, on the mainland. In season, there's a daily ferry from Pessáda to Skinári (Zákynthos), and two ships a day from Póros (℘ (0674) 72460) to Kilíni. The ferry betwen Argostóli and Lixoúri goes at least once an hour and costs around 300dr. In Lixoúri, sail boats can be rented with or without skipper (but only with the appropriate licence) by the day or by the week, ℘ 91 541. **Port authority**, ℘ (0671) 22 224.

By road: From Athens, **buses** 3 times a day (*see* p.11). Bus services to the main centres of the island are fairly good if not frequent; next to the KTEL station near the bridge on the waterfront in Argotóli there's a local KTEL tourist office to help you plan excursions—some go as far as Olympia in the

Peloponnese. For information, call ✆ (0671) 22 276/22 281. To really see the island, however, you need your own transport, readily available in the towns: try to avoid any mileage restrictions. Many **taxi** drivers specialize in trips around the island, and caiques go to the more popular beaches. A **car ferry** crosses the Gulf of Argostóli once an hour from Argostóli to Lixoúri.

Tourist Information

NTOG, Argostóli, on the waterfront ✆ (0671) 22 248, ✆ 24 466; pick up freebies like 'Kefalonia Tourist News', 'Trails of Cephallonia' and info on the Kefalonian Marine Turtle Project. **Tourist police**, see regular police, Argostóli ✆ (0671) 22 200. Also very helpful are **Filoxenos Travel**, 2 Vergoti, ✆ (0671) 23 055 and in Fiskárdo, **Fiskardo Travel**, near the post office, ✆ /✆ (0674) 41 315, and **Nautilus Travel**, down on the waterfront, ✆/ ✆ (0674) 41 500.

Festivals

21 May, Festival of the Radicals (celebrating union with Greece) in Argostóli; **21 May**, Ag. Konstantínos near Argostóli; carnival celebrations on the **last Sunday and Monday before Lent**; **Easter** festival in Lixoúri; **23 April**, Ag. Geórgios; **23 June**, Ag. Ioannis, at Argostóli; **15 August**, Panagías at Markópoulo; **16 August** and **20 October**, Ag. Gerásimos; **first Saturday after 15 August**, Robóla festival of wine in Fragáta.

Argostóli (ΑΡΓΟΣΤΟΛΙ)

Argostóli (pop. 10,000), magnificently set on a thumb of the great bay in the south, is a big, busy Greek town. It started life as the port of the great citadel of Ag. Geórgios and a smuggler's hamlet under the Orsini and gradually, when the threat of piracy diminished, grew up around warehouses full of raisins, where ships from all over Europe would dock to fill their holds; the port of Argostóli is especially deep and safe and to this day is used for winter-berthing of yachts and larger ships. As Ag. Geórgios, the Venetian capital, declined, the inhabitants petitioned Venice to make Argostóli the capital and in 1759 got their wish, to the eternal disgust of archrival Lixoúri. After the earthquake, the Kefalonians abroad lavished money to rebuild the town in a style worthy of a provincial capital. As a result, Argostóli has more public buildings than most island capitals, grouped neatly around the large, central and palmy **Plateía Vallianóu**. Pre-earthquake Argostóli was famous for its bell towers, two of which have been rebuilt—there's something vaguely German Expressionist about the one by the Catholic church near the square.

Argostóli has two museums: the **Koryalenios Historical and Folklore Museum** below the library on Ilía Zervoú Sreet (*open 9–2, closed Sun; adm*) is one of the best of its kind and gives great insight into the island's history and the devastation wrought by the 1953 earthquake. Many of its books were donated from private collections after the disaster; its also contains the Venetian records of the island, incuding its Libro d'Oro listing the local nobility, photos of old Kefaloniá icons and of Argostóli pre-1953, a traditional bedroom, memorabilia recalling Kefaloniá's early love affair with opera and theatre (of all the Ionian islanders, the Kefalonians were considered the most cultivated) and a carved ebony desk that belonged to Ferdinand Lesseps, the mastermind behind the Suez Canal, whose father, under the French occupation, was the grand master of the Ionian Freemasonry. The library itself is the ground floor of an elegant mansion rebuilt since the quake. The **Archaeology Museum** on G. Vergóti (*open 8.30–3, closed Mon; adm*) contains ex-votos to the god Pan from the cave of Melissáni, a room of Mycenaean finds—bronze swords, vases with spirals, and gold and ivory jewellery—coins from the four ancient cities of Kefaloniá, and a startlingly modern bronze bust of a man from the early 3rd century AD. The island's first theatre, the **Kéfalos**, has been reconstructed above the museum.

The one structure to survive the earthquake in one piece was the 800m **Drapanós Bridge**, built by De Bosset in 1813 over the shallowest part of the bay, punctuated with a commemorative obelisk that originally read: 'To the Glory of the British Nation'. In 1858, during their Ionian island tour, Gladstone and his wife took a stroll over the bridge when they were surprised by a mass demonstration of Kefalonians demanding union with Greece. The British inscription survived after the union with Greece, but was effaced by the Italians in the Second World War, who meant to replace it with an inscription to Ugo Foscolo. Take it to join the road to Sámi; a few minutes on by car, the picturesque church of **Ag. Barbára** peers from the rockface over a little bridge. A few kilometres further, at Razáta, a dirt road leads up to ancient **Krani** (Paleókastro), where the huge stone blocks of the 7th-century BC Cyclopean walls snake through the trees. There are some fragments of a Doric temple to Demeter, and a rectangular hollow carved out of the top of the hill called the Drakospilia, or Dragon's Lair, although it was probably really just a Roman tomb.

The Lassí Peninsula

One thing to do in Argostóli is to shoot the loop by foot, bike or car—there's no bus—around the little Lassí peninsula, just north of the city. There are a number of sandy beaches, and a clutch of bars, tavernas and discos around the **Katavóthres** or swallow holes, where the sea is sucked into two large tunnels deep under the ground. Where the sea water actually went was a big mystery until 1963, when Austrian geologists poured 140 kilos of green dye into the water. Two days later the dye appeared in the lake of the Melissáni cave and at Karavómylos, near Sámi, on the other side of the island. The rushing water of the Katavóthres was harnessed by two sea mills to ground Argostóli's wheat, the first built by a certain Mr Stevens at the beginning of the British Protectorate, the second by a Greek; once a major tourist attraction, both were destroyed by the earthquake (which also greatly diminished the suction).

One has been reconstructed, for decoration more than anything else; the mill is now used as a lobster nursery. At the tip of the Lassí peninsula is the lovely **lighthouse of Ag. Theódori**, a Doric rotunda built by one of Kefaloniá's great benefactors, British Resident Charles Napier, and reconstructed to its original plans after the 1875 earthquake. A 20-minute walk inland is a memorial to the Italian troops who hid nearby but were found and slaughtered by the Germans.

The coastal strip just south of Argostóli with its huge beaches, **Platís Gialós** and **Makris Gialós,** was once a place of great natural beauty, a sandy paradise for the town dwellers. Now the locals steer clear and leave it for the razzle-dazzle of package tourism, but since Kefaloniá is hardly lacking in beautiful places to swim, don't feel deprived if you give it a miss.

Argostóli ✉ *28100,* ☎ *(0671–)*   **Where to Stay**

Two of the island's swankiest hotels are bang in the middle of the coastal strip decribed above: **Mediterranée**, on the beach at Makris Gialós, ☎ 28 760, 🖷 24 758 (*A; exp*) caters for the fat wallets of a youngish crowd; all mod-cons and a variety of land and sea sports. **White Rocks**, at Platís Gialós beach, 3km from Argostóli, ☎ 23 167, 🖷 28 755 (*A; exp*) appeals to a slightly older clientele and is just as pricey, well-equipped and glam.

In town, **Hotel Ionian Plaza**, in central Plateía Valliánou, ☎ 25 581, 🖷 25 585 (*C; exp–mod*) is a stylish hotel, each room with a balcony.

Olga, ☎ 24 981, 🖷 24 985 (*C; exp–mod*) is clean, tidy and agreeable; most rooms have pretty balconies and fantastic views across the bay to the distant mountains.

Cefalonia Star, at 50 Metaxá St, ☎ 23 180 (*C; mod*) is at the quieter end of the waterfront.

For a little less, cosy, family-run **Irilena**, ☎ 23 118 (*C; mod*) is a pleasant choice on the Lassí peninsula, near a little beach. *Open May–Oct.*

You can get basic rooms at **Hara**, 87 Leof. Vergotí, ☎ 22 427 (*D; inexp*). **Camping Argostoli**, ☎ 23 487, is 2km north on the Lassí peninsula.

O Mezes, in Lauranga St and **Sto Psito**, two streets up from the Folklore Museum, are both set in a pretty gardens and excel in traditional grills, *mezédes* and Cypriot specialities like *sheftália* (minced meatballs on a spit, served with pitta bread) (*3500–4500dr*). In the main square, **Kefalos** serves a large menu of Greek favourites on pretty pink tablecloths; **El Greco** and **Caliva** are also good choices. **Taverna Diana** on the waterfront near the fruit market does good moussaka and *kreatópita* (*see* above). If you have a hankering for charcoal-grilled chicken with a lemon marinade or lamb *kléftiko*, washed down with a house wine, get a table at **Psitaria Elliniko**, near Hotel Olga, ⓒ 23 529. Locals enjoy **Patsouras** on the waterfront near the NGTO and **Phaedra** on the Lassí peninsula; those in the know go for good, robust lunches at **Tzivras** on a side street by the fruit market (*2000 dr*).

Kreatópita (Kefalonian meat pie)

Argostóli's restaurants (*see* above) are a good place to try *kreatópita*. Many families prepare it for Apokreás (Carnival), and for Analipsos (Ascension Day). The following recipe serves 12. You'll need:

> *1 leg of lamb, cut into one inch chunks (keep the bones to one side)*
> *juice of one lemon*
> *¼ cup olive oil or butter*
> *1 chopped onion*
> *3 potatoes (parboiled in their jackets, then peeled and diced)*
> *1 large carrot (parboiled and diced)*
> *3 cups cooked rice*
> *2 tbspns tomato purée*
> *1 cup feta cheese, crumbled*
> *½ cup parsley, chopped*
> *1 tb. dried oregano*
> *3 cloves of garlic, chopped*
> *3 sprigs fresh mint, chopped*
> *1 tbspns cinnamon*
> *1 orange or lemon peel, grated*
> *salt and pepper to taste*
> *16 shop-bought filo sheets*
> *8 tbspns melted butter*
> *3 hard-boiled eggs, cut in quarters*

Preparation:

Cover the lamb bones with cold water in a pot and simmer for 1 hour, keeping the pot covered. Strain, boil down to 1 cup of stock, and set aside. Sprinkle the lamb with lemon juice. Heat the oil or butter in a pan, add the onions and lamb, and sauté the meat until the onions are soft but not brown. Empty pan into a large bowl and add the potatoes, carrot, rice, tomato purée, cheese, oregano, garlic, mint, cinnamon, parsley, and grated peel. Season with salt and freshly ground black pepper. Add enough lamb stock to keep the filling moist while the pie bakes.

Butter a 9 x 12 x 3 inch pan. Add a base of 8 filo sheets, brushing the melted butter in between each sheet, making sure the filo fits the sides and bottom of the pan. Add filling and spread evenly. Arrange the quartered eggs on top and cover with the remaining filo sheets, brushing each layer and the top with butter. Score the top 3 filo sheets into square or diamond shapes with a sharp knife. Bake for 40 to 50 minutes at 325° F (gas mark 3) until golden brown on top. Remove from the oven; let stand for 15 minutes, then cut into diamonds or squares and serve warm.

Lixoúri and the Palikí Peninsula

Ferries trundle across the bay from Argostóli to the easterly, bulging Palikí peninsula and **Lixoúri** (ΛΗΧΟΥΡΙ), Kefaloniá's second city, all new houses on wide streets and in itself not terribly interesting, even if it's the home of the Pale Philharmonic. Lixoúri is known for its sense of humour, and in its central square near the waterfront the town has put up a **statue of Andréas Laskarátos**, the city's most famous native son, a dapper fellow holding his top hat. Sometimes known as the 'Greek Voltaire', Laskarátos (1811–1901) was a minor aristocrat, poet and satirist who was a product of one of the several English schools founded on the Ionian islands by Lord Guilford. Laskarátos was a supporter of the British protectorate and directed most of his savage broadsides at local politicians and the Orthodox church; he heckled the clergy so much in his 1856 attack on Ionian morals, called *The Mysteries of Cephalonia* that they finally excommunicated him—in Greek, *aforismós*, meaning that the body will not decompose after death. When Laskarátos found out he hurried home, collected his innumerable children's decomposing shoes and returned to the priest, asking him to please excommunicate the footwear, too. On a more serious note, Laskarátos was found guilty of libel and fled to England before he returned to serve his sentence in Charles Napier's model prison. The Kefalonians forgave him even while he was alive for his complete honesty and integrity.

You can get a glimmer of what pre-earthquake Lixoúri was like on the west end of town at the **Iakovátos Mansion**, a rare survival and now a library and icon museum (*open 8–1.30 Mon–Fri; 9.30–12.30 Sat*); one of the works is attributed to Mikális Damaskinós. Fresco fragments and iconostases salvaged from the earthquake have been installed in the town's newer churches. North of Lixoúri, the unexcavated ancient city of Pali (or Pale) stood on the hill of Paliókastro.

The Palikí peninsula is well endowed with beaches. Closest is **Ag. Spyrídon**, just north of town and safe for children, while 4km south are **Michalitsáta** and **Lépeda**, both sandy, the latter near the abandoned cave-monastery, now church, of Ag. Paraskeví. In the same area, **Soulári**'s church of Ag. Marína has fine icons and a handsome Venetian doorway; the next village, **Mantzavináta**, has good frescoes in its church of Ag. Sofía.

From here a dirt road leads south to the lovely beach of **Ag. Geórgios** (or **Miá Lákko**), a long stretch of golden-red sand, which merges to the west with the Palikí's best known beach, simply known as **Xi**, a long crescent of pinkish sand, with sun beds and a taverna.

Just south of it is the famous **Kounópetra**, a huge monolith a few inches from the shore that rocked to and fro, pulsating at the rate of 20 times a minute. The earthquake of 1953 fouled up the magic by stabilizing the sea bed beneath and likewise destroyed the houses on pretty, deserted **Vardianá islet** off the coast. Another by-road to the west passes the abandoned monastery of **Tafíon**, en route to a second monastery, **Kipouríon**, rebuilt as it was before the earthquake in the 1960s, perched on the west cliffs, with spectacular sunset views and guest rooms where you can spend the night. The peninsula is full of caves: the most interesting, **Drákondi Spílio**, 40m deep, can be reached from the monastery with a guide.

The sparsely populated northern part of the Palikí has a scattering of pretty villages such as **Damoulináta**, **Delaportáta**, and **Kaminaráta**, the latter famous for its folk dances, and more beaches: the large, lovely white sands of **Petáni**, rarely overcrowded and known as Paralía Xouras, 'Old Geezer beach', for the old man who used to run the seaside taverna. Even more remote—accessible by a minor road—is another beach called **Ag. Spyrídon**, a stretch of sand tucked into the northernmost tip of the Palikí peninsula.

Lixoúri ✉ *28200,* ✆ *(0671–)*   **Where to Stay and Eating Out**

Cefalonia Palace Hotel, next to Xi beach, ✆ 91 111, winter bookings, ✆ 92 555, 🖅 92 638 (*A; exp*) is a brand new hotel with a pool, all rooms with sea view and balcony. **Pension Bella Vista**, ✆ 91 911 (*A; mod*) is small, modern and comfortable, all rooms with bath and simple kitchen and sea view. Although used by tour operators, the **Summery** in Lixoúri, ✆ 91 77 (*C; mod*) is a pleasant place to stay. **Akroyiali** has good fish in season and **Zorbas** has a nice garden; neither costs an arm and a leg.

Most of Kefaloniá's rural population is concentrated in the fertile region of valleys, gardens and green rolling hills called the Livathó, southeast of Argostóli. After Platís Gialós beach, emerging free from the tourist tinsel is **Miniés**, home of a ruined Doric temple of the 6th-century BC and some of Greece's finest white wine.

Kefaloniá in a Glass

Kefaloniá is one of the most important islands for wines, especially Robóla, a grape variety introduced by the Venetians in the 13th century that ferments into distinctive lemony dry white wines. Lately it's been better than ever: the Robóla from Gentilini, a small vineyard in Miniés owned and operated by Nichólas Cosmetátos, has been something of a revolution in the country, demonstrating just how good Greek wines can be when made with the latest techniques and *savoir faire*, even when starting from scratch. In 1978 Cosmetátos purchased an estate in these limestone hills, planted his first vines, built a small but ultra-modern winery, and carved a cellar out of the cliffs to attain the perfect storage temperature. Each year his vintages improve; pale gold Gentili Animus, 100 per cent Robóla, is a crisp, delicious wine well worth looking out for; Gentili Fumé is a Robóla aged in oak casks, with an oaky fragrance. Gentili also does a fine Muscat fortified dessert wine (Amando) and a lovely aperitif wine (half Muscat, half Robóla) called Dulcis, which goes perfectly with fresh fruit. Another label to look for, Calligas, was founded in the early 1960s, and produces lovely Robólas and other dry whites and reds and occasionally the very rare Thiniatikó, which yields a velvety port-like wine. In fish tavernas, the common house wine is Tsoussi, made from a white grape unique to Kefaloniá. You may also see Mavrodáphni Kefallinías, another sweet wine.

The coastal road south of Miniés continues to **Svoronáta,** where the church has pretty icons and a ship ex-voto, and where the red sands of **Avithos beach** (with a *cantina* and taverna) look out to the tiny islet of Días. This is named after a similarly tiny islet off the coast of Crete, and like that one had an altar to Zeus, or Días: sacrifices were coordinated by smoke signals with those on Mount Aínos. **Domáta,** the next village east, boasts Kefaloniá's oldest olive tree (able to squeeze 20 people in the hollow of its ancient trunk) and the beautiful church of the **Panagía,** with a pretty reconstructed Baroque façade and an enormous 19th-century carved and gilded iconostasis that cost 12,000 gold sovereigns—all melted down. It too has an naval ex-voto, the relief of the ship that was sailing through the Bosphorus when the sailors spotted the coffin containing the body of Patriarch Gregorius, martyred by the Turks in Constantinople in 1821. His body is now in Athens' cathedral, but the Kefalonians got to keep the coffin. Another church worth looking out for in the area is at **Kaligata** with its silver throne and grandiose iconostasis, and bell tower decorated with carvings of the Byzantine eagle, lion and crocodile. A road from Kaligata leads down to one of the prettiest beaches on this coast.

Nearby **Kourkomeláta** was rebuilt by the wealthy Kefalonian shipowner Vergotís; everything is as bright, new and pastel-coloured as a suburban southern California. The neoclassical cultural centre and surrounding vineyards add to the effect. At **Metaxáta**, where printing was introduced to Greece, Byron (along with a retinue including his faithful Venetian gondolier Tita) rented a house for four months in 1823, finished his satirical rejection of romanticism, *Don Juan*, and dithered over what to do as the representative of the London Committee, while each Greek faction fighting for independence jostled for the poet's attention—and especially his money—before he died his pathetic death from fever in Missolóngi.

Just below Metaxáta a battle of some consequence took place in 1564, when three fat galleys owned by the Chief Eunuch of Sultan Suleiman the Magnificent, sailing from Venice with a rich cargo and a number of ladies from the harem, were pounced upon and seized by the Knights of Malta. For Suleiman, it was the last straw in the Turks' long-running battle with the privateering Knights, and in 1565 he retaliated by sending a massive Ottoman fleet to beseige Malta and obliterate the knights once and for all: the first Great Siege of Malta. After four months of pounding, the Turks finally gave up, and Suleiman died the following year. It was the first great defeat of the Ottomans by the west.

Just west, **Lakídra**, rebuilt by French donations after the earthquake, is the most important village of the Livátho and believed by some archaeologists to be the site of Odysseus's palace; in the suburb of Kallithéa, near the plain little of church of **Ag. Nikólaos ton Aliprantídon**, four Mycenaean tombs yielded a good deal of pottery from 1250–1150 BC. Byron used to come here and sit on a rock, inspired by the views, and a line from the poem he wrote is inscribed on a plaque: ΑΝ ΕΙΜΑΙ ΠΟΙΗΤΗΣ ΤΟ ΟΦΕΙΛΩ ΕΙΣ ΤΟΝ ΑΕΡΑ ΤΗΣ ΕΛΛΑΔΟΣ ('If I am a poet, I owe it to the air of Greece').

Inland: Ag. Andréas, Ag. Geórgios, Ag. Gerásimos

North of Metaxáta is the Byzantine convent of **Ag. Andréas**, originally known as Panagía Milapídia (the Apple Virgin) after an icon discovered on an apple tree trunk. Perhaps the one and only good deed done by the quake of 1953 was to shake loose the whitewash on the walls, revealing frescoes that date back to the 13th century (in the chancel) and the 17th and 18th centuries (along the nave).

The church, now the **Ag. Andréas Monastery Museum** (*open Mon–Fri 9–1.30 and 5–8, Sat 9–1.30, closed Sun*), houses icons, fresco fragments and saintly relics orphaned by the eathquake, among them the Veneto-Byzantine icon of *Panagía Akáthistos*, painted in 1700 by Stéfanos Tsankárolos from Crete. Since the earthquake, a new Basilica of Panagía Milapídia was built next door to house the convent's bizarre prize possession: the sole of St Andrew's right foot, donated in the 17th century by Princess Roxanne of Epiros.

Above the church looms the tree-filled **Castle of Ag. Geórgios** (*open Jun–Oct 8.30–7, Sun 8.30–3, closed Mon*) spread over a 1056ft hill and commanding a wonderful view of the surrounding plains and mountains. Cool even on the hottest days, the citadel was founded by the Byzantine emperors, and later served as the residence of the Orsini and Tocco families during the days of the County of Kefaloniá, but it had to be completely rebuilt by the Venetians and Greeks under Nikólaos Tsimarás after the fierce seige of 1504 dislodged the Turks. With the rebuilding of the fortress, the nearby town of Ag. Geórgios became the Venetian capital, with a population reaching 14,000 living in or just outside the polygonal walls. A huge earthquake caused heavy damage to the village of Ag. Geórgios in 1636, and in 1757 was abandoned, and its port, Argostóli, became the new capital. Storerooms, prisons, Venetian coats-of-arms, a ruined Catholic church, and a bridge built by the French during their occupation crumble away within the battlements; of the 15 churches, the **Evangelístria** with Byzantine icons and five by Kefaloniá's greatest painter Andréas Kavatínos (1660–1740) still stands in the present-day little village.

To the east lies the green **plain of Omalós** and the **monastery of Ag. Gerásimos**, where the bones of Kefaloniá's patron saint rest in a silver reliquary, in a small church built over his little grotto hermitage. Gerásimos was a native of Lixoúri, and was canonized a century after his death, but he was so neglected by the sinful people that one day without warning he relocated his relics to Argóstoli, before they found their final place here. If half of the male population of Corfu are named Spíros after St Spyrídon, then 50 per cent of the Kefalonians are named Gerásimos. The saint's speciality is intervening in mental disturbances and exorcising demons, especially if the patient keeps an all-night vigil at his church on 20 October, his feast day, but pilgrims from all over Greece pour in all year round; a small hostel allows 20 to stay overnight. The monastery is dwarfed by an enormous plane tree and its tall pseudo-Rococo freestanding belfry. Opposite is a local winery, **Si.Ro.Ke**, sometimes open for tastings.

Mt Aínos National Park

From the Argostóli–Sámi road, a branch winds up the summit to **Mégas Sóros** (1628m), the highest point of majestic Aínos range, the loftiest in the Ionian islands, and covered with snow from December to March. The road goes as far the tourist pavilion, 1300m up, and from there you can easily hike the rest of the way, an impressive stroll among the tall, scented trees seemingly on top of the world. On a clear day, the Peloponnese, Zákynthos, Ithaca, Lefkáda, the Gulf of Pátras and Corfu are spread out below as if on a great blue platter.

Originally all the mountains were blanketed with its unique indigenous species of black fir—*Abies cefalonica*—with a distinctive bushy appearance and upward-pointing branches; the forests were so dense that Strabo and other ancient writers called the island Melaina, 'the Dark'. Since ancient times timber was the main source of Kefaloniá's prosperity; recent studies at Knossós show that the Minoans imported Kefaloniá's firs for the pillars of the labyrinth. Much prized for the construction of triremes in Odysseus' times and later by Venetian galley-builders, two disastrous fires, in 1590 and 1797, share the blame for destroying nine-tenths of the forest; the latter burned for three months. In 1962 what had survived of the forest was made into Mount Aínos National Park. A handful of wild horses, the last survivors of an ancient breed who lived in the park, are sadly near extinction. Hesiod mentioned the 8th-century BC temple of **Aenesian Zeus**, the foundations of which are just below Mégas Sóros; you can see the bones from the great animal sacrifices that took place there.

The South Coast: Beaches and the Virgin's Little Snakes

The south coast of Kefaloniá is bursting with good sandy beaches shielded from the north winds by Megás Sorós. There are good beaches at **Spartiá**, under sheer white cliffs, and **Trapezáki**, 1½km from the tiny harbour of **Pessáda** (ΠΕΣΑΔΑ)—Kefaloniá's chief link to Zákynthos (with a summer *cantina* but no telephone for the unwary foot passenger to ring for a cab, so be first off the boat and grab one that's waiting). East, below **Karavádos**, is another pretty little sand beach with a taverna perched above and plane trees and reeds spread behind.

The beach at **Lourdáta** (ΛΟΥΡΔΑΤΑ), is the longest and most crowded. Lourdáta's name is said to derive from the English lords who spent time here in the 19th century, perhaps attracted by the village's warm microclimate; its main square, with a spring and an enormous plane tree, is the beginning of Kefaloniá's first nature trail, blazed with funds from the WWF. It takes about 2½ hours to walk and passes through a sample of the island's flora—orange and olive groves, macchia shrubs and scrubby phyrgana, pine woods and kermes oaks, and masses of wild flowers in the spring. The path goes by the ruined **Monastery of Síssia**, founded in 1218 by St Francis of Assisi (hence its name) on his return from the Crusades in Egypt; converted to Orthodoxy in the 16th century, a new monastery was built just above after 1953.

Káto Kateliós is a small resort, a pretty place with springs, greenery and a beach that curves along Moúnda Bay. Just east, Potomákia beach below Ratzaklí is a favourite nesting place of loggerhead turtles (*see* 'Zákynthos', pp.206–7); from June to September volunteers for the British charity Care for the Wild mark the nests and carefully take visitors to see the turtles and their babies; don't go looking on your own as it's crucial not to disturb the nesting mothers.

Just inland, Kefaloniá's most unusual religious event takes place in the village of **Markópoulo**, set over the sea on a natural balcony. During the first 15 days of August, small harmless snakes 'inoffensive to the Virgin Mary', with little crosses on their heads, suddenly appear in the village streets. Formerly they slithered into the church (rebuilt in exactly the same place after the earthquake) and mysteriously disappeared near the silver icon of the Panagía Fidón ('Virgin of the Snakes'). Nowadays, to keep them from being run over, the villagers collect them in glass jars and bring them to the church, where they are released after the service and immediately disappear as they did in the past. Although sceptics believe that the church is simply along the route of the little snakes' natural migratory trail, the faithful point out that the snakes fail to appear when the island is in distress—as during the German occupation and in 1953, the year of the earthquake. Some of the locals may try to tease you into believing the island was the birthplace of Marco Polo (it's just barely possible; Polo was born *c.* 1254, when Kefaloniá was nominally under Venice).

Skála (ΣΚΑΛΑ) with its long beach and low dunes is the biggest resort in this corner, with plenty of watersports, sunbeds, bars—the works, but still relatively low-key. The Romans liked the area; near Skála a Roman villa was excavated, with 2nd-century AD mosaic floors, one portraying Envy, tied to a stake and being devoured by leopards and tigers, and another of two men making sacrifices at an altar. Two km north of Skála, a 7th-century BC temple of Apollo has also been discovered, though most of its porous stone was cannibalized to build the nearby chapel of Ag. Geórgios.

Pronnoi, one of the four ancient cities of Kefaloniá, was located inland, above the village of **Pástra**, although only a necropolis and some walls of the acropolis have survived. In 1992, in the nearby hamlet of **Tzanáta**, Danish and Greek archaeologists uncovered a huge 12th-century BC domed tomb seven metres under a vineyard, which is said to be the most important ever discovered in Western Greece. The bones, gold jewellery and seals discovered inside are now being studied at the University of Pátras, but the discovery (the Kefalonians immediately declared it the tomb of Odysseus) has added new fuel to the 'Where Was Ithaca Really?' debate.

The scenery between Skála and Póros is magnificent; from Tzanáta the road descends through the wild and narrow 'Póros Gap', carved, according to myth, by Heracles who ploughed his impatient way through the mountains. **Póros** (ΠΟΡΟΣ), with direct ferry links to Kilíni, was originally the ancient port of

Pronnoi. The rich and fertile Valley of Pronnos, just behind Póros, was the site in the 1820s of Charles Napier's model farm, worked by Maltese farmers with the aim of teaching good husbandry to the Kefalonians. Officially called New Malta, or just the 'Colony', it began full of promise, and failed through lack of support from the High Commissioner on Corfu, and the fact that the recruiter on Malta thought it was a good chance to export the costly sick and infirm rather send Napier any real farmers. Now Póros, with its clear turquoise waters, abundant fresh fish and beach, is rapidly developing as a resort.

✆ (0671–)   ***Where to Stay and Eating Out***

Pessáda ✉ 28082

> **Sunrise Inn**, 1½km from the port, ✆ 69 586, 📠 69 621 (*B; exp*) is comfortable and air-conditioned, set in the trees, with a pool and children's activities. In nearby Spartiá, **Poseidon**, ✆ 86 475, 📠 69 649, book in Athens, ✆ (01) 895 9899 (*mod*) has apartments with sea view balconies, a tennis court and a large garden. **Karavados**, ✆ 69 400 (*B; exp*) has a pool near Ag. Thomas beach.

Skála ✉ 28082

> **Aliki**, ✆ 83 427, 📠 83 426 (*B; mod*) overlooks the sea, has a large garden and is good value. **Ostria's House**, 600m from Ratzaklí, ✆ 83 383, book in Athens, ✆ (01) 202 4555 (*mod*) is a small and attractive pension. Up the coast at Póros, the first taverna on the waterfront is particularly agreeable and known for good home-cooking.

Lourdáta ✉ 28083

> **Lara**, ✆ 31 157, 📠 31 156 (*C; mod*) is a pleasant moderate-sized hotel, set in greenery a few minutes from the sea. *Open May–Oct*. Two of the best tavernas in the village, **To Thalassíno Trifilli** and **Klimatis** are run by members of Archipelagos, the local environmental group, who can inform you about any new nature trails and activities on the island. If it's on offer, try the *prentza* cheese made in nearby Simotáta.

North Kefaloniá: Caverns and Castles

Directly before the famous Battle of Lepanto, the Christian fleet under Don Juan of Austria was anchored in the Bay of **Sámi**. Now the port for ships to Pátras, Corfu and Italy, Sámi, with its little hotels and campsite, makes a half-hearted attempt at being a resort in its own right. Although the bay, with mountainous Ithaca as a frontdrop, is not unattractive, the town and its beach are of little interest. However, 4km east you'll find **Andisámos**, one of the most exquisite pebble beaches on

Kefaloniá, set in a bay of exceptional beauty with lushly forested hills spilling down to the postcard-clear water; and because facilities don't stretch beyond a simple *cantina*, the crowds stay away.

On the two hills behind Sámi are the town's **ancient walls**, which according to the chroniclers once enclosed 18,000 houses. Although the citizens, like those of Kefaloniá's other three ancient cities, initially agreed to surrender to Titus Quintius Flaminius, they changed their minds and put up a heroic four-month resistance to the Romans in 187 BC before their inevitable defeat, destruction of their city, and sale into slavery.

Sámi is also close to Kefaloniá's magnificent grottoes (*both open sunrise–sunset in summer, but closed after October*). **Drogaráti cave** (*adm*), near the hamlet of Chaliotáta, is a lugubrious den of orange and yellow stalactites and stalagmites; one of its great chambers has such fine acoustics that Maria Callas came here to sing, and concerts are occasionally held in the summer. The other, the more magical steep-sided **Melissáni** ('purple cave'; *adm exp*), is a half-hour walk from Sámi; small boats wait to paddle you across its mysterious salt-water lake (supplied by the swallow holes near Argostóli), immersing you in a vast shimmering play of blue and violet colours, caught by the sun filtering through a hole in the roof of the chasm, 100ft overhead. According to the school of thought that believes that Homer's 'Ithaca' consisted of both Itháki and Kefaloniá, this was the Cave of the Nymphs, where the Phaeacians deposited Odysseus. There are other, undeveloped caves for spelunkers only in the vicinity of Sámi, many with lakes and dangerous, precipitous drops, best of which is **Angláki cave**, near Pouláta.

At the base of Kefaloniá's northernmost peninsula, pretty **Ag. Evfimía** (ΑΓ. ΕΥΦΗΜΙΑ) is the port for Ithaca and Astakós, and a far cosier resort base than Sámi. There's good swimming off a scattering of white pebbly beaches along the Sámi road. A mosaic uncovered in Archeotíton Street is believed to have been the floor of the early Byzantine church of Ag. Evfimía, and the pretty village of **Drakopouláta**, a few kilometres above the port, was spared by the earthquake. Further west, scattered across the slopes of Mount Ag. Dinatí, are more of Kefaloniá's most traditional villages and goats with silver-plated teeth—caused by the high mica content in the soil.

✆ *(0674–)*   ***Where to Stay and Eating Out***

Sámi ✉ 28080

> **Pericles**, ✆ 22 780, 🖷 22 787 (*B; exp*) is a largeish unexceptional complex on the edge of town, with two round pools, tennis and nightclub. **Melissani**, ✆ 22 464 (*D; mod*) is set back in greenery on the edge of Sámi, a small hotel

with a pool and tennis. *Open May–Oct.* **Kastro**, ℘ 22 656 (*C; mod*) has sea view balconies and is convenient for the ferry. **Karavomilos Beach Camping**, 1km from town, ℘ 22 480, is well-equipped. The taverna selection is unexciting though Delfini, Adonis and Port Sámi are pretty reliable. Look out for local specialities such as octopus pie and meat cooked in a ceramic *stámna* and expect to pay around *2500dr.*

Ag. Evfimía ✉ 28081

For the moment there are only two hotels here, though one or two more may be in the offing. Newest and smartest is family-run **Hotel Gonatas**, ℘ 61 500, 🖾 61 464 (*C; exp–mod*) with a pool and sea views, at Paradise Beach, a five minute amble from the the little port. Paradise Beach is also blessed with a taverna, **Paradise**, which has earned itself a big reputation for Greek and international dishes. Stick to the Greek. **Moustakis**, ℘ 61 030 (*C; mod*) is in town. *Open April–Sept only.*

Up the Northwest Coast: to Mýrtos, Ássos and Fiskárdo

The journey from Argostóli north to Fiskárdo is magnificently scenic—perhaps a good reason to take the bus, so you don't have keep your eyes on the road, although there are some very tempting stops along the way. The first good beach, white pebbly **Ag. Kiriakí**, with several bars and tavernas, rims the crotch of land linking the Palikí peninsula to the rest of Kefaloniá, a few kilometres under the village of **Zóla**. An unpaved road links Zóla to **Angónas** (it's also on the main the Argostóli road) where local folk artist Razos has decorated the village square with paintings. Eight kilometres to the north and 2km below **Divaráta** (though the signpost indicates 4km), curves the U-shaped bay of **Mýrtos**, where sheer white cliffs carpeted with green maquis frame a stunning crescent of tiny white pebbles and patches of sand against a deep sea so blue it hurts. There are sunbeds, but if you want to make a day of it, bring provisions (and a hat—there's no shade in the afternoon) or settle for a pricey sandwich at the beach café.

The road winds along a corniche to another famous, stunning view over **Ássos** (ΑΣΟΣ), where the Venetian citadel and colourful little fishing hamlet tucked under the arm of the isthmus look like toys and sweetly belie the horror that happened here in September 1943, when 1500 Italian prisoners were ordered by the Germans to march over the cliffs to their deaths.

Ássos was rebuilt by the French after the earthquake and, though its sleepy charm may get a bit frazzled by day-trippers during the day, it becomes a friendly little Greek village in the evening; there are only a handful of rooms to rent and a couple of tavernas. The **Venetian fortress**—a favourite sunset destination, by foot or, much easier, by car—dates from 1585, when the Turks occupied Lefkáda and began raiding this coast; it was the seat of the Venetian provveditore until 1797. His house survives in ruins, along with the church of San Marco and a rural prison, used until 1815. The venerable olive tree in main Plateía Paris is said to have shaded the open-air sermons of St Cosmás the Aetolian, an 18th-century missionary; at one point, the story goes, his words were being drowned out by the buzzing cicadas. Cosmás told the insects to hush up, and they did.

East of the main road, an unpaved road rises up the inland villages of the peninsula. One, **Varí**, has by its cemetery a late Byzantine church called Panagía Kougianá, with rare and curious frescoes painted by a folk artist, who decorated the left wall with scenes from hell, and the right one with scenes of paradise until the villagers applied a coat of whitewash. The church is usually locked; ask in the village for the key.

Continuing up to Cape Ather, the northernmost tip of Kefaloniá, the road passes a white rocky beach of **Chalikéri**, where people come to soak in the exceptionally briny water and leave pleasantly pickled. In **Ántipata Erissóu**, the unusual Russian church of 1934 was built by a Kefalonian who made a fortune in the Soviet Union. **Fiskárdo** (ΦΙΣΚΑΡΔΟ) is by a landslide the prettiest and trendiest village on the island, its 18th-century houses gathered in a brightly coloured apron around a yacht-filled port. A fluke in its innermost geological depths spared it from the 1953 earthquake, and it's a poignant reminder of the architecture Kefaloniá once had, now all turned to dust. Some of the old houses have been fixed up for guests (*see* below); others are decorated with folk paintings of mermaids and ships. Four carved stone sarcophagi and the ruins of a Roman bath are fenced off by the Panormos Hotel.

Genius and Extrovert

The name Fiskárdo is derived from Robert Guiscard, the *terror mundi* of the 11th century, whose very name once made popes, emperors and kings tremble in their boots. Born near Cherbourg in in 1017, in a village now called Hauteville-le-Guichard, the 6th of 13 sons of minor Norman nobleman Tancred de Hauteville, Robert and three of his brothers found employment as mercenaries working mostly for and sometimes against the Lombards in Italy, who were revolting against their Byzantine overlords. None was a match for mounted Norman knights. By a mix of adroit military leadership, an eye for the main chance and cunning (his nickname *Guiscard* means 'crafty' or 'wizard') Robert set out to conquer southern Italy for himself, and was made Duke of Apulia and Calabria in 1059 by Pope Nicholas II. Other Hauteville brothers came to join him; the most successful was the youngest, Roger, who married a cousin of William the Conqueror, defeated the Arabs of Sicily and founded an extraordinary dynasty of Norman-Sicilian kings with the Guiscard's aid, in 1072.

Robert Guiscard could leave Sicily to his little brother because his ambitions were of a rather larger scale: he wanted the throne of Constantinople itself. With the excuse that Byzantine Emperor Michael VII had locked his empress (Guiscard's daughter) up in a convent, the Guiscard had just defeated the new emperor Alexius Comnenus I at Durazzo and was on his way west to invade Byzantium. His plans were interrupted in 1083 when he was summoned by Pope Gregory VII (Hildebrand) to expel Holy Roman Emperor Henry IV from Rome. To pay for their troubles, the Normans sacked Rome; to establish a base for his next campaign, Robert sent his son Bohemund to take Corfu.

In 1085 the Normans had just scored a major victory at Corfu over the Venetians, Byzantium's allies, when a typhoid epidemic at last laid low the 68-year-old warrior; the Guiscard was brought ashore and died in the arms of his Lombard warrior wife, Sichelgaita. His body was preserved in salt and sent back to Italy to be buried next to his brothers; the coffin was washed overboard in a storm, but later recovered off Otranto and the messy remains of the Guiscard were buried at Venosa. As John Julius Norwich wrote in *The Normans of the South*: 'He was that rarest of combinations, a genius and an extrovert...a gigantic blond buccaneer who not only carved out for himself the most extraordinary career of the Middle Ages but who also, quite shamelessly, enjoyed it.' Such was the power of his name that the old pirate was granted a posthumous and completely false reputation as a virtuous Crusader; two centuries after his death Dante installed him in *Paradiso*.

✆ (0674–)

Where to Stay and Eating Out

Ássos ✉ 28084

There are more than 200 beds in private rooms, but they fill up fast in the summer. Try **Linardos Apartments**, ✆ 51 563 (in winter, call Athens ✆ (01) 652 2594), **Cavos** ✆ 51 564, **Pension Yerania** ✆ 51 526 or **Kanakis Apartments**, ✆ 51 631 with its own tiny pool. There are five tavernas, of which **Kokolis** is the most established.

Fiskárdo ✉ 28084

In bijou Fiskárdo, where everybody likes to stay, four typical houses have been renovated by the NTOG; for reservations, write to **Paradosiakós**

Ikismós Fiskárdou, Kefaloniá, ✆ 41 398. There are two pensions, which are renovated and done out in traditional style: the **Filoxenia**, ✆ 41 319, and the **Dendrinos**, just out of town, ✆ 41 326. Self-contained apartments include **Porto Fiskardo**, ✆ 41 257, **Stella**, ✆ 41 211 and **Kaminakia**, ✆ 41 218. **Tassia**, ✆ 41 205, is a fine fish restaurant in the harbour, serving up ample portions of the day's catch to landlubbers and yachters who like to drop in (*3500dr*), and **Gaeta,** run by the same family, is a good grillhouse. Five kilometres away in Máganos, **Ionio** is an excellent traditional café and taverna.

Kýthera (ΚΥΘΗΡΑ)

Tucked under the great dangling paw of the Peloponnese, Kýthera, the isle of the goddess of love, is on the way to nowhere, and owes a good part of its attraction to the fact. The opening of the Corinth canal doomed even the minor commercial importance Kýthera once had by virtue of its position between the Ionian and Aegean seas; even today, unless you take the small plane from Athens, getting there is usually awkward, time-consuming and expensive, requiring a long overland drive and ferry or a long hydrofoil ride. Although sentimentally it continues to be one of the Eptánissa, or Seven Ionian Islands, with whom it shares a common history of Venetian and British occupation, politically it now belongs, rather bizarrely, not to any district in the adjacent Peloponnese, but to Attica; Piraeus is the centre of its administration.

In this century Kýthera's population has decreased dramatically, most emigrating to the other side of the world; some 100,000 people of Kýtheran origin now live in Australia or 'Big Kýthera' as the 2500 who still live on Kýthera call it. All the emigrants who possibly can return each summer, constituting its main tourist rush. Nor are many of them interested in developing the island's tourist potential; they like it fine the way it is. The non-Aussies who do visit are usually Italians or hardy Hellenophiles anxious to escape their own countrymen, or the wealthy who have scattered their villas all over Kýthera.

The tourist season is unusually short for a Greek island—mid-July to mid-September—and off season the island is uncannily quiet and shut down. Whatever the time of year, Kýthera is certainly not without its charms, although it can hardly hope to match the shimmering luxuriance of Watteau's sumptuous painting, *Pèlerinage à l'Ile de Cythère*. Much of the landscape has the look of abandoned farms and orchards, but in summer it is lent a golden sheen by the *sempreviva*, which when dried keeps 'forever', or at least a few years, rather like love itself.

History

Minoans from Crete were the first to settle Kýthera during the early Copper Age, founding a small colony near Kastri. Located at the crossroads between Crete and the mainland, and the Aegean and Ionian Seas, it soon became a key trading station. The Minoans also were the first to make use of what became the island's prize commodity in antiquity: murex sea shells, the source of a reddish purple dye, which they used to colour their ceramics, and for royal garments—hence the Kýthera's other early name, Porphyrousa. Abandoned by the Cretans in the mid 15th century, the settlement at Kastri was later taken over by a Mycenaean colony. Other early visitors to Kýthera were the Phoenicians, who according to Herodotus (I,105) introduced the cult of Astarte, their goddess of love, whom the Greeks called Aphrodite. The story goes that when Zeus took his golden sickle and castrated his father, Cronos, he cast the bloody member into the sea at Corfu. This gave birth to Aphrodite, who rose out of the foam on her scallop shell at Kýthera (as painted so memorably by Botticelli). She apparently found Kýthera far too puny for her taste and moved to Paphos, Cyprus, but throughout antiquity both places remained sacred to her. The sanctuary of Kytherian Aphrodite was up on the fortified acropolis of Paliokástro, and according to Pausanius was the most sacred of all such temples in Greece, but scarcely a trace of it remains today.

In the Peloponnesian War, Kýthera, as a sailing station between the seas and enjoying views of every passing ship, was essential to the defence of Sparta's home territories, and just as essential to the Athenian fleet, and it frequently changed hands: Kýthera would be attacked and invaded 80 times in recorded history. In the 5th century BC Kýthera gave birth to a lyric poet, Philoxenes, who ended up working in the mines when he couldn't stop laughing when he heard the pompous verses of Dionysos, the Tyrant of Syracuse, a lesson not lost on later poets.

In the early Byzantine period, life was so precarious that at times the only inhabitants on Kýthera were hermits and saints; the Saracens based on Crete were so ferocious that in the 10th century the island was all but abandoned until Nikephóros Phokás reconquered Crete for Byzantium. It marked the beginning of Kýthera's prosperity in the Middle Ages, under the Eudhaemonoyánnis family from Monemvássia. The Venetians occupied the island in 1204; the nobleman Marco Venier claimed it, and got it, on the basis that his family, like Julius Caesar's, was descended from Venus.

Venieri was soon distracted by quarrels on Crete, and left the island in the hands of its old lords, the Eudhaemonoyánnis; when Venier's descendants and other members of the Venetian nobility on Crete revolted against Venice, the Republic took the island under its own wing. The Venetians called it 'Cerigo' or the 'Eye of Crete'; the Venetian governor spent most of his allocated budget on operating a state of the art messenger service to Heráklion, Crete, to keep the governor there

To Gythion, Peloponnese

To Neapoli, Peloponnese

To Piraeus

Kýthera

Platia Ammos

Karaves

Gerakido

Ag. Anastasia

Ag. Pelagia

Potamos

Palio Chora

Trifilanika

Aronidika

Friligianika

Makronesi

Diakofti

Kato Chora

Mylopotamos

Mitata

Mt. Paliokastro (213m / 700ft)

Ag. Sofia

Dokana

Mermingaris (457m / 1500ft)

Viaradika

Temple of Aphrodite

Paliopolis

Avlemonas

Kournani

Kastri

Peripou

Fratsia

Korvounades

Mirtidion Monastery

Ag. Minas

Kaladi

Kontolianika

Drimonas

Livadi

Firi Ammos

5km
3 miles

KYTHERA (CHORA)

Kalamos

Kapsali

Vroulea

Venetian Fortress

Chalkos

N

To Gythion, Peloponnese

To Antikythera and Kastelli (Crete)

informed of Turkish movements in the area. In 1537, Barbarossa stopped on his way home from his unsuccessful siege of Corfu and destroyed the island, taking 7000 captives; raids continued and the population declined until the Battle of Lepanto in 1571. After Crete fell in 1669, Kýthera became a refuge for Greeks from the Peloponnese and Crete, and only once in 1715, during the incessant wars between Venice and Turkey, did the Venetian commander on the island surrender to the Turks; but in 1718, under the Passarovic Convention, the Turks had to give it back. Like the other Ionian islands, after 1797 it was occupied by the French, Russians, French and British, and in 1864 it was ceded to Greece.

Getting There and Around

By air: At least one flight a day from Athens, which takes 40 minutes; airport information, ✆ (0735) 33 297, tickets from the Olympic Office at El. Venizélou 49, Pótamos, ✆ 33 688.

By sea: From the end of June through September, there are **hydrofoils** to Ag. Pelagía 5 times a week from Gýthion; 5 times a week from Piraeus (it takes 5–6 hours), by way of Hýdra, Spétses Porto Cheli and Monemvássia; another sails once a week from Chalkidíki in Macedonia. For information contact **Ceres**: ✆ (01) 428 0001 in Pireaus, ✆ 31390 on Kýthera.

Regular Miras **ferry** services run from Neápolis daily (50 minutes, ✆ (0734) 22947); 5 times a week with Gýthion (3 hours, ✆ (0733) 22996/22410/24501), twice a week with Monemvássia, (✆ (0732) 61219), Kastélli (Crete) and Piraeus (7 hours, ✆ (01) 417 4459/427 4060); there are also links once a week with Antikýthera. In the low season, services are greatly reduced. Even in high season, the hydrofoils are very susceptible to rough seas south of Monemvássia and cancellations are not uncommon. For ferry information on Kýthera, ring Ag. Pelagia ✆ 33 490/33 890 or Kapsali ✆ 31 301 **Port authority**: ✆ 33 280.

By road: **Buses** leave Chóra and Ag. Pelagía only once a day for the major towns and villages of the island; expect to rely heavily on **taxis,** which charge set fees. At Ag. Pelagía, Pótamos and Kapsáli there are cars and mopeds to **hire**.

✆ (0735–)   ## Tourist Information

For **tourist police** see regular police, ✆ 31 206. In **Ag. Pelagía**, hotels and rooms are listed on a large noticeboard near where the ferry docks. For help with accommodation in the south of the island try Yannis Fatseas at **Kytheros International** ✆ 31 790, ✉ 31 688, or **Porfyra Travel** ✆ 31 888, both in Livádi.

The tourist guide *Kythera* is freely available and full of interesting titbits, and there's a very pleasant 'unofficial' homepage on the island at *www.geocities.com/Athens/Delphi/3728/cerigo.htm.*

Festivals

29–30 May, Ag. Trias at Mitáta; **15 August**, Panagías Mirtidíon; **24 September** Mirtidión Monastery.

Chóra (XΩPA), the capital of the island, is a pretty-as-a-picture-postcard blue and white Greek village, 275m above the port of Kapsáli, and guarded by a mighty if ruined fortress furnished by the Venetians in 1503. Its location was supposedly selected by pigeons, who took the tools of the builders from a less protected site; the views of the sea and surroundings are worth the climb up. Ten old **Venetian mansions** in Chóra still retain their coats-of-arms, and a small two-room **museum**, generally open in the mornings, contains artefacts dating back to Minoan times. Below, a 20-minute walk down the hill, the port and mini-resort of **Kapsáli** (KAΨAΛI) has a few restaurants and two picturesque pebble and sand beaches, one very sheltered and boaty, the other only a tiny bit more exposed; pedaloes will take you to other pebbly strands. The little 'egg islet', Avgó, offshore here is said to be the spot where Aphrodite was born.

Kálamos, just east, is within walking distance. One of its churches, Ag. Nikítas, has a pretty bell tower, and there is a *kafeneíon* by the square. Dirt roads continue across the rugged landscape to various beaches; nearest is pebbly **Chalkos**, set in a beautiful, almost enclosed, bay with a small summer snackbar.

Northwest of Chóra

From Chóra, the paved road heads north to **Livádi** (ΛIBAΔI), where there's a stone bridge of 13 arches, built by the British in 1822 and proudly heralded as the largest in Greece. If you ring ahead (© 31 124) you can visit the Roússos family's ceramic workshop, where the ancient tradition of Kýthera pottery is kept alive, now into the fourth generation. Heading east from Livádi, a 4km dirt road leads to the dramatic beach and tiny snack shack of **Fíri Ámmos** ('red sands'), popular with snorkellers; in an ordinary car, the final descent is manageable, if a little hair-raising. West of Livádi via Drimónas is the important **Monastery of the Panagía Mirtidíon** with a tall carved bell tower, magnificently set on the wild west coast among cypresses, flowers and peacocks. The monastery is named after a gold-plated icon of the Virgin and Child, whose faces have blackened with age—a sign of special holiness that attracts huge numbers of pilgrims. Two small islets just off-shore are said to be pirate ships that the Virgin turned to stone for daring to attack the monastery. Pilgrims can stay in the very simple hostel.

North of Drimónas, **Milopótamos** (MYΛOΠOTAMOΣ) is the closest thing to Watteau's vision of Kýthera, a pretty village criss-crossed by tiny canals of clear water—so much water, in fact, that the toilet in the valley is in a constant state of flush. The stream valley through the middle of town is called the Neraída, or Nymph; an old watermill lies along the somewhat overgrown path to the waterfall at Foníssa, surrounded by the ancient plane trees, flowers and banana plants; on quiet evenings you can hear the nightingales sing. The ghost town **Káto Chóra** lies just below Milopótamos, within the walls of a Venetian fortress built in 1560. Above the gate there's a bas-relief of the winged lion of St Mark gripping his open book reading the angelic words '*Pax Tibi, Marce, Evangelista Meus*' that meant that Kýthera was on good terms with Venice (a closed book signified a less cordial relationship). The lion welcomes you to a desolation of empty 16th-century stone houses and churches, although some are slowly being restored. A road descends steeply down to one of the island's best secluded beaches, white sandy **Limiónas**.

Signs from Milopótamos lead down to the cave **Ag. Sofía**, Kýthera's most impressive, at the end of a rugged, declining track (*usually open summer afternoons 3–8, but check in the village or call © 34 062*). In the past, the cave was used as a church, and inside there are frescoes and mosaics, as well as stalactites and stalagmites and small lakes that go on and on; some say it tunnels all the way under Kýthera to Ag. Pelagía. And at Ag. Pelagía a sign does indeed point down a rocky hill to a mysterious Ag. Sofía.

The East Coast

From both Fratsiá and Frilingianiká, winding roads branch east to **Paliópoli** (ΠΑΛΑΙΟΠΟΛΙΣ), a tiny village on the site of **Skandeia**, the port mentioned by Thucydides. The Minoan trading settlement was here, from 2000 BC until the rise of the Mycenaeans; their long-ago presence (ruins of the settlement may be seen at a place called **Kastrí**) has bestowed archaeological status on the long and lovely beach, which has kept it pristine except for a good taverna.

In ancient times, devotees would climb to the temple of Urania Aphrodite, 'Queen of the Heavens', to pay their respects to the goddess. Urania Aphrodite was often known as the 'eldest of the Fates', the daughter of the Great Goddess Necessity, whom even the great Zeus could not control. Pausanius wrote that her temple was one of the most splendid in all Greece, but the Christians destroyed it and built the church of Ag. Kosmás (with the temple's Doric columns). Travellers once commented on the presence of a bath belonging to Menelaus, known as the Bath of Helen, but now only the acropolis walls remain at the site, called **Paliokástro**.

From Paliópoli the coastal road descends to **Avlémonas** (ΑΒΛΕΜΟΝΑΣ), a fishing village with good restaurants. By the sea is a small octagonal fortress built by the Venetians, who left a coat-of-arms and a few rusting cannon inside. A short drive and walk from the village is one of the island's finest beaches, **Kaladí**, featured on many a tourist office poster. Follow signs marked ΠΡΟΣ ΚΑΛΑΔΙ—2km of dirt road which leads past a blissful little chapel and abruptly stops; from here there's a steep, but mercifully short, climb down to the glorious double-coved pebbly beach. Definitely not for the faint-hearted, but well worth it in the end. Another dirt road leads north of Avlémonas, 7km to **Diakófti** (ΔΙΑΚΟΦΤΙ), a scrap of a resort popular with Greek families, which is taking over as the island's main port and has a strip of white sand, protected by a pair of islets, Makronísi and Prasonísi. The main road from Diakófti passes the airport; to the south, near the centre of Kýthera, **Mitáta** is a great place for picnics, surrounded by lovely green countryside and lemon trees; the cool clear water of its spring is delicious. It's also a good spot to purchase delicious thyme honey, at about half the price of the rest of Greece—3500dr a kilo; one source is George and John Protopsáltis, ℂ 33 614.

Palio Chóra and the North

Palio Chóra (or Ag. Dimitríou), is Kýthera's Byzantine ghost town, founded by the noble Eudhaemonoyánnis clan in the Monemvassian style. Set high on the rocks, it was carefully hidden from the sea in a magnificent gorge—according to legend, the terrible Barbarossa found it only by capturing the inhabitants and torturing them until they told him where it was. Beside the ruins of the fort is a terrible 330ft abyss, where mothers threw their children before leaping themselves, to avoid being sold into slavery by Barbarossa. Most of the island's ghost stories and legends are centred here. The dirt road drive and the scramble up are rewarded not only by views over the precipice, but a few frescoes in the haunted churches.

Palio Chóra is near **Potamós** (ΠΟΤΑΜΟΣ), which, despite its name, has no river. It is the largest village in the north, all blue and white like the new Chóra. It has a bank and an Olympic Airways office, and the largest building at the edge of town is Kythera's retirement home. Come on Sunday if you can, when the village hosts the island's biggest market. West of Potamós, **Ag. Eleftheríos** is a lovely secluded beach, and a pretty place to watch the sunset.

At **Gerakári** to the northwest you can see yet another tower, this time built by the Turks in the early 18th century. From the pretty village of **Karavás**, the road continues to the fine beach and good taverna at **Platiá Ámmos**. **Ag. Pelagía** (ΑΓ. ΠΕΛΑΓΙΑ), Kýthera's northern port, also has a long pebble beach and a few more facilities, if not a lot of soul. There are some excellent beaches to the south including one by the name of **Fíri Ámmos**.

Kýthera ✉ 80100, ℂ (0735–)   ***Where to Stay and Eating Out***

When it comes to finding a place to stay on Kýthera you may be hard pressed to find anything luxurious.

Chóra (Kýthera)

Margarita, tucked away off the main street ℂ 31 711, ✆ 31 325 (*B; exp–mod*) is a nice old pension in a building that was once a bank, with an impressive wooden spiral staircase. **Castello**, ℂ 31 069, ✆ 31 869, has three studios and six rooms leading off a walled garden near the fortress; immaculate and well-designed, rooms all have telephone, fridge and overhead fans. There are a number of typical, simple tavernas offering straightforward Greek food up in Chóra, notably **Zorba's**, in the main street. Chóra is also well endowed with shops selling local arts and crafts; at **Nikolaou**, on the road coming into town from the north, you can see rugs being woven and a fine selection of ceramics, gifts and ethnic-style jewellery. **Stavros** is known the island over for stocking well-presented local produce—wine, jam, honey, chutneys, oils, vinegars, freshly baked sweets and an eclectic selection of books. **Ta Kythera**, just inland at Manitochóri, ✆ 31 563, has clean, pleasant double rooms. *Open June–Aug only.*

Kapsáli

One of the nicest places to stay on Kýthera, Kapsáli is the chosen spot for **Greek Islands Club**'s fine selection of villas and apartments, ✆ UK (01932) 220 477, 🖷 229 346. Also here, the **Raikos** hotel ✆ 31 629 (*B; exp*) is the island's biggest and most expensive with air-conditioned rooms and a pool. *Open May–Sept.* **Kalokerines Katikies**, ✆ 31 265 (*C; mod*), have furnished apartments. Taverna **Magos**, ✆ 31 407, and the lone taverna at the far western end of the beach, have lovely views of Kapsáli, and serve all the usual Greek specialities.

Livádi

There are two places to stay here: **Aposperides**, ✆ 31 790 or 31 656 (*B; exp*), a pristine, hotel-like pension, or **Rousos**, in Káto Livádi, ✆ 31 124, with apartments. **Taverna Pierros** is probably the oldest and most traditional taverna on Kýthera, with authentic home-cooking and kind prices. **Faros,** near the 'British bridge', is a favourite for *mezédes*. Three km north, the **Lokanda** in Karvoynádes is a good place for a pizza or snack.

Avlémonas

There are plenty of self-catering apartments here, among them **Poppy's**, ✆ 33 735; **Roulas**, ✆ 33 060; **Christoforos**, ✆ 33 057, **Manolis Stathis**, ✆ 33 732 and **Mandy's**, ✆ 33 739 (*all mod*). **Taverna Sotiris**, ✆ 33 722, prettily set in a small square overlooking the sea, prepares excellent seafood as fresh as can be, caught by the owners themselves. Just outside nearby Paliópoli, try the **Skandia**, serving Greek specialities served under an enormous elm tree—a great place for lunch.

Diakófti

For peace and quiet you can't beat **Sirene Apartments**, right on the sea, ✆ 33 900, or winter in Athens ✆ (01) 481 1185 (*A; exp*), with their big verandas and kitchens. Also try **Kythera Beach Apartments**, ✆ 33 750 (*C; mod*), within spitting distance of the sea. *Open April–Oct.*

Mitáta

People come from across Kýthera to eat at **Michalis** (ΜΙΧΑΛΗΣ) an informal taverna in the village's main square, with panoramic views of the surrounding hills and valleys; Michális' wife cooks a number of island specialities, including cockerel and rabbit, prepared with vegetables from their own garden.

Ag. Pelagía

Filoxenia, ✆ 33 800 (*B; exp*) has 54 furnished apartments and a pool. The 10-roomed **Kythereia** pension, ✆ 33 321 (*D; mod–inexp*) is nearest the pier and serves breakfast. **Aphrodite**, ✆ 33 926, is clean with sea views.

There's a limited selection of tavernas: the popular **Kaleris**, ✆ 33 461, has tables right on the sand. In the evening a lot of people end up inland at Karavás, at the **Amir Ali** piano bar, apparently named after a Turk, but no one knows why.

Elafónissos (ΕΛΑΦΟΝΗΣΟΣ) and Antikýthera (ΑΝΤΙΚΥΘΗΡΑ)

From Ag. Pelagía you can look out across the Lakonian sea to the islet of **Elafónissos**, which until the 17th century was a part of the Peloponnese, and is now connected daily in the summer by caique every 40 minutes from Neápolis in July–September or less often from Ag. Pelagía (✆ (0734) 61177 for info).

The one village is mostly inhabited by fishermen and sailors, but the main reason for visiting is 5km south of the village, **Katá Nísso**, a twin bay endowed with two gorgeous white sandy beaches that go on and on, as yet hardly discovered by tourists (a caique from the 'capital' makes the trip). There are two tavernas and two small B-class pensions in the village, if you want to play Robinson Crusoe with a roof over your head: **Asteri tis Elafonissou**, ✆ (0734) 61 271 and **Elafonissos**, ✆ 61 268, *open June to September.* Rough camping on the beach is another possibility.

Another islet, the utterly remote **Antikýthera**, lies far to the south of Kapsáli, midway between Kýthera and Kastélli, Crete. If the *meltémi* isn't up, as it often is, ships call once a week en route between Kýthera and Crete. Fewer than 150 people live in Antikýthera's two villages, **Potamós** and **Sochória**, and the rest is very rocky with few trees; curiously, like west Crete, the island is slowly rising. By Potamós, ancient **Aígilia** has walls dating back to the 5th century BC.

There's a small beach at **Xeropótamo**, 5 minutes from Potamós by boat, or 30 minutes on foot. Water is a luxury, and the few rooms available are quite primitive; running water and toilets are rare. Food can also be scarce.

The World's Oldest Computer

Antikýthera is just a tiny smudge on the map, but thanks to the wild winds that churn the surrounding sea it is also a name familiar to any student of ancient Greek art. For here, on the 22nd day of the ancient Greek month of Mounichon, in the first year of the 180th Olympiad (5 May, 59 BC), a Roman ship sailing from Rhodes, laden with booty that included the magnificent 4th-century BC bronze statue known as the *Ephebe of Antikýthera* (one of the celebrities of the National Archaeology Musem in Athens), went down off the coast of Antikýthera. Now you might ask: how is it that anyone could even begin to know the precise date of a 2000-year-old shipwreck? Pinpointing even the century of ancient finds is more often than not just an archaeological guessing game. The answer is that part of the booty from Rhodes included the world's first computer, and its timekeeping mechanism was stopped forever on the day the ship went down.

The wreck was discovered by chance in 1900 by sponge divers from Sými, who in a storm sheltered off the inaccessible coast of Antikýthera. After the storm, a few divers donned their weighted belts and went down to see if this remote seabed might in fact shelter a sponge or two. Instead they were startled to see a man beckoning to them—the famous Ephebe. The Greek archaeological service was notified, and sent down a small warship to haul up the bronze and marble statues, vases, and glass—the world's first underwater archaeological dig. One of the items was a lump; as the months passed and the sea mud dried, a wooden cabinet about a foot high was revealed. This quickly deteriorated on contact with the air, leaving a calcified hunk of metal that broke into four bits. Archaeologists were astonished to see that they belonged to a mechanical device inscribed with ancient Greek script.

At first dismissed as a primitive astrolabe, the Antikýthera Mechanism, as it was known, soon proved to be much more complex. In 1958, a young British science historian, Derek de Solla Price, was allowed to examine it and was the first to recognize it as an astronomical computer, which, by its setting, was made on the island of Rhodes in 82 BC. The days of the month and the signs of the zodiac were inscribed on bronze dials, with pointers to indicate the phases of the moon and position of the planets at any given time, operated within by a complex mass of clockwork: bronze cog wheels with triangular teeth, connected to a large four-spoke wheel (the most prominent part visible at the National Archaeology Museum in Athens) driven by a crown gear and shaft, which probably had some kind of key for winding. A moveable slip ring allowed for Leap Year adjustments and alignments.

As far as anyone can judge, it was last set by the Roman sea captain on the day his vessel went down. He may have been bringing it to Rome on the special order of Cicero, who knew of the 'future-telling astronomical' device from his school days at Rhodes' famous School of Rhetoric. 'It is a bit frightening to know,' concluded Derek Price, 'that just before the fall of their great civilization, the Ancient Greeks had come so close to our age, not only in their thought, but also in their scientific knowledge.' The next similar device to be noted anywhere was in 11th-century India, by the Iranian traveller al-Biruni. (For all the details, pick up a copy of Victor Kean's *The Ancient Greek Computer from Rhodes*, Efstathiadis Group, 1991).

Lefkáda (ΛΕΦΚΑΔΑ)

On Lefkás you feel very strongly the bond of the land with the depths, with the spirits of the cosmogony, with the dynamism of the earth.

Ilias Venezis, Lefkas

The island of Lefkás (more popularly known in Greece by its genitive form Lefkáda) was named for the whiteness (*leukos*) of its cliffs. It barely qualifies as an island; in ancient times Corinthian colonists dug what is now the 20m (66ft) wide Lefkáda ship canal, separating the peninsula from the mainland. This is kept dredged by the Greek government and is easily crossed by a swing bridge; beyond the canal a series of causeways surrounds a large, shallow lagoon, where herons and pelicans figure among the migratory visitors.

Lefkáda is not always a love-at-first-sight island; the approach from land is unpromising, and first impressions may be disappointing. As on Kefaloniá, Ithaca and Zákynthos, a series of earthquakes—most devastatingly in 1946—destroyed nearly all the buildings. Appearances change once you make your way down the coast, where Lefkáda's long sandy beaches, mighty mountainous ridge and high plateaux, stunning sea cliffs and off-shore islets more than compensate.

Of all the Ionian islanders, the people of Lefkáda, not too surprisingly, have the most in common with the mainlanders; their faces are stronger and bonier, their women famed for being the most dignified and beautiful. In the mountain villages they still make fine laces and embroideries and weavings on looms in the back rooms of their houses. The island is just as famous for its perfect windsurfing at Vassilikí and sailing through the enchanted isles off Nídri. Dolphins seem to like it as well: there are more varieties seen off the coasts of Lefkáda than any where else, including the rare *Delphinus delphis*.

History

Although inhabited at least as far back as the late Paleolithic era (8000 BC), Lefkáda first enters recorded history as 'the peninsula of Epirus' in Homeric times, part of ancient Akarnania and site of the city Nerikus, located at modern Kallithéa. Nerikus is recorded as being huge, but over the years farms and houses have almost completely overtaken all the remains. In 640 BC, the Corinthians used a ruse to snatch the island from the Akarnanians, and founded the city of Lefkáda where it is today. One of the first things they did was dig the channel through the shifting sands that separated Lefkáda from the mainland, to better protect their shipping, and they built the first fort at the northern tip, which throughout history would be the key to the island. During the Peloponnesian War, Lefkáda, as a loyal ally of Corinth, sided with Sparta and was devastated twice, by the Corcyraeans (435 BC) and the Athenians (426 BC). Lacking any resources to maintain the channel, it silted up during this period, and Lefkáda rejoined the mainland.

The biggest blow to ancient Lefkáda came with the war between Macedonia and Rome in the mid 3rd century BC, when the island was the capital of Akarnania and had to pay the price for siding with Macedonia; in 230 BC the Romans thoroughly devastated it, then came back and reopened the channel. Another dark moment was the Battle of Actium, where Augustus outmanoeuvred and defeated the fleets of Mark Antony and Cleopatra, and won the Roman Empire as his prize. To celebrate his victory, Augustus founded a new city, Nikopolis (near modern Aktion) which drained away Lefkáda's wealth and population. In later years, Augustus and Virgil came to visit the island on their short-lived Greek tour. In the 4th century the island is recorded as being the seat of a bishopric; then, as far as the historical record goes, it dropped into total obscurity.

Although Lefkáda was granted to Venice after the Fourth Crusades, the island, like Corfu and Paxí, spent the next century under the Byzantine Despot of Epirus. The inhabitants, exasperated by the fights and pirates, received permission from Venice to built the fortress of Santa Maura, a name that the Venetians used to refer to the entire island; the Duke of Lefkáda held court here. When Constantinople fell in 1453, the mother of the last Emperor Constantínos XI, Helene Palaeológos, founded a monastery within the walls of Santa Maura. When the Turks took Lefkáda in 1479, they turned the monastery into a mosque, and, meaning to stay, they built a causeway and aqueduct to supply the fortress.

Venetian influences on Lefkáda were never as strong on the other Ionian islands, partly because they could never decide if they really wanted it. In 1500 the combined forces of Spain and Venice under the Gran Capitan Gonzales de Cordoba captured Santa Maura, but the very next year Venice made a treaty with Turkey and the senate at Corfu returned Lefkáda to the Turks. In 1684, the future doge of Venice, Francesco Morosini, angry at losing his own fortress at Herákleon, Crete,

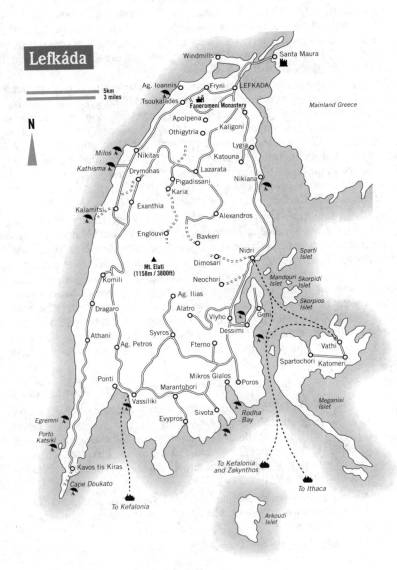

Lefkáda

5km
3 miles

N

Windmills
Santa Maura
Ag. Ioannis
Fryni
LEFKADA
Tsoukalades
Faneromeni Monastery
Mainland Greece
Apolpena
Kaligoni
Othigytria
Lygia
Milos
Nikitas
Katouna
Kathisma
Drymonas
Lazarata
Pigadissani
Nikiana
Karia
Kalamitsi
Exanthia
Alexandros
Englouvi
Bavkeri
Nidri
Sparti Islet
Dimosari
Mt. Elati
(1158m / 3800ft)
Neochori
Mandouri Islet
Skorpidi Islet
Komili
Skorpios Islet
Ag. Ilias
Dragaro
Alatro
Vlyho
Geni
Athani
Syros
Dessimi
Vathi
Ag. Petros
Fterno
Spartochori
Katomeri
Ponti
Mikros Gialos
Poros
Meganisi Islet
Marantohori
Vassiliki
Sivota
Rodha Bay
Evypros
Egremni
Porto Katsiki
To Kefalonia and Zakynthos
Kavos tis Kiras
To Ithaca
Cape Doukato
To Kefalonia
Arkoudi Islet

and, seeing the Turks bogged down and defeated outside the walls of Vienna by Jan Sobieski (1683), launched an offensive at Lefkáda, defeating the Turks with the help of an army of Greek priests and monks under the Bishop of Kefaloniá; from Lefkáda Morosini went to re-conquer the whole of the Peloponnese for Venice—the Republic's last great victory. The Turks took it back during their last great siege of Corfu in 1715, until the hero of the hour, Count von der Schulenberg, arrived and systematically took it back for Venice.

With the fall of Venice, the French and then the Russians grabbed Lefkáda, but it was Ali Pasha, the tyrant of Epirus, who really wanted it. Believing the island had been promised him by the British in 1799 in exchange for his support of Russia, he tried to purchase it outright from Russia in 1807, but was held back by the diplomatic efforts of Russian foreign secretary, Count John Capodístria of Corfu; Ali Pasha then sent in an army to grab it but was repulsed militarily by the same Capodístria. In the fervor of a Greek-led victory, Capodístria is said to have sworn to support the cause of independence with the Greek captains who had taken refuge on the island, among them Kolokotrónis.

In 1810, the British, led by the Duke of York's Light Greek Infantry, attacked the French, who were still holed up in the island's fortress of Santa Maura; when the Greek mercenaries working for the French saw their fellow Greeks, 1600 immediately changed sides, although it still took a month to dislodge the French. Under the British Protectorate, there was an initial uprising against Maitland, protesting the new taxes he levied to pay for the reopening of the channel, but otherwise Lefkáda seems to have been a peaceful place, especially under the island's Resident, Charles Sebright, one of the few who bothered to learn modern Greek. British travellers noted that the proximity of the once malarial Gulf of Arta tended to afflict the island with fever—but only the temperate islanders; British soldiery notably escaped coming down with anything at all.

Getting There and Around

By air: Flights once a day from Athens and regular charters from England (Monarch, Air Ferries, and Air Caledonian among them), to Aktion, the nearest airport, 26km away on the mainland; from May–mid Oct there are bus connections to Lefkáda from the airport. Another charter, Britannia, flies to Préveza.

By sea: In summer, **boats** from Nidrí and Vassilikí to Sámi, Fiskárdo and Póros (Kefaloniá) and Kióni (Ithaca). Daily boat from Nidrí to Meganísi. **Port authority:** ✆ 22 176.

By road: There are **bus** connections with Athens (see p.11), Arta and Préveza; Athens is about six hours' drive by car, Préveza about an hour.

The main island **bus station** is located on the north end of Lefkáda Town; for information call ✆ 22 364. Routes aren't very frequent, and to really see the island you need at least a moped; there are plenty to hire at Vassilikí and Nidrí.

✆ *(0645–)*

Tourist Information

See regular police, Lefkáda Town, ✆ 22 346; Vassilikí, ✆ 31 218 and Vlychó, ✆ 95 207.

For help with anything from travel to accommodation, the first travel agent to set up on the island, **George Kourtis**, is still on Nidrí's main street, ✆ 92 494, ✉ 92 297.

Festivals

50 days after Easter, Faneroméni Monastery; **26 July**, Ag. Paraskeví near Ag. Pétros, carnival festivities, with a parade; in **August**, the Arts and Letters Festival and large International Folklore Festival, in Lefkáda Town; throughout the **first two weeks of August,** Karyá, which is well-known for its handmade lace and woven carpets, puts on a stream of festivities including a clarinet festival on the **11th** and 'Riganada', the recreation of a traditional wedding, where everyone wears their finest old costumes; **11 November**, Ag. Minás in Lefkáda.

Lefkáda Town

Approaching Lefkáda over the floating bridge, the first thing you'll see as you cross the causeway over the lagoon is the massive **Fortress of Santa Maura**, dipping its feet in the sea near Akarnania (as the region is still known) on the mainland. Santa Maura 'the black saint' was a virgin martyr worshipped by the first Christians of Lefkáda—one whom emperor Julian the Apostate tried to discredit when he passed through, saying she was just Aphrodite in disguise. First built by the Crusaders, most of what stands dates from the Venetian and Turkish reconstructions. Although the buildings within the walls were blown to smithereens in an accidental powder explosion in 1888, the fortress continued to serve as a military camp, and, for 10 years after the 1922 Asia Minor Disaster, as a refugee camp. In 1938 everything within the walls of the fortress was sold off as building stone, leaving only a little church and the tomb of a certain Enrico Davis, General Minister of the Armies of His Britannic Majesty in Sicily, a member of the troops who occupied the fortress from 1810–64.

Santa Maura has survived the periodic earthquakes that rattle Lefkáda better than the capital, **Lefkáda Town**, which collapsed like a house of cards in the earthquake in 1948, and was hit hard again in 1971. The people of Lefkáda, however, have learned to take the tremors in stride, and since Venetian times gave up trying to build in stone and mortar. Their anti-seismic town is like no other in Greece: narrow lanes lined with brightly painted houses, the ground floor built in a flexible wooden frame, filled with stones and bricks, topped by a wooden second floor, the whole sometimes given a coat a stucco or more often covered with corrugated metal sheets, to keep the hard core from falling out of the frames during a severe shock. Another unusual feature of the town is its iron bell towers, rearing up like oil derricks. The whole is a friendly, bustling market town with more genuine Greek atmosphere than anything you'll find in the resorts.

The causeway enters town at **Bosketo Park**, a large shady square displaying busts of Lefkáda's three great contributors to letters: Valaorítis, Sikelianós (for more on both, *see* pp.184 and 186), and Patrick Lafcadio Hearn (1850–1904), whose Irish surgeon father and Kytheran mother named him after his birthplace. He went on to become a journalist in the States, and in 1890 went to Japan, where he became an expert on Japanese language and culture, teaching the Japanese about Western literature and vice versa; every now and then Japanese tourists make the pilgrimage to the island to honour the man they know as Yakomo Kuizumi.

Lefkáda's churches, built mostly in the 18th century under the Venetians, are square, domeless and solidly built of stone, and have largely survived the tremors, although the chances of finding them open aren't always good; try going in the late afternoon, or ask around for the key. Some of the finest examples of the Ionian school of painting are in **Ag. Minás** (1707), built on the order of the Venetian governor of the island and dedicated to the patron saint of Heraklíon, Crete, whose icon appeared when a tree on the site was struck by lightning; with a superb carved golden iconostasis and icons of the Four Evangelists and the Decapitation of Ag. Minás, by Nikólas Doxaras, and others by Koutouzis.

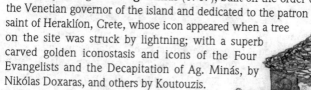

Ag. Dimítrios (1688), just east of the town centre, holds three icons by Nikólas' father, Panagyótis Doxaras, including an excellent St John the Baptist, holding his head on a platter with an expression of infinite compassion; the icons of Christ and St Dimitrios show the softer touch the painter acquired after his travels in Italy. Another, the **Pantokrátor**, is a little basilica founded by Francesco Morosini to celebrate his victory over the Turks in 1684. It has a pretty façade, last reworked in 1890, with an original curved roofline, and inside a very Italian painted ceiling and also some very Italian portraits of the Apostles on the iconostasis. Lastly, **Ag. Spyrídon** (17th century) has a fine carved wooden screen.

There are four small museums in Lefkáda Town: near Ag. Spyrídon, the **Orpheus Folklore Museum** (*follow the little signs; open 10–1 and 6–9; winter Mon–Wed, 10–12 and 6–8*) has four rooms displaying the beautiful embroideries and weavings made on the island, dating back to the last century; there are also old maps, including a precious original map of Lefkáda made by the Venetian mapmaker Coronelli in 1687. The **Archaeology Museum**, in Fanerománis Street, houses mostly the finds from cave sanctuaries and the 30 12th-century BC tombs discovered by Dörpfeld in Nidrí; the **Icon** (or **Post-Byzantine**) **Museum**, with works of the Ionian school, is housed in the municipal library (© 22 502), and, appropriately for the town that established the first municipal brass band in Greece (1850), the **Lefkáda Phonograph Museum**, beyond the square at 12–14 Kalkáni Street (*open 10–1 and 6–8.30pm or as late as 11pm, depending on season*), founded by a local collector. The only museum of its kind in Greece, it contains old gramophones sent over by relatives from the United States, records of Cantades and popular Greek songs of the 1920s, and one of the first discs recorded by a Greek company, 'Orpheon' of Constantinople, founded in 1914. A cemetery dating from 600 BC was discovered a few years ago on the outskirts of town, and is in a permanent state of excavation, and still not open to the public.

Just Outside Town

The closest place to town for a swim is the **Gýra**, the long, sandy, if often windy, lido that closes off the west side of the lagoon, with a few tavernas. On the other side of the windmills, a second beach, good for surfing, **Ag. Ioánnes Antzoúsis**, is tucked under a chapel, supposedly named for the Angevin Knights who founded it during the Crusades. In the opposite direction, by the cemetery, stop at the Café Pallas for a refreshing glass of almond milk, or *soumáda*, and watch the old men in the olive grove opposite play *t'ambáli*, Lefkáda's unique version of boules, played with egg-shaped balls on a concave ground, which as far as anyone knows is played nowhere else in the world. Two km south, set among the ruins of the monastery, the stone church of the **Panagía Odhigýtria** (1450) is the oldest on the island, the only one to have withstood all the earthquakes.

To the southwest, just above town is the 17th-century **Fanerománi Monastery**, rebuilt in 1948 after a fire. It is a serene place in the pine woods, with bird's-eye views over the town, lagoon and the walls of Santa Maura—a view sketched by Edward Lear. On the islet with the ruined chapel of **Ag. Nikólaos** was a cottage where Angelos Sikelianós and his wife Eva would spend their summers.

Sikelianós and the Delphic Idea

> *'...Lefkadas thunders within,*
> *the rainstorm gathers,*
> *bursts in the godly olive grove*
> *stirs up the sea...*
> *Oh my island—*
> *I will not find anywhere a nurture*
> *like my nurturing*
> *another soul like my soul*
> *another body like my body.'*

Angelos Sikelianós

Angelos Sikelianós, born on Lefkáda in 1884, was as romantically handsome as a poet should be. Although he duly followed his parents' wishes by going off to law school in Athens, he abandoned higher education after a couple of years to join a theatre company with two of his sisters, Helen and Penelope. Penelope married the brother of Isadora Duncan and, through him, Sikelianós met his own American spouse, Eva. All shared an interest in reviving the mythic passion and power of ancient Greece in active artistic expression rather than in the dusty, pedantic spirit of the time. Sikelianós did his part by writing startling lyrical poetry, infused with the spirit of Dionysian mysticism, in a longing to join the world of the gods to the world of men.

In the 1920s, Sikelianós and Eva came up with the idea of reviving the 'Delphic Idea' of learning and the arts, in the same spirit as the revival of the Olympics. Their goal was to create an International Delphic Centre and University, and stage a Delphic Festival of drama, dance, music, sports, and crafts; this actually took place in 1927 and 1930, funded in part by a mortgage on the Sikelianós house and Eva's inheritance. But the Depression closed in, and the following years were bitter; Eva went back to America, and, although they divorced, she continued to support the 'Delphic Idea' and send Sikelianós money. Sikelianós remarried and sat out the war years in a small flat in Athens, in declining health; his finest moment came when he gave the funeral oration of his fellow poet Palamas, and declared 'In this coffin lies Greece' and boldly led the singing of the banned Greek national anthem, even though he was surrounded by German soldiers. The dark years of the war and Greek civil war added a tragic power to his poetry, but his progressive ideas barred him from membership in the Athens Academy, and, as they will tell you in Lefkáda, from winning the Nobel Prize, although he was twice nominated. In 1951 he died when he mistook a bottle of Lysol for his medicine.

Lefkáda ✉ *31100,* ✆ *(0645–)* **Where to Stay**

Hotel Lefkas, ✆ 23 916, 🖷 24 579 (*B; exp*) on the water-front, is comfortable, if a bit workaday; all rooms have a balcony, and the hotel also supplies a minibus service. Most rooms at the **Niricos Hotel**, ✆ 24 132 (*C; mod*) face the water. **Byzantion Hotel**, ✆ 21 315 (*E; inexp*) is a basic but well-kept pension at the waterfront end of the main shopping street.

Lefkáda ✆ *(0645–)* **Eating Out**

Restaurants are numerous and reasonably priced on Lefkáda and portions seem to be larger than elsewhere in Greece. If it's on offer, try the increasingly rare local wines *vartsámi*, *kerópati*, or *yomatári*. In central Plateía Antistási, there are plenty of colourful cafés and tavernas, good for people-watching. In Dimaríou Verrioti, near the Folklore Museum, **Taverna O Regantos** is blue and white and cute, with solid fare for around *2500dr*. On the edge of town, towards Ag. Nikítas, **Adriatika** enjoys a pleasant garden setting, is pricier, but has some good Greek specialities and excellent service (*3000dr*).

The East Coast

The east coast of Lefkáda is as lovely, green and bedecked with beaches as the choice coasts of Corfu, and not surprisingly most of Lefkáda's tourist facilities have sprung up here. Just a few kilometres south of Lefkáda Town, at Kaligóni on a hill near the shore, are the scant ruins of **ancient Nerikus**, the pre-Corinthian city, where Dörpfeld (*see* below) found Cyclopean walls, traces of roads, arches, a water-tank, and a pre-Roman theatre, as well as some early Byzantine ruins, which can be located after some scrambling through the olives. Further along is the once cute fishing village of **Lygiá**, now a sprawling commercial resort with narrow beaches; **Nikiána**, spread out more attractively, has striking views of the mainland.

Further south is **Perigiáli**, with a fine beach and some new hotels, and, two kilo-metres further on, **Nidrí** (ΝΥΔΡΙ) Lefkáda's busiest resort town. Nidrí looks out over lovely Vlýcho Bay, closed in like a lake by the Géni peninsula, its still waters dotted with the privately owned wooded islets of **Mandourí**, **Sparti**, **Skorpídi** and **Skórpios**.

The last, where Aristotle Onassis wed Jackie Kennedy in 1968, still belongs to what remains of the Onassis family—Aristotle's little granddaughter. From the sea you can spy Aristotle's tomb, and excursion boats now have permission to land on the beaches if no one is in residence. You may notice a little red caique taking over a small army of workers who maintain the island; Onassis stipulated in his will that they must be from Nidrí. His obsession with privacy and payoffs in the right places kept tourist facilities at Nidrí (pop. 300 in 1968) at a bare minimum during his lifetime, but the locals have since made up for lost time. By Lefkáda standards Nidrí is cosmopolitan, commercial and smack on the main road; the tavernas are mostly lined up along the seafront, all of which can get very very busy and noisy in the summer. Much of the old beach was sacrificed for the building of a quay, so most people head up to Perigiáli for a swim.

Sit at a café in Nidrí at twilight—there's one so near the shore you can sit with your feet in the sea—and, to the sound of croaking frogs, watch Mandourí, 'the poet's island' as the locals call it, float above the horizon on a magic carpet of mist. The Venetian villa on Mandourí belongs to the family of the poet Aristotélis Valaorítis (1824–79). Like many intellectuals from the Ionian islands, Valaorítis studied abroad, and when he returned it was first to serve as a member of the Ionian Parliament, and later the Greek Parliament, where he was renowned as a public speaker. Highly romantic like his friend Sikelianós and as patriotic as any in his day, he was one of the first to write verse in the demotic language of the people.

One of the nicest excursions from Nidrí is the 45-minute walk by way of the hamlet of Rachí to the **waterfall**, at the end of the Dimosári gorge. In the spring it gushes forth with enthusiasm; in the summer it is little more than a high altitude squirt, but it's wonderfully cool and refreshing, and there's a pool for a swim.

Vlychó, the next village south, is a quiet charmer, famous for its traditional boatbuilders. Sandy **Dessími** beach, with a campsite, lies within walking distance, as does the **Géni peninsula**, covered with ancient, writhing olive groves. Wilhelm Dörpfeld, Schliemann's assistant in the excavation of Troy, found a number of Bronze Age tombs behind Nidrí and instantly became a local hero when he announced that they proved his theory that Lefkáda was the Ithaca of Homer. He died in 1940 and is buried near the house in which he lived, by the Géni's white church of Ag. Kyriakí. Further south, **Póros** is near the very pretty white pebble beach of **Mikrós Gialós**, set under the olive trees. **Sívota**, the next town south, has an exceptionally safe anchorage that draws yacht flotillas; many use it for winter berthing. The nearest swimming is at **Kastrí**, to the west.

Lefkáda ✉ *31100,* ☎ *(0645–)*　　**Where to Stay and Eating Out**

Nikiána

The hotel apartment complex, **Red Tower** ☎ 92 951 (*B; exp*) sits high like a castle with wonderful views over the water. **Porto Galini** ☎ 92 431, 📠 92 672 (*B; exp*) provides luxurious furnished apartments among the cypresses and olives, and watersports down on the beach.

Aliki ✆ 71 602, 📠 72 071 (*C; exp–mod*) is a top-notch new small hotel in a superb location; pool and air-conditioned rooms overlooking the sea and its own small beach. For a little less, try the **Pension Ionian,** ✆ 71 720 (*B; mod*), a stone's throw from the sea, or **Hotel Pegasos,** ✆ 71 669 (*B; mod*). The **Hotel Konaki,** at Lygiá ✆ 71 126, 📠 71 125 (*B; exp–mod*) has a garden setting, overlooking a large pool. Just north of Lygiá, **Kariotes Beach Camping,** ✆ 71 103, ironically has a pool but no beach in sight.

Nidrí

Ta Niksakia, 1km from Nidrí, ✆ 92 777, book in Athens 📠 (01) 764 5440 (*A; exp*) are studio apartments with commanding views, 200m above the sea. The **Nidrí Akti** pension, ✆ 92 400 (*B; mod*) also has good views. Two km north in Perigiáli, **Scorpios,** ✆ 92 452 (*exp*) is an apartment complex with pool; **T'Aremno Beach,** ✆ 92 112, 📠 92 018 (*B; exp*) has modern air-conditioned rooms right on the beach. **Bella Vista,** ✆ 92 650, is set in a garden 500m from Nidrí and two minutes from the beach; studios have pretty views of Vlýcho Bay.

There are plenty of restaurants in Nidrí: **Kavos** has consistently good food for *2500dr.* Just out of town, **Haradiatika** is popular with locals for its good quality meat and *mezé;* and the **Olive Tree** and **Paliokatouna** towards Neochóri are also well-liked.

Póros/Sívota

In Póros, **Okeanis** at Mikrós Gialós, ✆ 95 399 (*exp*) is a relatively quiet place on the beach, with comfortable rooms. *Open May–Sept.* You can camp in the lap of luxury at **Poros Beach,** ✆ 95 452, with 50 sites, some bungalows, a bar, restaurant and pool. Sívota has rooms to rent, but is better known for its excellent fish tavernas, where you can pick lobster from the sea cage.

Inland Villages: Lace and Lentils

At least once while on Lefkáda, venture inland, where traditional farming villages occupy the fertile uplands framed in mountains, and where it's not unusual to encounter an older woman still dressed in her traditional costume of brown and black, with a headscarf tied at the back, sitting with distaff in hand, or at her loom, or over her embroidery. Although many villages are facing the usual rural exodus of their young people for the bright lights and easier money to be made on the coast, **Karyá** is one large village to aim for, the centre of the island's lace and embroidery cottage industry, where the ethnographic **Museum Maria Koutsochéro** (*open 9–8 in high season*) is dedicated to the most famous embroiderer of them all, a woman from Karyá whose works were in international demand around 1900. Most of the women sell their goods direct, although don't come looking for bargains: look for signs reading KENTHMATA. Another well-known traditional lace and embroidery town is **Englouví**, the highest village on Lefkáda (730m), tucked in a green mountain valley; it is even prouder of its lentils, which win prizes at Greek lentil competitions. In the interior there are several notable churches with frescoes, among them the Red Church (Kókkini Eklisía) and Monastery of Ag. Geórgios (from around 1620) near **Aléxandros**, a nearly abandoned village crumbling to bits, and the 15th-century church of Ag. Geórgios at **Odhigytría** (near Apólpaina), its design incorporating Byzantine and Western influences. **Drymónas** to the west is a pretty village of stone houses and old tile roofs.

Down the West Coast

The much less developed west coast of Lefkáda is rocky and rugged, and the sea is often rough—perfect for people who complain that the Mediterranean is a big warm bathtub. For under the cliffs and mountains are some of the widest and most stunning stretches of sand in the Ionian, that are only just beginning to be exploited. The road from Lefkáda Town avoids the shore as far as the farming village of **Tsoukaládes**, from where a 2km road leads down to narrow pebbly Kalímini beach and the most turquoise water imaginable (take provisions and swimming shoes). The long sandy beach of **Pevkóulia** begins under the mountains and stretches around the coast to **Ag. Nikítas** (ΑΓ. ΝΙΚΗΤΑΣ). With only a cluster of hotels at the top, the nucleus of the village, with its pretty tile roofs and old tavernas, is off limits to developers; the narrow streets are overhung with flowers and vines. Beware that parking is a major headache, especially on summer weekends. With nothing between here and Italy, the sea is clean, but cold. Don't let your windsurfer run away with you, though—the odd shark fin has been spotted off the coast. Just south of here, 2km off the main road, **Káthisma** is another good, wavy place to swim with a taverna and cantinas on the wide beach of golden sand, dotted with places to dive and little caves to explore. An unpaved road leads to yet another beautiful sandy beach below the village of **Kalamítsi**; set among giant rocks, with rooms and tavernas that make it a good quiet base.

The Original Lovers' Leap, Vassilikí, and Windsurfing

> *At length Leucate's cloudy top apppears,*
> *And the sun's temple, which the sailor fears.*
> *Resolved to breathe awhile from labour past,*
> *Our crowded anchors from the prow we cast.*
>
> Aeneid, book III

To reach Lefkáda's southwest peninsula, a secondary road from Kalamítsi crosses to the pretty leafy village of **Chortáta** and **Komíli**, where the road forks. Buses continue down the coastal road only as far as **Atháni**, a tiny village that struggles to meet the demands of tourists heading further south to the superb beaches along the peninsula. The first, long and undeveloped **Gialós**, can be easily reached by a path from Atháni; the next, glorious golden **Egrémni**, requires a labour of love to reach from land—a long unpaved road followed by 200 steep steps. Sandy **Pórto Katsíki** ('goat port') further south is magnificently set under pinkish white cliffs, reached by another long walkway-stair from the road (*500dr for parking*) and is a popular excursion boat destination; there's a taverna too.

At the end of the road are the famous 190ft sheer white cliffs of **Cape Doukáto** or **Kávo tis Kyrás** (Lady's Cape), topped by the scantiest of ruins of the famous temple of Apollo Leucas 'of the Dolphins'. It was here that Sappho, rejected by Phaon (a man) hurled herself into the sea below; one old tradition says that she was only imitating the goddess Aphrodite, who took the plunge in despair over the death of her lover Adonis. Later, Romans rejected by their sweethearts would make the leap—with the precaution of strapping on feathers or even live birds and employing rescue parties to pull them out of the sea below.

Before becoming a cure-all for unrequited love, the leap was made annually by unwilling sacrifices to stormy Poseidon—prisoners or criminal scapegoats, sent over the edge in the hope of driving evil from the island. But death was to be averted if possible: Strabo wrote that all kinds of birds would be tied to the victims, to lighten the fall, and the sea below would be full of rescuers in boats who would grab the scapegoat to take him safely beyond their territory. In later years, priests serving at the temple of Apollo would make the jump safely as part of their cult, called *katapontismós*, 'sea plunging', rather like the divers at Acapulco, one imagines; no doubt the leaps were accompanied with animal sacrifices—read barbecues—for a pleasant ancient Greek outing. Young Greeks still soar off the edge, but now use hang-gliders instead of feathers. The white cliffs, now topped by a lighthouse, are a famous and long dreaded landmark for sailors, who until recent times would never fail to toss some money into the sea here, in lieu of the ancient sacrifice. Byron, sailing past in 1812 during his first visit to Greece, was strangely moved, and set down the experience in *Childe Harold* (canto II).

> But when he saw the evening star above
> Leucadia's far-projecting rock of woe
> And hail'd the last resort of fruitless love,
> He felt, or deem'd he felt, no common glow
> And as the stately vessel glided slow
> Beneath the shadow of that ancient mount,
> He watch'd the billow's melancholy flow,
> And, sunk albeit in thought as he was wont,
> More placid seem'd his eye, and smooth his pallid front.

The left-hand fork in the road at Komíli passes by way of the pretty farming village of **Ag. Pétros** through citrus groves, on the way to **Vassilikí** (ΒΑΣΙΛΙΚΗ), one of the very best places in Europe to windsurf and Lefkáda's second biggest resort after Nidrí, although not half so compromised by package tourism. A shady, charming village, Vassilikí has a little tree-rimmed port with pleasant cafés and shops that specialize in all types of boards for sale or hire. The long beach running north of town isn't the best for swimming, full as it is with surfers whizzing around the bay, their brightly coloured sails like butterflies skimming the water. On most days a gentle breeze blows up by mid-morning, perfect to teach beginners the fundamentals, and by mid-afternoon it's blowing strong for the experts; by evening, the wind, like a real gent, takes a bow and exits, allowing a pleasant dinner by the water's edge before the discos open; the nightlife is almost as exhilarating as the wind. Caiques from Vassilikí round the white cliffs of Cape Doukáto for the beach of Pórto Katsíki (*see* above) and the pretty white beach of **Agiofýlli**, accessible only by sea.

Lefkáda's highest peak, Eláti (1158m) cuts off the inland villages of the south, which can only be reached from Vassilikí or the Póros-Sívota road in the southeast. The road rises from the plain of Vassilikí, covered with olives and fields of flowers (flower seeds for gardeners are an important local product) to **Sývros**, one of the larger villages in the interior, with places to eat and Lefkáda's largest cave, **Karoucha**. From here the road tackles the increasingly bare slopes of Eláti to lofty little **Ag. Ilías**, with magnificent views.

Kolokytholouloutha Yemista

One of the nicest appetizers in the spring are stuffed courgette (or zucchini) blossoms; although they don't often appear on restaurant menus, they're not too hard to make if you're self catering. To serve 6 you need:

> *1 cup long-grain rice*
> *1 smallish onion, finely chopped*
> *1 large tomato, peeled, seeded, and chopped*
> *one third of a cup of olive oil*
> *3 tbs fresh parsley, minced*
> *3 tbs fresh mint, finely chopped*
> *18 large zucchini blossoms, gently washed and drained*

Combine the rice, parsley, mint, onion, oil, tomato, and mix well; season with salt and freshly ground black pepper. Using a small spoon, stuff mixure into the blossoms. Arrange in a shallow saucepan, add ¾ cup warm water, and cover. Bring to a boil and simmer until the rice is cooked (approximately half an hour); serve warm.

Karyá ✉ 31080

The Karyá Village, ✆ 41 030 (*B; mod*) has pleasant rooms if you want to get away from the beach crowds. There are also some tavernas and traditional lazy *kafeneíons* under the plane trees.

Ag. Nikítas ✉ 31080

Odyssia ✆ 99 366 (*C; exp*) is one of the island's nicest hotels, with a roof garden. **Hotel Kalypso**, ✆ 99 332, 📠 97 333 (*B; exp*) is clean and pleasant and **Ag. Nikítas**, ✆ 99 460 (*C; exp*) is a decent small hotel at the top of the village. Generally, rooms with private bath and overlooking the sea cost *6–10,000dr* depending on season.

Vassilikí ✉ 31082

Smartest here is **Ponti Beach**, ✆ 31 572 (*B; exp*), above the bay, air-conditioned and with a pool and fabulous views. **Lefkatas**, ✆31 229 (*C; mod*) is a pleasant choice. **Christina Polete**, ✆ 31 440, has newly converted rooms and two small apartments in a beautiful house, one field back from the sea. Or try **Billy's House**, ✆ 31 418 (*mod*), with nice rooms, private baths and kitchen, 70m from the beach. **Katina's Place**, ✆ 31 262, (*mod–inexp*) is a simple, clean and tremendously hospitable pension with great views over the village and port. **Vassilikí Beach** campsite is well-located halfway along the bay, ✆ 31 457, 📠 31 458. **Miramare** and **Mythos** are among the better tavernas and, depending on how raucous you're feeling, there's a terrific choice in the way of nightlife. **Zeus** is the crazy late-night bar for young windsurfers while **After Eight** attracts a slightly gentler crowd, with a pool table and '60s–'80s music.

Meganísi (ΜΕΓΑΝΗΣΙ)

Spectacular rocky and wild Meganísi, an hour and a half by daily ferry or excursion boat from Nidrí, lies off the southeast coast of Lefkáda. Believed to be the island of Taphos mentioned in the *Odyssey*, it was the main base of the semi-mythical Teleboans, sailors and pirates who at one point were powerful enough to take on the King of Mycenae. The population of 1800 is still employed in traditional occupations—seafaring for the men, embroidery and lacemaking for the women. Ferries call at **Váthi**, a pretty port with lots of good fish tavernas, rooms to rent and a campsite, packed to the gills for the *panegýri* of Ag. Konstantínos on 21 May. A road leads up to the cheerful flowery hamlet of Katoméri, where a track heads down to the beach of Polistafíon in narrow Athéni Bay and there's even a small, nice, moderately priced hotel (**Meganisi**, © (0645) 51 639). The paved road continues around to **Spartochóri**, with a couple of good tavernas.

Excursion boats from Nidrí usually call at the yawning 90m-deep **Papanikólaos' Grotto**, said to be the second largest in Greece and named for the daring Greek resistance submariner who used to hide here and dart out to attack Italian ships, and at the sandy beach of **Ag. Ioánnis** with a summer cantina.

Paxí (ΠΑΞΟΙ)

The island of 20 fabled secrets, Paxí is the tiniest and yet one of the most charming of the canonical Seven Islands. Together with its little sister Antípaxi it has long served as a kind of gently upmarket, small-is-beautiful escape from the mass package tourism on Corfu, and yet, in July and August, is certainly not without its share of tourists, mostly Italians and yachting types, straining the limited accommodation to its limits. Paxí (or Páxos) is so small that you can easily walk its 8km length in a day, twisting and turning through the immaculate groves of olives that brought the islanders most of their income before tourism.

Paxí's golden olive oil has long been considered among the best produced in Greece and has won many international medals; you can note from the start that, unlike olives grown on Corfu, trees are rarely sprayed against the dreaded dacus fly, but are protected with ecologically sound sticky traps in plastic bags. Besides the beauty of the silvery trees (there are some 300,000—each family owns at least 500) and the tidy stone walls, the little island has some of the friendliest people you'll find anywhere in Greece, notwithstanding Edward Lear's limerick of 1863:

> There was an old person of Paxo
> Which complained when the fleas bit his back so,
> But they gave him a chair
> And impelled him to swear,
> Which relieved that old person of Paxo.

History

Paxí was happily shunned by history. Mythology tells us the island was created by a blow of Poseidon's trident as a love nest for his mistress, far from the gaze of his wife Amphitrite. What mention it received in antiquity referred to its seven sea caves—Homer describes Ipapanti as having rooms of gold. Another cave was used by Papanikólaos (*see* 'Meganísi', above) to ambush passing Italian ships, a trick unfortunately copied by German U-boats the following year.

Exolitharo
Lakkas

Ipparandi
Lakka
Apergatika
Kastanitha
Ag. Charalambos
Petratika
Dendiatika
Cave
Grammatiko
Longos
Magazia
Anemoyiannatika
Panagia
Islet
Boikatika
Platanos
Ortholithos Cave
Ag. Ioannis
Boudanatika
GAIOS
Kastro
Vlachopoulistika
Ag. Nikolaos
Makratika
Fanariotika
Oxias
Mongonissi
Islet
Ag. Spiridou
Katsionissi
Islet

To Corfu

To Parga,
mainland

To Ithaca,
Kefalonia
and Patras

Voutoumia
Beach

Antipaxi
Ag. Emilianos
Agrapidias

ANTIPAXI

Daskalia
Islet

N

3km
2 miles

Getting There

By boat: Almost daily connections with Corfu, and with Sívota and Párga (on the mainland; in the summer buy your ticket a day or two in advance), also infrequent connections with Pátras, Kefaloniá and Ithaca. Connections are far less frequent in the off season. In the summer you may well be asked to have a room reservation before boarding a **ferry** to the island, which is small, wooded, and fearful of campers and their fires. The Paxos Express **excursion boats** circle the island, offering a look at the caves and dramatic cliff scenery, stopping at the better pebbly beaches and Antípaxi. **Port authority:** ✆ 32 259.

See regular police in Gáios, ✆ (0662) 31 222.

10 February, Ag. Charálambos; **Easter Monday** procession from Gáios to Velliantítika; **11 August**, Ag. Spyrídon; **15 August**, Panagía.

Why the Oracles Are Silent

Plutarch, in his essay 'Why the Oracles Are Silent', recounts an incident of great moment that took place here at the beginning of the 1st century AD. A ship was sailing from Asia Minor to Italy, and as it passed Paxi all the passengers heard a loud voice from the island calling out the name of Thamus, the ship's Egyptian pilot. The voice commanded him: 'When the ship comes opposite Palodes, tell them the Great God Pan is dead.' Thamus did so at the designated spot, and great cries of lamentation arose, as if from a multitude of people. This strange story went around the world, and even came to the attention of Emperor Tiberius, who appointed a commission of scholars to decide what it might mean.

What they determined was never entirely disclosed, but any astronomer, mythographer or priest (as Plutarch was) in that period would have been aware that times, as measured on the great dial of the firmament, were changing—a new World Age was at hand.

Now that we're only a century or two from 'the Dawning of the Age of Aquarius', as the song goes, this calls for a slight digression. If you've ever watched a child's top spin, you'll have noticed its axis tends to wobble a bit, so that the point on top traces a slow circle through the air while the whole thing is spinning much more rapidly. The earth, in its rotation, does this too—only each gyration of its axis takes about 26,000 years. (This is why the pole stars move; in 13,000 years the northern pole will point towards Vega in the constellation of the Lyre, 50° away from our current pole star Polaris.) Another effect of this phenomenon is the 'precession of the equinoxes'. The *equinoctial points* are the places where the celestial equator crosses the ecliptic, the plane of our solar system (or as we see it from Earth, the path of the sun, moon, and planets across our sky); another way to explain these points is that they are the positions of the sun at the equinoxes, the first day of spring and the first day of autumn. As the earth slowly wobbles, these equinoctial points move around, too, passing slowly through the signs of the zodiac. So every 2160 years or so, the sun on March 20 (New Year's Day for many cultures) finds itself in a new sign. Since the remotest times, at least some cultures on the earth have kept track of this movement. In Plutarch's day, the spring equinox fell in Aries, but it was about to move into Pisces. Today, it's at the end of Pisces and about to move into Aquarius. Each of these periods is a 'World Age'—in case you ever wondered what that term meant. The transition is officially marked by a great conjunction of the planets; that's what the Christmas star of the Magi was, according to modern interpretations. The men of Plutarch's time and later had no shortage of explanations for what their New Age was to portend. Astrologers heralded it as the birth of a new Golden Age, ruled by Saturn; the creation of the Roman Empire under Augustus, bringing the end of a long period of civil strife, seemed to be part of heaven's decree. Later, Christians would claim that theirs was the true faith of the Age of Pisces, as represented in one of the most widespread early Christian symbols, the cold, chaste fish. It was a time of confusion and loss of faith, when the old pagan oracles really did fall mysteriously silent, and when new philosophies and cults of every stripe were battling for hearts and minds in the Mediterranean world. And so today we live among our own confusions, with our own legions of dubious 'New Agers', waiting, as Yeats put it in 'The Second Coming', to see:

> ...what rough beast, its hour come round at last,
> Slouches towards Bethlehem to be born.

Gáios (ΓΑΙΟΣ)

Legend has it that St Paul landed on Paxí and like St Patrick sent all the snakes into exile, but it was his disciple Gaius who actually brought Christianity to the island, and is buried in **Gáios**, the pretty toy capital of the island that took his name. Most of the islanders live in Gáios, and it's where you'll find a small sandy beach and all of Paxí's facilities, a fleet of yachts and on the harbour-front even a tiny **aquarium** of sea critters who are released and replaced pot-luck every year, so there's no telling what you'll see. The streets of Gáios are fortunately too narrow for cars (so narrow that people can lean out of their windows and shake hands) although human traffic jams occur during the day in the summer, especially on the worn flagstones of the handsome waterfront square, when day-trippers from Corfu and cruise ships sail into the little port. For a fine overview of Gáios harbour, walk past the Governor's House (although the Venetians lumped Paxí and Corfu together, the little island always had a resident governor) and continue to the New Port and the new road. If you bring your own bottle, several shops sell draught olive oil from the barrel; it's so good that you can almost drink it straight.

On a rocky islet facing the harbour is the well-preserved **Kástro Ag. Nikólaos**, built by the Venetians in 1423, and an old windmill, and beyond it, the islet of

Panagía, which on 15 August is crowded with pilgrims. In the evening they come back to Gáios and dance all night in the village square. **Mongoníssi**, another islet, is connected by boat taxi—belonging to a pretty little family-run restaurant—which brings customers over for dinner and music and dancing in the evening.

Sea Caves and Forests of Olives

If it's not windy, rent a boat to explore Paxí's seven sea grottoes of brilliant blue. Most are located among the sheer limestone cliffs on the wind-beaten west coast of Paxí, including the impressive **Kastanítha**, 600ft high. Another distinctive cave, **Orthólithos**, has a monolith standing sentinel at its entrance; caiques can enter about 5m inside. Homer's wild cove and cave **Ípapanti** does not have the golden rooms he mentions, although it used to shelter monk seals. **Grammatikó** is the largest cave of them all. When sailing around the island, you can also see the **Moúsmouli Cliffs** and their natural bridge **Tripitos**.

The main road from Gáios that crosses the island was donated by Aristotle Onassis, a great fan of Paxí. The minibus (everything on Paxí is mini) runs north to **Lákka** (ΛΑΚΚΑ), a tiny port where the boats from Corfu usually call and sometimes cause traffic jams. Lákka is within easy reach of small, shady pebble beaches, and the Byzantine church in the village has particularly musical Russian bells, which you can ring if you find the villager with the key. Walk inland to the church of Ípapanti, topped by two odd stumpy, flat-topped domes, with a massive free-standing campanile on one side, crowned by an onion dome. The Venetian stone **Grammatikoú mansion** near Lákka is fortified with a tower.

Laid-back **Longós** (ΛΟΓΓΟΣ), Paxí's third minute port, is about midway between Gáios and Lákka, and gets fewer visitors; there's a pleasant rocky beach (and others within easy walking distance to the south) and a few bars. In tiny **Boikatiká** village the church Ag. Charálambos contains an old icon of the Virgin and in nearby **Magaziá** are two churches of interest, Ag. Spyrídon and Ag. Apóstoli; the latter's churchyard affords an impressive view of the Eremitis cliffs. At **Apergatiká** the Papamárkou mansion dates from the 17th century.

Paxí ✉ *49082,* © *(0662–)*   ***Where to Stay and Eating Out***

Be prepared for prices a little above the norm; transport costs add to the tariff, and essential supplies from the outside world can be cut off without warning whenever the wind kicks up. Restaurants and cafés take full advantage of the day-trippers who come from Corfu and the yachting set berthed in Gáios. Official accommodation is extremely limited, rather expensive, and block-booked by tour operators in the summer. Everyone else stays in private rooms, which are invariably clean, pleasant, tidy and double, and average *4000–5000dr*.

Gáios

Paxos Beach Bungalows, ✆ 31 211 (*B; exp*) has some very pleasant, comfortable chalet bungalows near the beach, but these are only available in the off season. You may have better luck with the **Paxos Club**, 1km from Gáios, ✆ 32 450, ✉ 32 097 (*exp*), with a large pool and very comfortable rooms. Take the caique to Mongoníssi for the excellent restaurant there (*3000dr*) and to while the day away on the beach.

There are a handful of tavernas in Gáios such as the **Taka Taka** serving solid Greek fare and fish, the former reasonably priced, the latter about *3500dr* for a meal; **Naïs** offers a wide variety of croissants and sandwiches. **Spiro's Taverna** and **Costa's Kafeneíon** are also good value.

Lákka

The **Ilios**, ✆ 31 808 (*E; inexp*), and **Lefkothea**, ✆ 31 408 (*E; inexp*) are both small and open all year, but fill up in season. You can eat well and for a reasonable price at **Sgarelios** and **Klinis** or the pretty little Italian **Rosa**, featuring a wide variety of pasta dishes.

Antípaxi

South of Paxí lies tiny Antípaxi, with only a few permanent residents. From June until September four or five caiques leave Gáios daily for the 40-minute trip to its port Agrapídias. Although both Paxí and Antípaxi were created with a resounding blow of Poseidon's trident, the two islands are very different in nature; the part of Antípaxi facing Paxí looks bare, almost as if it had been bitten off by a Leviathan. Rather than olive oil, Antípaxi produces good white and red wines, and rather than little pebble beaches, Antípaxi's gentle side is graced with fine sandy beaches: **Voutoúmi** and **Vríka** are 'softer than silk'. There are two tavernas in the itty bitty village and port at **Ormós Agrapídias**, but no accommodation on the islet; if you want to stay bring a sleeping bag, for Voutoúmi has a small campsite. This could well be the uncontaminated paradise you've been seeking.

Zákynthos/Zante (ΖΑΚΥΝΘΟΣ)

> Fair isle, that from the fairest of all flowers,
> Thy gentlest of all gentle names dost take!
> How many memories of what radiant hours
> At sight of thee and thine at once awake!
> How many scenes of what departed bliss!
> How many thoughts of what entombed hopes!
> How many visions of a maiden that is
> No more—no more upon thy verdant slopes!
> No more! alas, that magical sad sound
> Transforming all! Thy charms shall please no more -
> Thy memory no more! Accursed ground
> Henceforth I hold thy flower—enameled shore,
> O hyacinthine isle! O purple Zante!
> 'Isola d'oro! Fior di Levante!'

Edgar Allen Poe, 1837

Of all their Ionian possessions the Venetians loved Zákynthos the most for its charm and natural beauty. *Zante*, 'the flower of the East', they called it, and built a city even more splendid than Corfu Town on its great semi-circular bay, all turned to rubble by the earthquake of 1953. Nevertheless, the disaster did nothing to diminish the soft, luxuriant charm of the landscape and its fertile green hills and mountainsides, the valleys planted with vineyards and currant vines, olive and almond groves and orchards, or the brilliant garlands of flowers and beautiful beaches (the flowers are best in spring and autumn, a time when few foreigners visit the island). And if the buildings are gone, the Venetians left a lasting impression—many islanders have Venetian blood, which shows up not only in their names, but in their love of singing. On the other side of the coin, the once politically progressive Zákynthos has bellied up to the trough of grab-the-money-and-run tourism that doesn't do the island justice, to the extent of sabotaging efforts to preserve the beaches where the loggerhead turtles breed.

History

Etymologists suggest the island's name comes from *kinthos*, or hill, although a strong tradition has it that Zákynthos was named for its first settler, a son of Dardanus from Arcadia. The Arcadians were famous from earliest antiquity for their love of music and festivals, and passed the trait on to their colony. According to Homer, Zákynthos' troops fought under the command of Odysseus at the Trojan War, although when he returned home and shot 20 local nobles—Penelope's

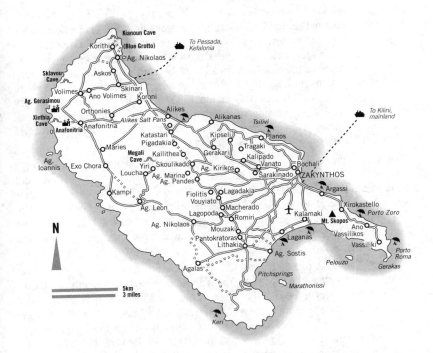

suitors—the island rebelled and became an independent, coin-minting state. It set up colonies throughout the Mediterranean, especially Saguntum in Spain, a city later to be besieged and demolished by Hannibal. Levinus took the island for Rome in 214 BC, and when the inhabitants rebelled, he burnt all the buildings on Zákynthos. Uniting with the Aeolians, the islanders forced the Romans out, although in 150 BC Flavius finally brought them under control.

In 844 the Saracens captured the island from their base in Crete, but the Byzantines were strong enough to expel them. The Norman-Sicilian pirate Margatone took Zákynthos in 1182; it later formed part of the County Palatine of Kefaloniá, with a Turkish interval between 1479 and 1483, before the Venetians, who had claimed it since 1204, took it in fact (paying the sultan 500 gold ducats and an annual tribute in return for his good will). The Venetians called Zákynthos 'the Golden' not only for its climate but for the riches they made from it; they enlarged its harbour to receive and water their galleys en route to Crete and exported its silks and cottons to Constantinople, along with a tithe of wheat for the Sultan; licorice and beeswax were important exports to England, Germany, and Russia. But the product that made the island's fame was its currants, plump and sweet, recognized as the best in the world. In the 16th century most of the crop went to the Dutch and English: a writer at the time noted that the English were right 'addicted to the liquorish stuff' and in 1583, to ensure constant supply, they set up the English Levant Company, headquartered in Zákynthos Town, although the Venetians taxed them so heavily that they eventually gave it up, and turned to the inferior product from Corinth, shipped out of Pátras.

Unlike the Corfiots, however, the people on Zákynthos revolted against the privileges of the Venetians and Zantiot nobility. In 1628, the wealthy business men and guilds rose up in 'the Rebellion of the Popolari' and seized control of the island for four years. It was an experience the islanders never forgot, even though they eventually surrendered. The guilds remained a force to be reckoned with, although from now on they devoted much of their energy into a competition to build and furnish the churches, each more beautiful than the next.

The end of Venetian rule on Zákynthos was messy and unruly. The government was weak, the nobles thoroughly corrupt. The rich had their own bodyguards to kill their rivals; in three years in the late 18th century, the courts recorded over 2000 assassinations. Amid the anarchy, the ideas of the French Revolution found fertile soil here; travellers wondered to see Greek priests reading Locke and the Enlightenment philosophers, encouraging the Zantiots to form their own Jacobin Club. After the fall of Venice, the French were more enthusiastically welcomed here than anywhere else, especially when they found numerous skeletons of poor souls chained to the walls of aristocratic cellars and publicly burned the Venetian *Libro d'Oro* in Plateía Ag. Márko and put an end to the rank of nobility. The ex-nobles appealed to the Tsar to restore order, and in 1798, after a siege of several months, the Russians forced the French garrison and the inhabitants to surrender.

The Septinsular Republic set up by the Russians was ruled by a Venetian-Zantiot noble, Count Giorgio Mocenigo, who re-established the aristocracy in 1801, provoking populist, high-spirited Zákynthos to revolt again. During the War of Independence many rebels on the mainland, notably Kolokotrónis, found asylum on the island, and in 1827, the combined British-Russian-French fleet called in Zákythnos for supplies before the Battle of Navarino and the resounding Turkish defeat that directly led to Greek independence.

Getting There and Around

By air: Daily flights from Athens, 2 or 3 times a week to and from Kefaloniá and Corfu; the Olympic office is at Alex. Róma 16, ✆ 28 611. There are several charters from major European cities; for airport information, call ✆ 28 688/28 322.

By sea: Ferry 6 or 7 times a day from Kilíni; once or twice a day from Pessáda, Kefaloniá to Skinári. **Port authority**: ✆ 28 117.

By road: All **buses** leave from the central station on Filíta Klavdianú in Zákynthos Town (✆ 42 656). The little station on the left offers direct ferry-bus links to Athens (*see* p.11); the main station has buses every hour to Laganás, 10 times to Tsilíví, 4 times a day to Alikés, 2 times to Volímes and 3 to Vassilikiós.

✆ *(0695–)*

Tourist Information

1 Tzoulati, off Plateía Solomoú, ✆ 27 307. For information in English about island happenings, pick up a free copy of *Zante Moments*, issued every 10 days in the summer. **Friendly Tours**, 5 Foscolos, ✆ 28 030, ✆ 23 769, live up to their name and can help with accommodation, excursions and rentals. Or try the homepage dedicated to the island at *www.zante.com/~gkallias/tour.info/links*. Even the bishop of Zákynthos has a web page, translated more or less into English at *www.ionian-islands.com/zante/church/indexen.htm*.

Festivals

A carnival initiated by the Venetians, known for its masked singers and dancing, remains strong in Zákynthos and lasts for **two weeks prior to Lent**; it's a good time to hear the island's special serenades, the *kantádes* (from the Italian *cantada*). During **Holy Week** the inhabitants also give themselves over to an infectious merriment. In **July** the Zakýnthia takes place with cultural activities; at the **end of August and beginning of September**, the International Meeting of Medieval and Popular Theatre, with daily performances takes place. For the major feast days of Ag. Diónysios on **23-26 August** and **16-19 December**, Zákynthos Town is strewn with myrtle and there are fireworks at the church. Slightly more modest is Zoodóchos Pigí in the town on **10 November**.

Zákynthos has some of the most interesting folk dances in Greece, many of which were introduced by Greek refugees or the Italians during the

Venetian period. At *panegýria* and weddings in the interior, you'll probably see the *yiaryitos*, in three-four and six-eight time, a variation on the ancient Cretan 'crane' or yerano dance, that Theseus supposedly invented after conquering the labyrinth. The *yiaryitos* is often accompanied by a dance with very small steps, the *galiantra*, which came from Italy. Another Italian dance, the *manfrena*, from the Italian *monferina*, is a dance in six-eight time and still quite popular. The Zákynthiots are famous for dancing the classic *syrtos* more slowly than another Greeks, but step lively enough in a *stavrotos*, accompanied by a local percussion instrument known as a *tambourioniakara*.

Zákynthos Town

For a week, beginning on 9 August 1953, what was by popular acclaim the most beautiful city in the Ionian islands, was decimated by earthquakes. Much of the damage happened with the first mighty tremor at 12 noon, when all the cooking stoves were lit to prepare the noonday meal, resulting in a fire that raged unchecked by their elementary fire-fighting equipment. British troops under Lord Mountbatten, soon joined by the Greek and American military, arrived on the scene to help. But there was little they could do as over the next five days 120 aftershocks rattled the island, punctuated by one explosion after another as the fires spread to barrels of oil and petrol and ignited all the dynamite and grenades that the local fisherman stored in their houses.

When the time came to rebuild, the Zantiots gamely tried to incorporate some of the old city's delight and charm into the dull lines of modern Greek architecture. They didn't fully succeed. But Zákynthos Town, or Chóra (pop. 10,000—down from 30,000 in the 17th century) is saved from anonymity by its superb setting—the ancient acropolis hovering above, crowned by a castle, and the graceful sweep of the harbour, punctuated off to the right by the unusual form of Mount Skopós. Wrapped along the waterfront, the streets of the long, narrow town are sheltered by arcades (as they were before the earthquake), where a few shops still sell the local speciality, *mandoláto* (white nougat with almonds) amongst the figurines of coupling turtles and other tourist foofaraws.

The rebuilders of Zákynthos failed where they should have done their best, in the town's front parlour, **Plateía Solomoú**, a seaside square with flowerbeds and statue of the portly Diónysos Solomós, raising a hand in greeting; the square is simply too large and open for comfort, and its pair of small cafés are overwhelmed by the solemn formal buildings: the town hall (with another statue of another homegrown poet, Ugo Foscolo, and the inscription 'Liberty Requires Virtue and Daring'), the Cultural Centre, and by the sea the church of sailors and corn merchants, **Ag. Nikólaos tou Mólou** 'of the Mole' (1561), its sandstone blocks carefully pieced together like a jigsaw after the quake. This is the only Venetian building in town to survive in any state, although in Venetian treatises on the island's architecture in the 18th century it wasn't even deemed worthy of mention. Originally occupying a small islet in the harbour, Ag. Nikólaos was the parish church of the painter priest Koutouzis (1741–1811), who shaved his beard and swanned around in a mini-cassock and red stockings and decorated the interior of his church with potted plants and rugs; when he wasn't painting, he wrote satrical verses about local bigwigs.

The **Neo-Byzantine Museum** (*open 8–2.30, closed Mon; adm; free Sun*) contributes to the sterile formality of the square, but can be forgiven for its contents: lovely paintings by the Ionian school, icons and other works of art salvaged from shattered churches across Zákynthos. There are marble fragments and ancient and Byzantine tombs, and excellent 16th-century frescoes from Ag. Andréa at Volímes, showing Jesus in the cosmic womb in the apse, New Testament scenes, nearly every saint in the Orthodox calendar on the side walls, and a *Last Judgement* on the back wall, with a great tree branch emanating from hell and the empty throne awaiting, cupped by the hand of God. Some of the most striking 16th-century icons are by Cretan Mikális Damaskinós, a contempory of El Greco who trained in Venice, although unlike El Greco he returned to Crete, stopping in Zákynthos on his way home. The 17th century was a golden age for art on the island, especially after the arrival of refugees from Crete, who joined the Ionian School (see **Topics**, p.61) leaving Zákynthos with some spirited, lovely works: the iconostasis of Ag. Dimitrioú tou Kollás and one from Pantokrátoras (1681), the latter further adorned with intricate wood-carvings. The icons range in style between the very oriental and the very western; there are works by Ioánnis Kýprios, the great Cretan-born painter-priest Emanuel Tzánes (who in 1659 went on to become the vicar of Venice's San Giorgio dei Greci), Nikólas Kallérgis, and Elie Moskos, who tried hard to adapt to western taste, with his rotund, sentimentalizing figures. In the 18th and 19th centuries, the school turned into Baroque candy floss, producing the awful kind of paintings that clutter up so many provincial museums in Italy—including some by the aforementioned priest Koutouzis. The last exhibit is a scale model of Zákynthos Town before the earthquake.

Inland from Plateía Solomoú, the smaller, triangular, marble-paved, pizzeria-lined **Plateía Ag. Márkou**—Zákynthos' Piazza San Marco—is as lively as the bigger square is sleepy. The social centre of town since the 15th century, before the earthquake it was the site of the Romianiko Casino, which everyone loved but no one rebuilt. The Catholic church of San Marco, now sadly devoid of all its art, occupies one end, near the **Solomós Museum**, founded by the local masons, with mementoes of the poets and other famous Zantiots, as well as photographs of the island before 1953. Adjacent are the mausoleums of Diónysos Solomós and Andréas

Kálvos (b. 1792); the latter lived in Paris and London for much of his life, and died in England, but in 1960 was granted the wish he expressed at the end of his romantic ode 'Zante': 'May Fate not give me a foreign grave, for death is sweet only to him who sleeps in his homeland.'

A Patriotic Perfectionist

Of the two poets, Solomós is the more intriguing character. Born in 1798, the son of a Count who owned the tobacco monopoly on the Ionian islands, young Diónysos was educated along with other Ionian aristocrats in Italy and wrote his first poems in Italian, when he decided that it was time for Greece to have a Dante of its own: like Dante, he rejected the formal scholarly language of the day (in Dante's day Latin, in Solomós' the purist Greek, or *katharévousa*) but chose the demotic language of everyday. Nearly as important, he broke away from the slavery to the 15-syllable line that dominated Greek poetry from the 17th century, and introduced Western-influenced metres and forms.

Solomós concentrated on perfecting lyrical verse until the War of Independence brought forth deeper, and increasingly spiritual works, especially in 'The Free Besieged', written after the heroic resistance of Missolóngi. Solomós' most famous poem, the *Ode to Liberty*, was written in 1824, after a visit to Zákynthos by Greek historian Spyridon Tricupis, who gave Byron's funeral oration at Missolóngi and urged the poet to write something inspirational in Greek. In October 1825, Tricupis wrote that the *Ode to Liberty* was being read in every civilized country in Europe—except Greece. Today the omission has been righted: the words are the lyrics to the Greek national anthem:

> Σε γνωρίζω απο την κοψυ του σπαθιου την τρομερη
> σε γνωρίζω απο την οψη που με βια μετραει τη γη...
>
> *I recognize you by the fierce edge of your sword;*
> *I recognize you by the look that measures the earth...*'

In a country of poets, Solomós has never lost the high esteem he enjoyed during his lifetime. His verse has a degree of beauty, balance and delicacy that rarely has been matched by other Greek poets—that is, whatever fragments have survived; highly strung and hyper-critical, he destroyed nearly everything he wrote in later years. He never married, quarrelled with his family, declared he hated Zákynthos, took to drink and moved to Corfu, where he often used his influence with the British to gain more lenient sentences for Greek nationalists on the Ionian islands.

Zákynthos' most important churches were reconstructed after the quake, among them little **Kyrá tou Angeloú**, in Louká Karrer street, built in 1687; inside are icons by Panagyótis Doxarás of Zákynthos and a pretty carved iconostasis. Near the Basilica tis Análipsis on Alex. Roma Street, is the boyhood **home of** Greek-Italian poet **Ugo Foscolo** (d. 1827), marked by a marble plaque and angel; he used to read by the light of the icon lamp in the shrine across the street before going off to study at the University of Padua and join Napoleon's army, with his head full of ideals. Like Kálvos, Ugo Foscolo died in self-imposed exile in England, but is buried in Italy.

Further south, the restored 15th-century **Faneroméni** church with its pretty campanile (on the corner of Lisgara and Doxarádou Streets) was, before the earthquake, one of the most beautiful churches in all Greece, decorated with frescoes by Panagyótis Doxaras and his son Nikolas.

At the south end of town, the huge **basilica and monastery of Ag. Diónysios** was rebuilt after the earthquake of 1893 by a special committee charged with rebuilding a new earthquake-resistant church, a task it completed in 1948, a few years before it faced the test it was designed for in 1953; the basilica is one of only three buildings left standing in town. Inside, the uncorrupted body of the island's patron Ag. Diónysos is stored in a fine silver reliquary. There are New and Old Testament paintings on the walls, an icon by Nikolas Koutouzis, and an array of gold and silver ex-votos are witness to his power that draws throngs of pilgrims every 24 August and 17 December for 24-hour litany services; the saint is said to spend most of his time on the road helping out local fishermen, so the pilgrims never forget to bring him a special present: a new pair of shoes. The monastery has a museum with four major paintings by Nicholas Koutouzis on the life and miracles of Ag. Diónysos, a Byzantine icon of the Virgin Thalassomahousa, and manuscripts from the beginning of the 16th century.

Up to Bocháli

Filikóu Street, behind Ag. Márkou, leads up to Bocháli, a suburb with gorgeous views over town and sea, where the church of Ag. Giórgios Filíkou was the seat of the local revolutionary Friendly Society. One road from the Bocháli crossroads leads to Lófos Stráni, where a bust of Solomós marks the spot where the poet sat and composed the 'Ode to Liberty' during the siege of Missolóngi. Another road from Bocháli leads up to the well-preserved Venetian **Kástro** (*open 8am–8pm; adm*), a short taxi ride or 45-minute walk up an old cobble path. Three gates, the last bearing the Lion of St Mark, guarded the medieval town. Ruins of churches still stand amid the pines up here, but a 16th-century earthquake rent the walls of the ancient acropolis.

Some neglected gardens in Akrotíri (take the north road at the Bocháli crossroads) recall the Venetian villas that once stood here, the centre of Zante society into the period of British rule; the one belonging to Diónysios Solomós' father was the residence of the High Commissioner. At Villa Crob nearby, the British laid out the first tennis court in Greece. Down in the north end of town, a romantically melancholy British cemetery is wedged next to the green cliffs (turn right at Bociari Street from N. Kolíva).

Beaches under Mount Skopós

The town beach isn't all that good—for better, cleaner swimming try the beaches along the beautiful rugged eastern peninsula under Mount Skopós, beyond **Argássi** (ΑΡΓΑΣΙ), with a somewhat soulless assembly line of hotels and tavernas along its waterfront. Heading further along, there's **Pórto Zóro**, **Banana Beach** (wide and sandy and strewn with sea daffodils, which send such a strong fragrance out to sea that they may have been the origins of the island's nickname *Fiore di Levante*), **Ag. Nikólaos**, **Mavrándzi** and the thinnish crescent strand at **Pórto Róma**, all with tavernas and at least minimum facilities. The 16th-century Domenegini tower by the sea was used for covert operations by the *Philikí Hetaireía*, or Friendly Society, especially in sending men and supplies over to the battles on the Peloponnese. To keep busybodies away they spread word that the tower was haunted, and installed a 'devil' at night to holler and throw stones at any passer-by. **Vassilikós** (ΒΑΣΙΛΛΙΚΟΣ) is a tiny village at the end of the bus line, but bear in mind that services are infrequent and you may have to get back to town by taxi. **Gérakas**, at the tip of the peninsula, has another long, lovely stretch of sandy beach, the finest of them all. Although popular with bathers, it's also popular with nesting loggerhead turtles and has been saved from any more hotels by its designation as a conservation area. Roads cross the peninsula for **Daphní** and **Sekánika**, two secluded, undeveloped beaches to the south, facing Laganás Bay, and both equally popular with the turtles.

Loggerheads over Loggerheads

A decade ago Zákynthos became the centre of an international stir when environmentalists themselves went at loggerheads with government ministries and the island tourist industry to protect Laganás Bay, nothing less than the single most important nursery of rare loggerhead turtles (*Caretta caretta*), hosting around 1000 nests a year on 4km of beach. These sea turtles are among the oldest species on the planet, going back hundreds of millions of years. As long as anyone can remember, they have gathered from all over the Mediterranean on the sands of Zákynthos every June until September, to crawl up on to the beaches at night, dig a deep hole with their back legs, lay between 100 and 120 eggs the size of golf balls and cover them up again before lumbering in exhaustion back to the sea. For 60 days the eggs incubate quietly in the warmth of the sands, and, when they hatch, the tiny baby turtles make a break for the sea. It is *absolutely essential* that the nesting zones remain undisturbed as much as possible—and everyone can help by staying away from the beaches between dusk and dawn, by not poking beach umbrellas in the sand, running any kind of vehicle over it, or leaving litter. Even then the odds for the turtle hatchlings aren't very good: the lights in the bay are liable to distract them from their all-important race to the sea, and they die of exhaustion.

Whether or not the turtles succeed in co-existing with the local tourist economy remains to be seen. At first the going was rough; uncompensated for the beaches they owned, some Zantiots did all they could to sabatoge the efforts of the marine biologists and even resorted to setting fires on the beaches to keep the turtles away. In 1983, when the steep decline in nests was noticed, the Sea Turtle Protection Society of Greece (STPS) was formed to monitor the loggerheads and mark their nests, and lead the fight for their protection. They have succeeded in improving public awareness, in limiting sea traffic in Laganás Bay, and in general making the loggerheads such a hip issue that the souvenir shops peddle little ceramic models of them. The probably unattainable goal of STPS is to create a Marine Park to control development, find alternatives for landowners and 'promote a sustainable tourism that respects the environment and the same time fully protects the nesting beaches'. Perhaps the mama loggerheads have already picked up the cue and for the past few years have avoided the main beach at Laganás.

Up Mount Skopós

From the edge of Argássi, a road leads up through the wildflowers, including several species of indigenous orchid, to the top of **Mount Skopós** ('look-out'), the Mount Hellatos of the ancient Greeks and the Mons Nobilis of Pliny, who wrote of a cavern that led straight to the Underworld. On the way note the picturesque ruins of the 11th-century **Ag. Nikólaos Megalomátis**, with a mosaic floor, built on the site of a temple to Artemis. Views from the summit not only take in all of Zákynthos, but the Peloponnese and the Bay of Navarino, where on 20 October 1827 the most famous battle of modern Greece was fought between the Turko-Egyptian navy and the Anglo-Franco-Russian fleet, leading directly to Greek independence. By the rocky lump summit or *toúrla* of Mount Skopós stands the venerable white church of **Panagía Skopiótissa**, believed to replace yet another temple to Artemis. The interior is decorated with frescoes and a carved stone iconostasis; the icon of the Virgin was painted in Constantinople, and there's a double-headed Byzantine eagle mosaic on the floor.

Zákynthos Town ✉ 29100, ☎ (0695–) *Where to Stay*

Outside August, accommodation in Zákynthos Town is usually feasible; if you have any difficulty, the tourist police off Plateía Solomoú have a list of rooms to let. **Hotel Palatino**, at Kolíva and Kolokotróni 10, ☎ 27 780, ✆ 45 400 (*B; exp*) is a stylish hotel near the town beach, with sea and mountain views from its balconies. In the same vicinity, **Alba** on Tertsetí Street, ☎ 26 641, has bungalows for about the same price. The much larger **Strada Marina** at 14 K. Lombárdou Street, ☎ 42 761, ✆ 28 733 (*B; exp*) is nicely located on the quay.

Little hotel **Reparo** at Roma and Voúltsou Street, ☎ 23 578 (*C; mod*) is clean, pleasant and friendly. **Lofos Strani**, on Kapodístrias ☎ 27 122 (*B; mod*) is a small pension up at Bocháli. Cheaper choices include **Ionion**, 18 A. Roma, ☎ 23 739 (*D; inexp*), and **Dessy**, 73 N. Kolíva, ☎ 28 505 (*E; inexp*).Along the peninsula, **Matilda**, at Pórto Zóro, ☎ 35 430, ✆ 35 429 (*B; exp*), 200m above the sea, is a real fancypants complex. *Open May–Oct.*

Aquarius, ☎ 35 300, ✆ 35 303 (*exp*) is prettily set in greenery, and advertizes itself as 'a place to forget the world'. **Locanda**, ☎ 45 563, ✆ 23 769 (*B; mod*) is a well-run family hotel by the beach at Argassi. For bungalows by the sea, **The Blue Cave**, on the small pebble beach of Ag. Nikólaos, by Vassilikó, ☎ 27 013, ✆ 26 288 (*exp*) is a good bet, with a pool, bar and disco. **Porto Roma**, ☎ 22 781 (*D; mod*) is small but perfectly adequate.

Zákynthos Town ☎ (0695–) *Eating Out*

You can dine well at **P. Evangelos** on Alex. Róma Street for *3000dr*; the food is freshly prepared and good. There are several expensive places on Plateía Ag. Márkos and one that's not, **O Zohio**, a greasy spoon on Psarón Street, with meals *under 2500dr*. On the road to Argássi, near the basilica of Ag. Diónysos, **Karavomilos** has the name for the best fish on the island (*3500dr and up*). In a similar direction, locals in the know go for lunch at delightful **Malanou**, 38 Athanásou ☎ 45 936. At night, they head to the **Quartetto di Zante** near Stavros and to **Arekia,** on the coast road north out of town, for live Greek music and traditional Zákynthos' *kantádes*, performed by male trios. The **Panorama** is in a lovely spot up by the castle, with live *kantádes* as well as traditional Zantiot dishes such as rabbit casserole, *skordaliá* (cod in a thick garlic sauce) or *moskári kokkinistó*, beef in tomato sauce (*3500dr*). At some point ask for a glass of the island's white Verdea wine, a favourite of the English since at least 1519, when a pilgrim described it 'as the strongest that ever I drank in my life'.

Laganás Bay and the South

On the map, Zákynthos looks like a piranha with huge gaping jaws, about to devour a pair of crumb-sized fish in Laganás Bay. These small fry are **Marathoníssi** and **Peloúzo**, the former is a popular excursion destinationwith a sandy beach and the latter was colonized in 1473 BC by King Zákynthos. Laganás Bay's most overripe tourist developments follow the sandy beaches step by step, starting at **Kalamáki**, on the east end of the bay, with a sandy beach under Mount Skopós, at the beginning of currant country. The next town, **Laganás** (ΛΑΓΑΝΑΣ) is Zákynthos' equivalent of Spencer's Blatant Beast, a resort that has long abandoned any sense of proportion and commerical decorum, set on flat hard sand beach that overlooks some curious rock formations by the sea. This brash Las Vegas on the Ionian is a favourite of British and German package tourists and about as un-Greek as it gets anywhere in Greece. At night its 'Golden Mile' of open bars, throbbing with music and flashing kinetic neon lights, are the joy of holiday revellers and ravers, but the dismay of the turtles. A bridge leads out to the pretty islet of **Ag. Sostís**, its limestone cliffs falling abruptly where the earthquake of 1633 cleaved it from the rest of Zákynthos. It's topped with pine trees and, this being Laganás, a disco.

The Belgian on the Beach

Not a few sunbathers at Laganás are keen students of the opposite sex's anatomy, so generously displayed and baked to a T. None, however, is as studiously keen as Vesalius (1514–64), the Renaissance father of anatomy, whose statue stands at the south end of the beach. Born in Brabant, Vesalius studied in Paris where he edited the 2nd-century AD anatomical works of Galen, the Greek physician to the gladiators and Emperor Marcus Aurelius. Vesalius went on to the medical university of Padua, and made it the leading school of anatomy in Europe, where in 1543 he published his milestone *De humani corporis fabrica*, the first thorough study of the human body since Galen's time. In 1555 Vesalius became the personal physician to Philip II of Spain, only to be sentenced to death by the Inquisition for dissecting a dead Spaniard. Philip commuted the sentence to a pilgrimage to the Holy Land, and on the way home the doctor's ship was wrecked off the coast at Laganás. Vesalius, realizing a return to Inquisition-plagued Madrid would mean an end to his studies anyway, decided to spend the rest of his life in the now ruined Franciscan monastery at Faneró, along the road from Laganás to Pantokrátoras; his epitaph is still intact.

A Gently Inclined Plain

Behind Laganás extends the lush plain of Zákynthos, a lovely, fairly flat region to cycle through, dotted with the ruins of old country estates wrapped in greenery. One still happily intact is the **Domaine Agria**, the oldest winery in Greece, run by the Comoutós family since 1638. The Comoutóses made their fortunes in raisin and currant exports, and were ennobled in the Libro d'Oro; today their estate is divided between olive groves, currants, and grape vines that yield excellent reds, rosés, whites, and old-fashioned, high-alcohol dessert wines. To visit their tasting room and museum of old winemaking tools, call ℰ 92 285.

The chief village to aim for is **Pantokrátoras**, near three fine churches: the beautiful **Pantokrátor**, founded by Byzantine Empress Pulcheria, and still retaining a number of Byzantine traits; **Kilíómeno**, restored after the quake, with beautiful icons; and the medieval church of the **Panagía**, with a pretty bell tower and stone carvings. The picturesque ruins of the Villa Loundzis, once one of Zákynthos' most noble estates, are in **Sarakína**. **Lithakiá**, south of Pantokrátoras, has another restored church, the 14th-century Panagía Faneroméni, containing works of art gathered from ruined churches in the vicinity.

From Lithakiá the main road continues south over the Avyssos Gorge—a rift made by the 1633 earthquake—the coastal swamp known as **Límni Kerióu**. If you look carefully at the roots of the aquatic plants, you can see the black bitumen or natural pitch that once welled up in sufficient quantity to caulk thousands of boats; both Herodotus and Pliny described the phenomenon and more recently an exploratory oil bore was sunk, but with negligible results. There are tavernas by the rather mediocre beach.

Just to the south, however, extends a second Mount Skopós. From the sea (there are caique excursions offered from Kerí Beach) this coast is magnificent, marked by sheer white cliffs as high as Dover's, deep dark blue waters and two towering natural arches at Marathía.

At the end of the road the mountain village of **Kerí** offers fine views, especially from its white lighthouse, and the cheapest rooms on the island. From the main road a secondary road winds westward to one of Zákynthos' more remote villages, **Agalás**, passing by way of the two-storey grotto called **Spiliá Damianoú**, where one formation resembles a horse; the legend goes that a giant named Andronia once lived in the area and pestered the good people of Agalás for food. His appetite was huge, and the people were at their wits' end when an old lady slipped him a poison pie. Down he fell at a place still called Andronia, where you can see twelve 15th-century wells with their old well-heads. His horse was so shocked it turned to stone.

Kalamáki ✉ 29100

Michelos, ✆ 48 080, one of the best tavernas in Zákynthos (and one of the most crowded), is just along the main Kalamáki–Zákynthos road. There's a convenient bar next door if you have to wait for a table. The **Cave Bar**, also away from the coast, up a little road lined with lights, is a romantic place of various levels, perfect for a troglodyte cocktail.

Heading Northwest

From Zákynthos Town the coastal road leads north, past the **Kryonéri Fountain**, built by the Venetians to water their ships. The red rock overhead was used for a suicide leap in a popular Greek novel, *Kókkinos Vráchos*. Beyond, the road turns abruptly west to reach a series of pretty sandy beaches, connected by short access roads and backed by orchards and vineyards. Holiday development is still fairly embryonic, calm and peaceful, especially when compared to the babylonian crud along Laganás Bay: long and narrow **Tsiliví** (ΤΣΙΛΙΒΙ), **Plános** (overlooking **Tragáki Beach**), little **Ámpoula** with golden sand, **Pachiámmos**, **Drossiá**, **Psaroú**, **Ammoúdi**, and **Alikanás**, where a wonderful long stretch of sand sweeps around the bay west to **Alikés** (ΑΛΥΚΕΣ), named for the nearby saltpans, an area popular with windsurfers.

The rich agricultural land inland from the coast is pleasant to explore, if directions can be a bit confusing. **Skoulikádo** rewards visitors with several interesting churches, among them the **Panagía Anafonítria**, decorated outside with stone reliefs and lovely interior and **Ag. Nikólaos Megalomáti**, named for a 16th-century icon painted on stone of St Nicholas, with unusually large eyes. **Ag. Marína**, a rare survivor of the earthquake, has a cell behind the altar where the insane would be chained in hope of a cure. Inland from Alikés, **Katastári** is the island's second-largest town, marking the northern edge of the plain; from here the main road divides, one branch spiralling into the mountains, while a newer offshoot follows the sea all the way to Korithí. In its early stages, this coastline is a sequence of beautiful pebbled beaches, such as **Makri Aloú** and **Makrí Giálos,** becoming more dramatic, volcanic and inaccessible as it wends northwards. The port of **Ag. Nikoláos** where the little ferry from Kefaloniá calls, nestles in a bay with beautiful views of its eponymous islet; sadly, the architecture doesn't live up to the natural setting. (Note there is no bus; and unless you find one waiting, taxis called in from afar can be pricey).

The white coast around here is pocked with caves, cliffs and natural columns and arches, and most spectacularly of all, one hour by boat from Skinári, **Kianoún**

Cave, the local version of Capri's Blue Grotto, glowing with every imaginable shade of blue; the light is best in the morning. Excursions from Ag. Nikólaos also run south to **Xinthia** with sulphur springs—evidence of the island's volcanic origins—and rocks and sand so hot that you need swimming shoes to protect your toes, and to the cave of **Sklávou.**

Zákynthos ✉ *29100,* ✆ *(0695–)*   ***Where to Stay and Eating Out***

Plagos Beach, at Ámpoula Beach, ✆ 24 147 (*A; exp*) is a big new hotel and bungalow complex, a stone's throw from the sea, with a pool and tennis court as well. **Caravel** at Tragáki, ✆ 25 261 (*A; exp*), sister to the one in Athens, will lighten your wallet, but has all the trimmings.

Orea Heleni, ✆ 28 788 (*C; mod*) is a nice choice at Tsiliví. **Cosmopolite**, ✆ 28 752 (*C; mod*) has 14 good rooms, 500 yards from the sea. There's also a good campsite, **Camping Zante**, on Ámpoula Beach, ✆ 44 754. On the coast road not far from Koroní and worth a detour, **Taverna Xikia**, ✆ 31 165, serves tasty Greek food in an idyllic clifftop setting.

Further north and well away from the block-booked beach resorts, the English-owned **Peligoni Club**, ✆ 31 482, or in the UK, ✆ (01243) 511499, is a little surf-and-sailing holiday haven set into the rugged volcanic coastline. Accommodation is in a sprinkling of villas within driving distance of the friendly clubhouse; the club caters just as well for watersports beginners and experts as it does for lazybones landlubbers with vast appetites and a talent for Scrabble.

It's also possible for some or all of the party to stay nearby at well-equipped **Camping Skinari**, ✆ 31 061, or pristine **Pension Panorama,** ✆ 31 013 (*mod–inexp*), and, for a fee, to use the club's facilities on a more ad hoc basis. At Ag. Nikoláos, **Hotel la Grotta**, ✆ 31 224 (*C; mod–inexp*) is handy for the ferry and the **Astoria** serves good fish overlooking the beautifully appointed harbour.

Up the Southwest Coast

Unlike the low rolling hills and plain of the east, the west coast of Zákynthos plunges steeply and abruptly into the sea, some 1000ft in places, and is a favourite place for caique excursions either from Zákynthos Town or Alikés. The last stop on the plain, taking the pretty road from Zákynthos Town, is **Macherádo**, in the centre of a cluster of farming villages. Its church of **Ag. Mávra** has a very ornate interior, with a beautiful old icon of the saint covered with ex-votos and scenes in silver of her life and martyrdom; the Venetian church bells are famous for their clear musical tones. Until recently it had a screen dividing the sexes. Also in Macherádo, note the fine reconstructed belfry of the 16th-century church of the Ipapánti. In the nearby wine-growing village of **Lagopóda** there is also the pretty crenellated Eleftherias convent, where the nuns do fine needlework.

From Macherádo the road rises to **Koiloménos**, with a handsome stone belltower from 1893, attached to the church of Ag. Nikólaos: unusually for Greece it is carved with Masonic symbols, and, if it looks stumpy, it's because it lacks its original pyramidal crown. A secondary road from here leads to the wild coast and the **Karakonísi**, a bizarre islet just off-shore that looks like a whale and even spouts great plumes of spray when the wind is up. At Ag. Léon (with another striking bell tower, this time converted from a windmill) there's another turn-off to the coast, to the dramatic narrow creek and minute sandy beach at **Limnióna**. Just before Exochóro, another road descends to **Kámbi**, where Mycenaean rock-cut tombs were found and two tavernas perched on the 650ft cliffs are spectacular sunset viewing platforms, although in summer you'll probably have to share them with coach parties from Laganás.

The main road continues to Anafonítria, site of the 15th-century **Monastery of the Panagía Anafonítria**, which survived several earthquakes intact along with its time-darkened frescoes and cell of St Dionysios—he was abbot here and his claim for sainthood was that he gave sanctuary to his brother's killer.

Below is **Porto Vrómi**, 'Dirty Port', because of the natural tar that blankets the shore, although the water is perfectly clear. Around the corner is a perfect white sandy beach, wedged under sheer white limestone crags set in perfectly clear azure water—the setting for Zákynthos' notorious '**shipwreck**'. The scene that graces a thousand postcards is a prime destination for excursion boats; although some tour guides let the punters fantasize that the wreck has been there for decades, the boat really belonged to cigarette smugglers in the late 1980s who ran the ship aground and escaped when they were about to be nabbed by the Greek coastguard. When word reached the inhabitants of the small villages above, immediate action was taken, and by the time the coastguard got back to the ship it was empty; the free smokes lasted for years. You can look down at 'shipwreck' beach from the path near the abandoned 16th-century monastery of **Ag. Geórgios sta Kremná**. The path, ever more overgrown, leads to the narrow cave-chapel of **Ag. Gerásimou**.

The road passes through an increasingly dry landscape on route to **Volímes** (ΒΟΛΙΜΕΣ), the largest village on the west coast, permanently festive with billowing, brightly coloured handwoven goods displayed for sale. Seek out the fine church of Ag. Paraskeví and the 15th-century Ag. Theodósios, with its stone carved iconostasis. On the village's main road, Dionysos's taverna is the place for top notch spit roast lamb and other excellencies. **Áno Volímes**, just above its sister town, is a pretty little mountain village.

The Strofádes

A couple of times a week caiques from Laganás sail the 37 nautical miles south of Zákynthos to the Strofádes (there are two, **Charpína** and **Stamvránio**), passing over the deepest point in the entire Mediterranean, where you have to dive 4404m down to reach Davy Jones' locker. Strofádes means 'turning' in Greek: according to myth, the Harpies, those composite female monsters with human heads, hands and feet, winged griffon bodies and bear ears were playing their usual role as the hired guns of the gods, chasing the prophet Phineas over the little islets, when Zeus changed his mind and ordered them to come back. They were still making a nuisance of themselves when Virgil's Aeneas sailed past on his way back from Troy:

> At length I land upon the Strophades;
> Safe from the danger of the stormy seas,
> Those isles are compassed by the Ionian main;
> The dire abode where the foul Harpies reign.

Aeneid III (trans. Dryden)

Although little more than flat, oval green pancakes in the sea, the Strofádes offered just the right kind of rigorous isolation Orthodox monks and mystics crave, and duly in the 13th century, the Byzantine emperor of Nicaea, Theodore Láskaris, found the **Pantochará** ('all joy') monastery on Charpína. Pirates soon proved to be a major problem, and in 1440, just before Constantinople itself fell to the Turks, Emperor John Palaiológos sent funds to build high walls around it, giving the monastery its current castle-like appearance; the monks could be drawn up in baskets whenever the alarm was sounded. As on Mount Áthos, no women or female animals were allowed, and the 62 monks of noble blood and 10 priests who resided there spent their days studying rare books. In 1530, however, the Turks managed to breach the walls, slew all the monks and plundered it.

In 1568, a certain Count Draganikos Sigouros of Zákynthos was ordained at the monastery, became its abbot two years later, lived an especially holy and useful life and at his request was buried at the monastery when he died on 17 December, 1622. When his body was dug up a few years later according to Greek custom, it was found intact; in 1717, another Turkish attack succeeded in killing all the monks except for two who managed to hide, and it was thought best for the body of the abbot, now canonized as Ag. Diónysos, to be removed to Zákynthos Town for safe-keeping. The evocative, desolate citadel of white stone belongs to the monastery of Ag. Diónysos in Zákynthos Town, although the population has been reduced to migratory turtle doves and quails. If you have your own boat and provisions and have been looking for an out-of-the-way, romantic destination you won't find a better one, although don't expect the monastery buildings to be open in the near future; it was rocked in an earthquake (6.6 on the Richter scale) on the 18 November 1997.

Greek holds a special place as the oldest spoken language in Europe, going back at least 4000 years. From the ancient language, Modern Greek, or Romaíka, developed into two forms: the purist or *katharévousa*, literally 'clean language', and the popular, or Demotic *demotikí*, the language of the people. But while the purist is consciously Classical, the popular is as close to its ancient origins as say, Chaucerian English is to modern English. These days few purist words are spoken but you will see the old *katharévousa* on shop signs and official forms. Even though the bakery is called the *foúrnos* the sign over the door will read ΑΡΤΟΠΟΛΕΙΟΝ, bread-seller, while the general store will be the ΠΑΝΤΟΠΟΛΕΙΟΝ, seller of all. You'll still see the pure form on wine labels as well.

At the end of the 18th century, in the wakening swell of national pride, writers felt the common language wasn't good enough; archaic forms were brought back and foreign ones replaced. Upon independence, this artificial construction called *katharévousa* became the official language of books and even newspapers. The more vigorous Demotic soon began to creep back; in 1901 Athens was shaken by riots and the government fell when the New Testament appeared in *demotikí*; in 1903 several students were killed in a fight with the police during a *demotikí* performance of Aeschylus. When the fury subsided, it looked as if the Demotic would win out by popular demand till the Papadópoulos government (1967–74) made it part of its 'moral cleansing' of Greece to revive the purist. *Katharévousa* was the only language allowed in schools and everything had to be written in the pure form. The great debate was settled in 1978 when Demotic was made the official tongue.

Greeks travel so far and wide that even in the most remote places there's usually someone who speaks English, more likely than not with an American, Australian or even South African drawl. On the

Language

other hand, learning a bit of Greek can make your travels more enjoyable. Usually spoken with great velocity, Greek isn't a particularly easy language to pick up by ear. But even if you have no desire to learn Greek, it is helpful to know at least the alphabet—so that you can find your way around—and a few basic words and phrases.

Greekspeak

Sign language is an essential part of Greek life and it helps to know what it all means. Greekspeak for 'no' is usually a click of the tongue, accompanied by raised eyebrows and a tilt of the head backwards. It could be all three or a permutation. 'Yes' is usually indicated by a forward nod, head tilted to the side. If someone doesn't hear you or understand you properly they will often shake their heads from side to side quizzically and say '*Oríste?*' Hands whirl like windmills in conversations and beware the emphatic open hand brought sharply down in anger. A circular movement of the right hand usually implies something very good or in great quantities. Women walking alone might hear hissing like a demented snake emanating from pavement cafés. This will be the local Romeos or *kamákis* trying to attract your attention.

Greeks also use exclamations which sound odd but mean a lot, like *po, po, po!* an expression of disapproval or derision; *brávo* comes in handy for praise while *ópa!* is useful for whoops! look out! or watch it!; *sigá sigá* means slowly, slowly; *éla!*, come or get on with you, *kíta!* look. Other phrases you'll hear all the time but won't find in your dictionary include:

paréa	gang, close friends	*listía*	rip-off
pedhiá	guys, the lads	*alítis*	bum, no-good person
ré, bré	mate, chum, slang for friends	*palikári*	good guy, brave, honourable
endáxi	OK	*pedhí mou/*	my boy/my girl
malákka	rude, lit. masturbator, used	*korítsi mou*	
	between men as term of endearment	*yasoo koúkla/os*	Hi doll, hello gorgeous
kéfi	high spirits, well-being	*etsi íne ee zoí*	that's life!
kaïmós	the opposite, suffering, sad	*ti na kánoume*	what can we do!
lipón	well, now then	*kaló taxídhi*	good trip, Bon Voyage!
hérete	formal greeting	*kalí órexi*	Bon appetit!
sto kaló	go with God, formal parting		

The Greek Alphabet

Pronunciation   English Equivalent

Α	α	*álfa*	short 'a' as in 'father'	Ν	ν	*ni*	n
Β	β	*víta*	v	Ξ	ξ	*ksi*	'x' as in 'ox'
Γ	γ	*gámma*	guttural g or y sound	Ο	ο	*ómicron*	'o' as in 'cot'
Δ	δ	*délta*	hard *th* as in 'though'	Π	π	*pi*	p
Ε	ε	*épsilon*	short 'e' as in 'bet'	Ρ	ρ	*ro*	r
Ζ	ζ	*zíta*	z	Σ	σ	*sígma*	s
Η	η	*íta*	long 'e' as in 'bee'	Τ	τ	*taf*	t
Θ	θ	*thíta*	soft *th* as in 'thin'	Υ	υ	*ípsilon*	long 'e' as in 'bee'
Ι	ι	*yóta*	long 'e' as in 'bee';	Φ	φ	*fi*	f
			sometimes like 'y' in 'yet'	Χ	χ	*chi*	German *ch* as in 'doch'
Κ	κ	*káppa*	k	Ψ	ψ	*psi*	*ps* as in 'stops'
Λ	λ	*lámtha*	l	Ω	ω	*oméga*	'o' as in 'cot'
Μ	μ	*mi*	m				

Diphthongs and Consonant Combinations

AI	αι	short 'e' as in 'bet'
EI	ει, OI οι	'i' as in 'machine'
OY	ου	*oo* as in 'too'
AY	αυ	*av* or *af*
EY	ευ	*ev* or *ef*
HY	ηυ	*iv* or *if*
ΓΓ	γγ	*ng* as in 'angry'
ΓΚ	γκ	hard 'g'; *ng* within word
NT	ντ	'd'; *nd* within word
ΜΠ	μπ	'b'; *mp* within word

Useful Phrases

Yes	*né/málista* (formal)	Ναί /Μάλιστα
No	*óchi*	Όχι
I don't know	*then xéro*	Δέν ξέρω
I don't understand... (Greek)	*then katalavéno...* (*elliniká*)	Δέν καταλαβαίνω...(Ελληνικά)
Does someone speak English?	*milái kanis angliká?*	Μιλάει κανείς αγγλικά?
Go away	*fíyete*	Φύγετε
Help!	*voíthia!*	Βοήθεια!
My friend	*o fílos moo* (*m*)	Ο φίλος μου
	ee fíli moo (*f*)	Η φίλη μου
Please	*parakaló*	Παρακαλώ
Thank you (very much)	*evcharistó* (*pára polí*)	Ευχαριστώ (πάρα πολύ)
You're welcome	*parakaló*	Παρακαλώ
It doesn't matter	*thén pirázi*	Δέν πειράζει
OK, alright	*endaxi*	Εντάξι
Of course	*vevéos*	Βεβαίος
Excuse me, sorry	*signómi*	Συγγνώμη
Pardon? Or, from waiters, what do you want?	*oríste?*	Ορίστε?
Be careful!	*proséchete!*	Προσέχεται!
Nothing	*típota*	Τίποτα
What is your name?	*pos sas léne?* (*formal*)	Πώς σάς λένε?
	pos se léne?	Πώς σέ λένε?
How are you?	*ti kánete?* (*formal/pl*)	Τί κάνεται?
	ti kanis?	Τί κάνεις?
Hello	*yásas, hérete* (*formal/pl*)	Γειάσας, Χέρεται
	yásou	Γειάσου
Goodbye	*yásas, hérete* (*formal/pl*)	Γειάσας, Χέρεται
	yásou, adío	Γειάσου, Αντίο
Good morning	*kaliméra*	Καλημέρα
Good evening/good night	*kalispéra/kaliníchta*	Καλησπέρα /Καληνύχτα
What is that?	*ti íne aftó?*	Τί είναι αυτό?

What?	ti?	Τί?
Who?	piós? (m), piá? (f)	Ποιός? Ποιά?
Where?	poo?	Ποιός?
When?	póte?	Πότε?
Why?	yiatí?	Γιατί?
How?	pos?	Πώς?
I am/ You are/He, she, it is	íme/íse/íne	Είμαι /Είσε /Είναι
We are/ You are/They are	ímaste/ísaste/íne	Είμαστε /Είσαστε /Είναι
I am lost	échasa to thrómo	Εχασα το δρόμο
I am hungry/I am thirsty	pinó/thipsó	Πεινώ /Διψώ
I am tired/ill	íme kourasménos/arostos	Είμαι κουρασμένος /άρρωστος
I am poor	íme ftochós	Είμαι φτωχός
I love you	s'agapó	Σ΄αγαπώ
good/bad/so-so	kaló/kakó/étsi kétsi	καλό /κακό /έτσι κ΄έτσι
slowly/fast/big/small	sigá sigá/grígora/megálo/ mikró	σιγά σιγά / γρήγορα / μεγάλο / μικρό
hot/cold	zestó/crío	ζεστό /κρίο

Shops, Services, Sightseeing

I would like...	tha íthela...	Θά ήθελα...
where is...?	poo íne...?	Πού είναι...?
how much is it?	póso káni?	Πόσο κάνει?
bakery	foúrnos/artopoleion	φούρνος /Αρτοπολείον
bank	trápeza	τράπεζα
beach	paralía	παραλία
church	eklisía	εκκλησία
cinema	kinimatográfos	κινηματογράφος
hospital	nosokomío	νοσοκομείο
hotel	xenodochío	ξενοδοχείο
hot water	zestó neró	ζεστό νερό
kiosk	períptero	περίπτερο
money	leftá	λεφτά
museum	moosío	μουσείο
newspaper (foreign)	efimerítha (xéni)	εφημερίδα (ξένη)
pharmacy	farmakío	φαρμακείο
police station	astinomía	αστυνομία
policeman	astifílakas	αστιφύλακας
post office	tachithromío	ταχυδρομείο
plug, electrical	príza	πρίζα
plug, bath	tápa	τάπα
restaurant	estiatório	εστιατόριο
sea	thálassa	θάλασσα
shower	doush	ντούς
student	fititís	φοιτητής
telephone office	Oté	OTE
theatre	théatro	θέατρο
toilet	tooaléta	τουαλέττα

Time

What time is it?	*ti óra íne?*	Τί ώρα είναι
month/week/day	*mína/evthomáda/méra*	μήνα /εβδομάδα /μέρα
morning/afternoon/evening	*proí/apóyevma/vráthi*	πρωί /απόγευμα /βράδυ
yesterday/today/tomorrow	*chthés/símera/ávrio*	χθές /σήμερα /αύριο
now/later	*tóra/metá*	τώρα /μετά
it is early/late	*íne norís/argá*	είναι νωρίς/αργά

Travel Directions

I want to go to ...	*thélo na páo sto (m), sti (f)...*	Θέλω νά πάω στό, στη...
How can I get to...?	*pós boró na páo sto (m), sti (f)...?*	Πώς μπορώ νά πάω στό, στη...?
Where is...?	*poo íne ...?*	Πού είναι...?
How far is it?	*póso makriá íne?*	Πόσο μακριά είναι
When will the... come?	*póte tha érthi to (n), ee (f), o (m)...?*	Πότε θά έρθη τό, ή, ό...?
When will the... leave?	*póte tha fíyi to (n), ee (f), o (m)...?*	Πότε θά φύγη τό, ή, ό...?
From where do I catch...?	*apó poo pérno...?*	Από πού πέρνω...?
How long does the trip take?	*póso keró pérni to taxíthi?*	Πόσο καιρό πέρνει τό ταξίδι?
Please show me	*parakaló thíkste moo*	Παρακαλώ δείξτε μου
the (nearest) town	*to horió (to pió kondinó)*	Το χωριό (το πιό κοντινό)
here/there/near/far	*ethó/ekí/kondá/makriá*	εδώ/εκεί/κοντά/μακριά
left/right	*aristerá/thexiá*	αριστερά/δεξιά
north/south	*vória/nótia/anatoliká/thitiká*	βόρεια/νότια/ανατολικά/δυτικά

Driving

where can I rent ...?	*poo boró na nikiáso ...?*	Πού μπορώ νά νοικιάσω ...?
a car	*éna aftokínito*	ένα αυτοκινητο
a motorbike	*éna michanáki*	ένα μηχανάκι
a bicycle	*éna pothílato*	ένα ποδήλατο
where can I buy petrol?	*poo boró nagorásso venzíni?*	Πού μπορώ ν'αγοράσω βενζίνη?
where is a garage?	*poo íne éna garáz?*	Πού είναι ένα γκαράζ?
a mechanic	*énan mihanikó*	έναν μηχανικό
a map	*énan chárti*	έναν χάρτη
where is the road to...?	*poo íne o thrómos yiá...?*	Πού είναι ο δρόμος γιά...?
where does this road lead?	*poo pái aftós o thrómos?*	Πού πάει αυτός ο δρόμος?
is the road good?	*íne kalós o thrómos?*	Είναι καλός ο δρόμος?
EXIT	*éxothos*	ΕΞΟΔΟΣ
ENTRANCE	*ísothos*	ΕΙΣΟΔΟΣ
DANGER	*kínthinos*	ΚΙΝΔΥΝΟΣ
SLOW	*argá*	ΑΡΓΑ
NO PARKING	*apagorévete ee státhmevsis*	ΑΠΑΓΟΡΕΥΕΤΑΙ Η ΣΤΑΘΜΕΥΣΙΣ
KEEP OUT	*apagorévete ee ísothos*	ΑΠΑΓΟΡΕΥΕΤΑΙ Η ΕΙΣΟΔΟΣ

Numbers

one	*énas (m), mía (f), éna (n)*	ένας, μία, ένα
two	*thío*	δύο
three	*tris (m, f), tría (n)*	τρείς, τρία
four	*téseris (m, f), téssera (n)*	τέσσερεις, τέσσερα
five	*pénde*	πέντε
six	*éxi*	έξι
seven/eight/nine/ten	*eptá/ októ/ ennéa/ théka*	επτά/οκτώ/εννέα/δέκα
eleven/twelve/thirteen	*éntheka/ thótheka/ thekatría*	έντεκα/δώδεκα/δεκατρία
twenty	*íkosi*	είκοσι
twenty-one	*íkosi éna (m, n) mía (f)*	είκοσι ένα, μία
thirty/forty/fifty/sixty	*triánda/ saránda/ penínda/ exínda*	τριάντα/σαράντα/ πενήντα/εξήντα
seventy/eighty/ninety	*evthomínda/ ogthónda/ enenínda*	εβδομήντα/ ογδόντα/ ενενήντα
one hundred	*ekató*	εκατό
one thousand	*chília*	χίλια

Months/Days

January	*Ianooários*	Ιανουάριος
February	*Fevrooários*	Φεβρουάριος
March	*Mártios*	Μάρτιος
April	*Aprílios*	Απρίλιος
May	*Máios*	Μάιος
June	*Ioónios*	Ιούνιος
July	*Ioólios*	Ιούλιος
August	*Avgoostos*	Αύγουστος
September	*Septémvrios*	Σεπτέμβριος
October	*Októvrios*	Οκτώβριος
November	*Noémvrios*	Νοέμβριος
December	*Thekémvrios*	Δεκέμβριος
Sunday	*Kiriakí/*	Κυριακή
Monday	*Theftéra*	Δευτέρα
Tuesday	*Tríti*	Τρίτη
Wednesday	*Tetárti*	Τετάρτη
Thursday	*Pémpti*	Πέμπτη
Friday	*Paraskeví*	Παρασκευή
Saturday	*Sávato*	Σάββατο

Transport

the airport/aeroplane	*to arothrómio/aropláno*	τό αεροδρόμιο /αεροπλάνο
the bus station/bus	*ee stási leoforíou/leoforío*	ή στάση λεωφορείου /λεωφορείο
the railway station/the train	*o stathmós too trénou/to tréno*	ό σταθμός τού τραίνου/τό τραίνο
the port/port authority	*to limáni/ limenarchío*	τό λιμάνι /λιμεναρχείο
the ship	*to plío, to karávi*	τό πλοίο, τό καράβι
the steamship	*to vapóri*	τό βαπόρι
the car	*to aftokínito*	τό αυτοκίνητο
a ticket	*éna isitírio*	ένα εισιτήριο

Finding your way round a Greek menu, *katálogos*, takes some doing, but there's a basic lay-out with prices before and after local tax. You begin with Orektiká, OPEKTIKA; dishes cooked in olive oil are known as Laderá, ΛΑΔΕΡΑ; main courses are Entrádes, ΕΝΤΡΑΔΕΣ; Fish are Psária, ΨΑΡΙΑ; dishes with minced meat, Kimádhes, ΚΥΜΑΔΕΣ and things grilled or barbecued to order are either Psitá, ΨΗΤΑ or Tis Oras, ΤΗΣ ΩΡΑΣ.

Ορεκτικά (Μεζέδες)	Orektiká (Mezéthes)	Appetisers
εληés	eliés	olives
κοπανιστι (τυροσαλατα)	kopanistí (tirosaláta)	cheese purée, often spicy
ντολμάδες	dolmáthes	stuffed vine leaves
μελιτζανοσαλατα	melitzanosaláta	eggplant (aubergine) dip
ποικιλια	pikilía	mixed hors-d'œuvre
μπουρεκι	bouréki	cheese and vegetable pie
τυροπιττα	tirópitta	cheese pie
αξινι	eahíni	sea urchin roe (quite salty)
Σούπες	**Soópes**	**Soups**
αυγολέμονο	avgolémono	egg and lemon soup
χορτόσουπα	chortósoupa	vegetable soup
ψαρόσουπα	psarósoupa	fish soup
φασολαδα	fasolada	bean soup
πατσας	patsás	tripe and pig's foot soup (for late nights and hangovers)
Λαδερά	**Latherá**	**Cooked in Oil**
μπαμιες	bámies	okra, ladies' fingers
γιγαντες	yígantes	butter beans in tomato sauce
μπριαμ	briám	aubergines and mixed veg
φασόλακια	fasólakia	fresh green beans
φακή	fakí	lentils
Ζυμαρικά	**Zimariká**	**Pasta and Rice**
πιλάφι, ρυζι	piláfi/rizi	pilaf/rice
σπαγκέτι	spagéti	spaghetti
μακαρόνια	macarónia	macaroni
Ψάρια	**Psária**	**Fish**
αστακός	astakós	lobster
καλαμαρια	kalamaria	squid
χταπόδι	chtapóthi	octopus
γαρίδες	garíthes	prawns (shrimps)
ξιφιας	ksifias	swordfish
μαρίδες	maríthes	whitebait
συναγρίδα	sinagrítha	sea bream
φαγρι	fangri	bream
σαρδέλλα	sardélla	sardines
σκουμβρι	skoumbri	mackerel
στρείδια	stríthia	oysters
λιθρίνια	lithrínia	bass
μιδια	mídia	mussels

Αυγά	Avgá	Eggs
ομελέττα μέ ζαμπόν	omeléta me zambón	ham omelette
ομελέττα μέ τυρί	omeléta me tirí	cheese omelette
αυγά τηγανιτά (μπρουγέ)	avgá tiganitá (brouyé)	fried (scrambled) eggs
άυγά και μπεικον	avgá kai bakón	egg and bacon
Εντραδεσ	**Entrádes**	**Main Courses**
κουνέλι	kounéli	rabbit
συκώτι	seekóti	liver
μοσχάρι	moschári	veal
αρνι	arní	lamb
λουκάνικο	lukániko	sausage
κατσυκι	katsíki	kid
κοτόπουλο	kotópoulo	(roast) chicken
χοιρινό	chirinó	pork
Κυμάδεσ	**Kymadhes**	**Minced Meat**
παστίτσιο	pastítsio	mince and macaroni pie
μακαρόνια με κυμά	makarónia me kymá	spaghetti Bolognese
μπιφτεκι	biftéki	hamburger, usually bunless
σουτζουκάκια	soutzoukákia	meat balls in sauce
μελιτζάνες γεμιστές	melitzánes yemistés	stuffed aubergines/eggplants
πιπεριές γεμιστές	piperíes yemistés	stuffed peppers
Της Ωρας	**Tis Oras**	**Grills to Order**
μρισολα	brisóla	beefsteak with bone
μπριζόλες χοιρινές	brizólas chirinés	pork chops
σουβλάκι	souvláki	meat or fish kebabs on a skewer
παιδακια	paidakia	lamb chops
κεφτέδες	keftéthes	meat balls
Σαλάτες	**Salátes**	**Salads and Vegetables**
ντομάτες	domátes	tomatoes
αγγούρι	angoúri	cucumber
ρώσσικη σαλάτα	róssiki saláta	Russian salad
σπανακι	spanáki	spinach
χοριάτικη	choriátiki	salad with *Feta* cheese and olives
κολοκυθάκια	kolokithákia	courgettes/zucchini
πιπεριεσ	piperiés	peppers
κρεμιδι	kremídi	onions
πατάτες	patátes	potatoes
μαρούλι	maroúli	lettuce
αγκιναρες	angináres	artichokes
Τυρια	**Tiriá**	**Cheeses**
φέτα	féta	goat's cheese
κασέρι	kasséri	hard buttery cheese
γραβιέρα	graviéra	Greek 'Gruyère'
μυζήθρα	mizíthra	soft white cheese
προβιο	próvio	sheeps' cheese
Γλυκά	**Glyká**	**Sweets**
παγωτό	pagotó	ice cream
μπακλαβά	baklavá	nuts and honey in fillo pastry
γιαούρτι (με μελι)	yiaoúrti (me méli)	yoghurt (with honey)

| ρυζόγαλο | rizógalo | rice pudding |
| μπουγάτσα | bougátsa | custard tart |

Φρούτα — Froóta — Fruit

πορτοκάλι	portokáli	orange
ρόδι	ródi	pomegranate
μήλο	mílo	apple
κερασι	kerási	cherry
ροδάκινο	rothákino	peach
πεπόνι	pepóni	melon
καρπούζι	karpoúzi	watermelon
ακτινιδι	aktinídi	kiwi
σύκα	síka	figs
σταφύλια	stafília	grapes
μπανάνα	banána	banana
βερύκοκο	veríkoko	apricot
φραουλες	fráoules	strawberries

Miscellaneous

ψωμί	psomí	bread
βούτυρο	voútiro	butter
μέλι	méli	honey
μαρμελάδα	marmelátha	jam
αλάτι	aláti	salt
πιπέρι	pipéri	pepper
ζάχαρη	záchari	sugar
λάδι	láthi	oil
λεμόνι	lemóni	lemon
πιάτο	piáto	plate
μαχαίρι	mahéri	knife
πηρούνι	piroóni	fork
κουτάλι	koutáli	spoon
λογαριασμό	logariasmó	the bill/check

Drinks

άσπρο κρασί	áspro krasí	wine, white
ασπρο /κοκκινο /κοκκινελι	áspro/kókkino/kokkinéli	white/red/rosé
ρετσίνα	retsína	wine resinated
νερό (βραστο /μεταλικο)	neró (vrastó /metalikó)	water (boiled/mineral)
μπύρα	bíra	beer
χυμός πορτοκάλι	chimós portokáli	orange juice
γάλα	gála	milk
τσάι	tsái	tea
σοκολάτα	sokoláta	chocolate
καφε	kafé	coffee
φραππε	frappé	iced coffee
παγος	págos	ice
ποτίρι	potíri	glass
μπουκαλι	boukáli	bottle
καραφα	karáfa	carafe
στήν γειά σας!	stín yásas (formal, pl)	to your health! Cheers!
στήν γειά σου!	stín yásou (sing)	

Glossary of Terms

acropolis — fortified height, usually the site of a city's chief temples

agíos, agía, agii — saint or saints, or holy abbreviated **Ag.**

ágora — market and public area in a city centre

amphora — tall jar for wine or oil, designed to be shipped (the conical end would be embedded in sand

áno/apáno — upper

caique — a small wooden boat, pronounced '*kaEEki*' now mostly used for tourist excursions

cella — innermost holy room of a temple

choklakía (or **hokalaía**) — black and white pebble mosaic

chóra — simply, 'place'; often what islanders call their 'capital' town, although it usually also has the same name as the island itself

chorió — village

dimarchíon — town hall

EOT — Greek National Tourist Office

epachía — Orthodox diocese; also a political county

exonarthex — outer porch of a church

heroön — a shrine to a hero or demigod, often built over the tomb

iconostasis — in an Orthodox church, the decorated screen between the nave and altar

kalderími — stone-paved pathways

kástro — castle or fort

katholikón — monastery chapel

káto — lower

kore — Archaic statue of a maiden

kouros — Archaic statue of a naked youth

larnax — a Minoan clay sarcophagus resembling a bathtub

límani — port

limenarchíon — port authority

loutrá — hot spring, spa

megaron — Mycenaean palace

metope — sculpted panel on a frieze

meltémi — north wind off the Russian steppe that plagues the Aegean in the summer

moní — monastery or convent

monopáti — footpath

narthex — entrance porch of a church

néa — new

nísos/nísi — island/islands

nomós — Greek province

OTE — Greek national telephone company

paleó — old

panagía — Virgin Mary

panegýri — Saint's feast day

pantocrátor — the 'Almighty'—a figure of the triumphant Christ in Byzantine domes

paralía — waterfront or beach

períptero — street kiosk selling just about everything

pírgos — tower, or residential mansion

pithos (pithoi) — large ceramic storage jar

plateía — square

skála — port

spilio — cave or grotto

stoa — covered walkway, often lined with shops, in an *ágora*

temenos — sacred precinct of a temple

tholos — conical Mycenaean temple

224

Index

Also Available from Cadogan Guides...

Country Guides

Antarctica
Belize
The Caribbean and Bahamas
Central Asia
China: The Silk Routes
Egypt
France: Southwest France;
    Dordogne, Lot & Bordeaux
France: Southwest France;
    Gascony & the Pyrenees
France: Brittany
France: The South of France
France: The Loire
Germany
Germany: Bavaria
Greece: The Greek Islands
Guatemala
India
India: South India
India: Goa
Ireland
Ireland: Southwest Ireland
Ireland: Northern Ireland
Italy
Italy: The Bay of Naples and Southern Italy
Italy: Lombardy, Milan and the Italian Lakes
Italy: Tuscany and Umbria
Italy: Three Cities—Rome, Florence and Venice
Japan
The Yucatán and Southern Mexico
Morocco
Portugal
Portugal: The Algarve
Scotland
Scotland's Highlands and Islands
South Africa
Spain
Spain: Southern Spain
Spain: Northern Spain
Syria & Lebanon
Tunisia
Turkey
Zimbabwe, Botswana and Namibia

City Guides

Amsterdam
Brussels, Bruges, Ghent & Antwerp
Florence, Siena, Pisa & Lucca
London
Manhattan
Moscow & St Petersburg
Paris
Prague
Rome
Venice

Island Guides

NE Caribbean; The Leeward Is.
SE Caribbean; The Windward Is.
The Caribbean: Jamaica
Crete
Cyprus
Mykonos, Santorini & the
Cyclades
Rhodes & the Dodecanese
Madeira & Porto Santo
Malta
Sicily

Lazy Days

Lazy Days Out across the Channel
Lazy Days Out in Tuscany
Lazy Days Out in Provence
Lazy Days Out in Andalucía
Lazy Days Out in the Loire
Lazy Days Out in the Dordogne & Lo

Plus...

Southern Africa on the Wild Side
Healthy Travel: Bugs, Bites & Bowel
Travel by Cargo Ship
Henry Kelly in the West of Ireland
London Markets
Mars
Hell